FEVER H

Adrian Bell

Juma

First published in 2001 by
Juma
Trafalgar Works
44 Wellington Street
Sheffield S1 4HD
Tel. 0114 272 0915
Fax. 0114 278 6550
Email: MLacey5816@aol.com

ISBN 1 872204 85 6

Printed by Juma.

cover design: IDFP (www.idfp.co.uk)

This book is dedicated to my dad. If you hadn't taken me to the Lane in 1971, I'd probably be relatively sane, spending mundane Saturdays shopping, but probably only half the person I became.

For Katrina. As the Roy Harper song goes, "Even though you drive me crazy..." You can probably guess the rest of it, Hon.

Acknowledgements:

Huge thank-yous must go to - Musical aka Andy Bonell, who bravely took on the role of my agent and is currently eating lard in an effort to get more Stella out of me; Alty aka Gary Taylor for planting the seed; Halfway aka Andy Nicolson and Webbo aka Step Firth for growing the seed; Martin Lacey and all at Juma for having faith where all other publishers neshed it, and helping me fulfil an ambition; Shiny Blade for coming up with the title of Fever Hitch, all those wonderful drivers who took the gamble of picking me up on the motorway systems of England, but especially Maidenhead and Maidenhead jnr, justoutsidestokeblade and josb jnr the younger, Bill, Stow Blade, Woodford Green Blade, the Family Glossop Blade, Luton Blade, Bert, Gleadless Valley Blade and Mouse, FBFD (Head of Security who came into his own with lifts this current season 2001/2002), Rob Kozluk's Lost Locks, Nick the ground-hopper (our win over Norwich Sept 2001 finally added Bramall Lane to his list), the Young Royals, Murdoch's Neighbour, Crouch End Blade, DC Blade and Miss DC, Warminster Blade (gosh, I did cheat a lot); Richard Littlejohn for allowing me to hijack 606; Martin Ross for those wonderful Sheffield Star features (and the phone call from Carly Bassett); Graham Boon for getting me in the Daily Star and the Evening Standard; Andy Pack for getting me to pretend to hitch with Monty; Matthew Bell at Flashing Blade; Father Dougal at The Red and White Wizaaard (RIP); all the London Blades not already mentioned above, i.e.: Soho Blade, the North London Blade, Radio Blade, Exiled Coal Astoner, Hammersmith Blade, Wimbledon Blade, Blackheath Blade, Stroud Green Blade, Windy, Billy D, N6 Blade, NW3 Blade, EC1 Blade, Lords Blade, Putney Blade, Camden Blade, Psycho Joe, Paris Blade, Champagne Blade, Architect Blade, Ealing Blade, Chiswick Blade, Israel Reds, Suze Blade, Foz, Hackney Wizard, Hackney Blade, Stratford Blade; the wider family of SUISA (now Viewpoints): Pommpey, Attila, Rob, Robby Blade, Donny Blade, Meersbrook Blade, Silent Blade, Sitwell, Halibut Tatlock, Born on Shoreham Street, Hightower, puppet, Lepps, Kirribilli Blade, Shinjuku, Freiberg Blade, Gannon's Right Foot (our Internet Blades manager), Dorset Blade and Mrs Dorset, Petrusha, Torcida, Ted Bovis, Stafford Blade, Radford Blade, Bradway Blade and sister, Young's Special Blade, Doc, Austin 1100 Blade, Hanover Blade, We Are Mark Beard, Greenhill Optimist, Oxspring Blade, Bob Hatton's Balding Bonce, Lampiao, Amsterdam Blade, Glasgow Blade, Bath Blade, Dublin Blade, Boozy Bladette, Scary Blade, Posh Blade, Barnette, Exiled Southern Blade, Copes, Asa, NickBlade, Horbury Common Bladesman (come back, we need you to add some balance to the site!), Trader Blade (we love you), Titanium, Bertie Blade, Concerned Blade, and I'm bound to have missed someone - if so, sorry (but if you all buy it, we might be able to pay the gas bill); Cheese Cake Truck; Chris at the Boardwalk; Human Oddities; JUB-Noise; Cardiacs; my entire family but especially mum and dad, Fiona, Julian, Alex and Deborah; the ladies in my life especially Katrina (thanks for the Word Processor, love), Jitka, Sarah, Clayre, Annette, Katrin, Spiky Em and Kirsty, Debbie, Alex, Leah, Fiona, Michaela, Annie; Ian and Veronika; Richard Caborn; all at Tesco Bishopsgate; and finally - Neil Warnock and those Red and White Wizards. We may have ended up mid-table, but all of you above helped make it the most memorable of seasons. And I really hope I didn't miss anyone out...

Foreword
By Richard Caborn MP, Minister for Sport.

I've always known that the Bell family can be a little eccentric. You see, I first came into contact with them when I became the apprentice of Rennie Bell (the author's father) at Firth Brown when I was all of 16 years of age. At his side I learned his unorthodox but effective style of working, as well as his tenacity on the football pitch as we played side by side in Inter-departmental matches at Firth Brown (Engineers v The Rest). When I became shop steward, we were on opposite sides, but it seemed to work as Rennie was a good boss, and he still tells me now that I was his favourite shop steward. But we were always on the same side in one respect - Sheffield United.

In the sixties we spent Saturday afternoons stood on the Kop (when we sent Harry Evans to get the tickets from the Lane), suffering together as only Blades fans can.

The Bell family connection was carried on in the eighties when Rennie's daughter Deborah spent a decade or so as my secretary. Again, a member of the family proved able to achieve and put things across to the public through a combination of the unorthodox and more tried and tested methods.

So, it came as no surprise when the youngest member of the family, Adrian, accosted me at Deborah's house warming party and thrust a chapter from his book into my hands. You see, I think to be a football fan in general, and especially a Blade, you need to be a little bit mad, and if you didn't have a sense of humour to start with, you soon develop one; gallows humour I think it's called...

So, give this book a read, as it shows to what lengths a truly dedicated Blade will go to in order to see his heroes in action, as well as giving a fascinating insight into what makes any football fan tick, striking a chord with us all, whether we be confirmed Unitedites, or just lovers of the beautiful game itself. I won't be joining Adrian myself on the slip roads of the M1, but as with all Blades of all ages, we're stuck with Sheffield United for life!

Introduction

Strange Behaviour

Remember what they say about people who show signs of strange behaviour in later life? "He must have been dropped on his head as a baby..." Well, to me, my activities have always seemed perfectly normal, but to others hitchhiking has always been regarded as a pastime of the barmy... And those that dislike football have always accused fans of the game of taking it all too seriously. Only a game, they say. As we say in Sheffield, "Gi' o'er!"

Well, here's a fascinating insight into why I turned out like I did. Indeed, I did take something of a tumble as an infant, and it took place during the greatest moment (so far, he says optimistically) in English football history. I'm not sure if I landed on my head, but why ruin a good story by checking the facts from my mum?

July 1966, and England had been taken into extra-time by West Germany in the World Cup Final. I was all of (nearly) 5 months old, and for some reason my mum decided it was time for my bath (the only reason I can think of for this is that my mum likes to keep to a strict timetable, and 5pm Saturday afternoon was obviously Adrian's bath-time, World Cup Final extra time or not). My mum, having been influenced heavily by my dad (a sports lover, and a lifelong Blade) over the years realised that she shouldn't miss this historic occasion, so the baby-bath was dragged in front of the TV, and I was given a good old soaping whilst England struggled to get ahead via the crossbar, the goal-line and a Russian linesman.

Then as Hurst leathered in that fourth England goal and Kenneth Wolstenholme uttered those words, the Bell family jumped up as one to celebrate, including my mum who promptly dropped me into the bath. I'm not sure how long I remained down there before I was picked up, but I bet was roarin' my head off (none-Sheffielders: that means crying) whilst they all cheered. No wonder I grew up like I did...

So, there you have it you see - outlandish behaviour explained. Yes, every time England play a World Cup match, I head for the nearest bath and dive in head-first whilst screaming, "They think it's all over. It is now!"... Okay, maybe not, but it may just explain why I decided at a tender age that hitching would be a great way to get about, and the football connection came about subliminally thanks to sinister BBC television-waves (or whatever they call them).

Well, it's a good story anyway...

Why Sheffield United?

Born in Sheffield to a sports daft dad (himself first taken to the Lane by his dad in 1938), the youngest child of five (two brothers and two sisters), and brought up in Ecclesall (definitely in the red-and-white half of the city), I didn't have much choice really. And if I had wanted to choose, it was going to be tough really, because my dad, as a lifelong Blade, was only going to take me to one ground, and that was Beautiful Downtown Bramall Lane.

With me aged 5, he did just that when, in October 1971, he took me to see Sheffield United against Liverpool. I can't remember too much about it, but I must have been hooked because I'm still going now.

For my sixth birthday I got my first United shirt (a lovely round red collar), and for my eighth I got another one (v-neck this time - I think my mum made the first shirt into dusters, which is quite a shame really).

Between 1971 and 1974 I was periodically allowed to go to the Lane with my dad and my brothers, but by the time the '74/75 season came along, trips were more frequent, and I was buoyed along by breathtaking performances from Woodward and Currie, and as an aspiring goalkeeper myself, Jim Brown became something of a hero to me, especially when he pulled off a penalty save from John Hollins of Chelsea that defied science... That was our best season in years, as we finished 6th, just one agonising point off Europe (I remember kneeling on the landing and uttering a quick prayer as we listened to the Radio Sheffield reports coming from that last game in Birmingham).

The following season saw me attending almost every home game, and boy, did I suffer. We finished bottom of the old first division, relegation a certainty by Christmas. Not that I was deterred, you understand.

The following season I was a season ticket holder for the first time, and this continued as we spiralled down the divisions. Any Blades that complain about the fare on offer at Bramall Lane these days never watched United struggling to survive in the old third division in 1980/81. When things are looking really bleak, I remember how we lost 1-0 at home to Brentford one cold, cold evening. Or the time we went 2-0 up against Millwall and still lost 3-2...

To me, part of being a Blade is as much about the disasters (losing 4-0 to Wednesday, Boxing Day 1979, relegation with the last kick of the season in both 1981 and 1994, relegation via the play-offs in 1988, losing to Wednesday - sod it, let's call them the pigs! - in a cup semi-final at Wembley in 1993, losing to Palace with the last kick of the play-off final in 1997) as it is about the triumphs (promotion with a 5-2 win at Leicester 1990, clinching the double over the pigs in 1992 by winning 3-1 at Hillsborough, FA Cup Quarter-Final penalty shoot-out wins against Blackburn in 1993 and Coventry in 1998).

And that, dear reader, is what makes us the wonderfully rounded personalities we are...

Why Hitching?

Back in 1984 I was a bit of a hippie. I had all the Gong albums, had just discovered Hawkwind, and wanted to go to Stonehenge Free Festival to see them. Not only that, that festival was the ultimate in hippie festivals, so I had to go. Much to my delight, I discovered that my 'A' levels would all be finished in time for me to go, and a friend of mine called Ben, a black guy who loved progressive rock, was wanting to go too. He was a serial-hitchhiker, and to him there was no other way to travel. If I wanted to go, and go with someone else, then I was going to have to hitch...

My mum wasn't too keen, but as I pointed out, I was 18 now, so could do as I pleased. So off I went.

When I'm feeling all dreamy and philosophical, I refer to my time at Stonehenge Free Festival in 1984 as "the defining moment of my life". And there may be something in that, because seventeen years on I'm still hitching, I still go to the 'Henge for Summer Solstice, and I still love Hawkwind...

Between 1984 and 1988 I hitched here and there, but not too frequently. However in 1988 I left Sheffield, and so hitching activity stepped up somewhat, especially as I never had any money because I was always spending it on records. In the meantime, things had happened with me and the Blades. For the second-half of the 1980s I'd been working in retail, so I worked every Saturday, thus making getting to see United quite hard. Very few matches were attended in this time, and to be honest I was more into my music at the time. But then I got a job in wholesale news (in Barnsley!), and I got Saturdays off. Dave Bassett had just taken over as manager at the Lane (early 1988), and I felt the urge to attend regularly again, so I came back on board just in time to see us go down one more time...

By October 1988 I had moved down south to Brackley in Northants (after two months training down there), and this only served to increase my passion for the Blades. The trouble was I was working back in retail again, so Saturday working reared its ugly head once more. The good thing was, it was convenience retail, and as a deputy-manager then store-manager, I had a say in the days off, so I managed to pick and choose what games I attended (to a certain degree). The increase in wages meant that I got the train up at first, but I soon decided I could buy more records if I hitched again, so in January 1989 I ventured out on my first football-hitch, to watch United draw 3-3 at home with Colchester in a rather bizarre FA Cup fourth round match.

Throughout my ten years living in Brackley, hitching was a regular activity, whether it was to see the Blades (home and away), go to Cardiacs gigs (or on one memorable occasion, the Wizards of Twiddly), or just a shopping trip to Banbury. Why, at one time I was even hitching to and from work every day!

By the time I got to London three years ago (summer 1998) and dipped out of the career rat-race (summer 1999), hitchhiking almost became a profession, especially as I went off to University and became an impoverished student... Mind you, I did have a part-time job with Tesco, and guess what? It involved Saturday working...

However, the last game of the 1999/2000 season saw us at home to Swindon on a Sunday, so off I went. As I looked through the programme, I realised that as a student I could get a very cheap season ticket indeed, so with cash burning a hole in my pocket, I strolled along to the box office at the end of the game and got one for £120! As I wandered light-headed away from the Lane I decided that the only way I was going to be able to do this next season was hitch rather a lot. Oh, and there was the small matter of telling Tesco they couldn't have me on a Saturday anymore...

Besides, thanks to meeting the London Blades, I now had a whole new load of chums to attend games with...

The London Blades and the Internet

In more clichéd moments, people refer to the Internet as being the thing that has changed the way we live our lives the most in recent years. Well, they have a point, especially in my case...

For the first year that I was living in London, I felt like I was the only Blade living there. I knew this couldn't be true, but when you go and watch United at Loftus Road, for some reason you just assume that everyone else has journeyed down from Sheffield. And how can you tell a London Blade anyway?

Anyway, like I said, after a year I ended up at the University of Greenwich studying MultiMedia Technology (as I write, I'm going through the process of transferring courses to Media Culture and Communications, as befits any self-respecting Media Whore), and this course taught me to find my way around a computer, including the wonders of the Internet...

During one late-night session in the library, I was surfing the 'net looking for stuff on Sheffield United when I came across an unofficial site. Included in there was an announcement from one Peter Salt saying that there would be a meeting of the London Blades on such-and-such a date. I'd missed that date, but Peter had an email address, so I mailed him saying I'd be happy to attend future meetings, and telling him a bit about myself...

He emailed me back saying that if I wanted to know when the London Blades were next meeting, I should check out the SUISA site message board, as the London Blades seemed to organise their social life on this.

So off I went to check it out, and sure enough, there was a posting from Peter saying that another London Blade had "crawled out of the woodwork". He went on to tell everyone that I was "Adrian Bell, studying at Greenwich University. Wonder what his alias will be? Greenwich Blade perhaps?"

Seemed good enough to me... I was living in Canning Town at the time, but felt an association with Greenwich would create a slightly friendlier image (anyone that's been to Canning Town will understand) so when I registered, Greenwich Blade it was...

Now, SUISA stood for Sheffield United Independent Shareholders Association, but by the time I came on board (I was never a shareholder by the way) SUISA wasn't exactly active. However, the message board certainly was rather busy, and over the next few weeks I observed from a distance, and marvelled at how a group of football fans could discuss all manner of things from music to politics, and even football from time to time. Some of the arguments that raged were thrilling and at times, bloody. Great stuff!

My first real contribution to a thread came when I hijacked one of Musical Blade's threads (he was inviting people to a gig in Camden, so I figured he was a London Blade), and ended up arranging to meet him and Alty in the World's End (after I rambled on about Industrial Hardcore Jazz for a while).

A fantastic night was had by all, and I realised that here were fellow Blades on a similar wavelength to myself. There soon followed my first London Blades day-out, at Charlton, February 2000 (we lost 1-0). I met most of the London Blades in the St. Christopher Inn, Greenwich, the first to introduce himself being Crouch End Blade who had a video of the League of Gentlemen for me. He called me Greenwich, which surprised me at first, but I soon got used to my new nickname...

Ah yes, Internet aliases... This is basically an adult's excuse to have a nickname, so whereas at school they rejoiced in such names as Belly (or indeed Belch, as I was known to 99% of my school mates), nowadays the aliases are mainly based on more "adult" themes. These are normally taken from where they live (Woodford Green Blade), where they work (Soho Blade), what they do (Musical Blade, Radio Blade), or where they study (Greenwich Blade!).

So, in rather rapid time I became an accepted member of the London Blades (even if I didn't drink) and the benefits were there for all to see. For a start, I had a group of mates to go to games with, something I'd not really had since I'd left school (and certainly not since I'd left Sheffield), then there were the events (such as the magnificent Fulham Monty where Musical booked a boat to take 200 Internet Blades on a cruise up and down the Thames before we watched Fulham stuff United 4-0), the trips to the pub midweek when we had no game, the curries...

Basically, it really is a community - not just the London Blades, but the SUISA and Internet Blades as a whole. The message board enabled me to meet up with Blades from not just all over the country (justoutsidestokeblade, FBFD - that is Fat B*stard From Durham, Stafford Blade, Radford Blade to name but a few), but all over the world (Copenhagen Blade, Kirribilli Blade, Lepps, Asa...). Why, there's even some from Sheffield (Rob, Attila etc).

We got ourselves an Internet Football Team, a regular pre-match pub, and I even got myself a few lifts out of it (Maidenhead, Luton Blade, Musical, Bill...). Hooray for the Internet.

And now you all expect me to give you the address for SUISA, don't you? Well, as of the start of the 2001/2002 season, the SUISA site folded, but the message board carried on in the form of Viewpoints, entirely independent, and providing we've all sent our subs to Webbo (who is also Webmaster for the official Blades site at www.sufc.co.uk), we can all still be found ranting and raving away at www.viewpoints.org.uk so see you there...

Oh, and by the way, I'm not really an anarchist. Voted labour all my life. That was just some tag the naughty London Blades put on me when they found out I went to Stonehenge. And I've *never* had a dog on a string...

Why the Book?

Well, I always thought I had a book in me, most likely to do with being a Blade in exile, but I never quite expected it to be all about one season (with me veering off into the past, like I do). However, after putting my first adventure up on the SUISA message board about the Preston match, the response was rather good. All the postings in reply were encouraging, and I started to get emails from Blades far and wide saying how much they enjoyed reading it and subsequent tales.

At the next home game, Alty suggested I should bring out the collected season's scribings as a book, and Halfway, aka Andy Nic, suggested likewise, offering another outlet for my tales via www.thebladesonline.com.

So the seed was planted, and it gave me something to focus on as I toiled my way up and down the motorways of England through the winter.

And this, kind people, is the result...

Note for Manchester United Fans

I'm sorry if this is confusing for you, but frequently throughout this book I refer to a team just as "United". I do actually mean Sheffield United by this because, you see, where I come from this is how we refer to our beloved team. At the same time, we do realise that there is indeed more than one United in the world, something you'd do well to remember yourselves.

Mind you, we were the first, I believe, so think about that for awhile the next time your team decides it's too big for the FA Cup - you know, that trophy that fans like me would die to see Sheffield United's captain holding aloft...

Prologue
Optimistic Visions of the Future

Saturday 12th August 2000: Sheffield United 2-0 Portsmouth

So, there we were - a happy bunch of London Blades meeting on the platform at St. Pancras station waiting to catch the 10.25am Midland Mainline Express to Sheffield. A new season was starting, and for that one marvellous day we can all allow ourselves to dream that this will be our year. Yep - by May we'd be promoted as champions and have secured both the Worthington Cup and the FA Cup, doing the double over our 'friends' from across the city along the way.

Alty caused the biggest stir by showing up wearing the new home shirt, and we all agreed that it was indeed rather splendid. Real red-and-white stripes for a start, although there were one or two comments that the stripes should be a centimetre thicker, or that the central stripe should be a red one, not a white one, and that collar would be better off round and red. In fact while were at it, let's replace the badge with the old Sheffield coat of arms and have it modelled by either a grey-haired number 7, or leave it untucked and sport flowing blonde locks and a nice big 10... Okay, so it wasn't perfect, but enough of us still made a beeline for the club-shop upon arrival and bought the damn thing...

Anyway, we were an excited crew on the train going up, reading the Guardian (courtesy of Crouch End) and the Mirror (provided by me), generally living it up in First Class... Erm, did I mention first class? Ah yes, you see you could get a pretty good deal from Midland Mainline, and travelling in the posh seats meant we didn't have to mingle with the riff-raff on the way up (apart from when venturing to the buffet bar). The thing is, one or two London Blades could remember where I was last May Day - ah yes, that was it, coming face to face with a riot shield at Trafalgar Square... What's more, many had read of my adventures hitchhiking to United matches in Flashing Blade, and before too long, comments were made...

"Some anarchist hitchhiker you are, travelling first class on the train!" exclaimed Soho.

So I looked out of the window, saw that the weather was fine, realised that there would only be a few weeks of fair-weather hitching available, looked at the fixture list and decided there and then that if I was indeed the greatest hitchhiker of all time, then Preston away was the time to prove it! But for now I wasn't about to take up the London Blades' challenge of getting off at Loughborough and thumbing-it the rest of the way.

"Look, I'm going to hitch to Preston next week, and I'll write all about it on SUISA. Satisfied?" I countered.

It kept them all quiet for a while, anyway...

Just to jeopardise my image even further, upon arrival in Sheffield I was seen getting into a taxi heading for the ground with three other London Blades. Like children let loose in a sweetie shop, we ran amok in the Blades Superstore, myself and Lords purchasing new home shirts (Lords even had his alias printed on the back of his - I preferred not to, as Greenwich has far too many letters), Crouch End (CEB to his Internet chums) was seen discreetly buying a purple-and-gold away shirt (and asking for a plain brown bag to carry it in) whilst Wimbledon bought everything in the shop with the words Sheffield, United or Blades on it...

On the pitch we all felt that United promised much, but as ever with the Blades gave not quite so much. Ahead 1-0 thanks to a Dev penalty, we should have been streets ahead, but with twenty minutes to go United decided to make a game of it, allowing Portsmouth to get a few shots in and look a lot better than they really were. Musical commented that for some reason we'd all missed this for three months, and surely we would have replied, but we were all too busy chewing our nails.

Then on the break, a lucky deflected own-goal sealed it for the Blades, and we all legged it back to the station, safe in the knowledge that the treble was still on, as was our aim to win all 46 league games.

Not even a wet-tissue fight with some bratty Pompey kids (wound up by the North London Blade) could dampen our enthusiasm, or the delay whilst the driver repaired a flat tyre (well, that was how the NLB reported it to us as he leaned out the window dragging on a fag).

Myself, I had to make the most of the fun, as I figured that I wouldn't be on the train very often for the rest of the season. Even if my fellow Blades weren't giving me such flak, I'd already decided at the start of the season that as a poor student with a season ticket, the only way I could afford to get through this season was by upping the hitching-ante...

And so I relaxed in the bar at St. Pancras with the LBs, before popping into the Stratford Tandoori on the way home. I polished off a Phal before retiring to my bed, dreaming of Lee Sandford struggling with all three trophies at the end of the season, dropping the Worthington Cup whilst behind him Neil Warnock was heard to say to the press, "We owe our success to our wonderful fans, especially those nutters that travel long distances, and can I just say that the standard of refereeing in this division is second to none..."

Hmmm...dream on!

Chapter 1
First Class Anarchist

Saturday 19th August 2000: Preston North End 3-0 Sheffield United

On the way up to the Portsmouth game, travelling first class on the train, I kept having feelings of guilt, reinforced by the London Blades asking me if the Anarchists' Society knew about this... And I thought to myself, "Am I not the greatest hitch-hiker in the known universe?" And verily the answer came to me through the trumpeting of the Star Wars theme.

"Yea, Greenwich, thou art. Now get off your fat lazy student backside and prove it once more..."

Trouble was, I didn't finish work until 10:30 Friday night, and previous attempts to hitch on a Saturday have proved difficult. There was only one thing for it, so straight after my shift I emerged from the Tesco staff toilets resplendent in my shiny new Blades top. It drew gasps of delight from the checkout chicks... (Perhaps I imagined this?).

The main problem that my bizarre start-time brought about was that it ruled out the attendance of the delightful Czech girl Andrea 2 (I know four of them, so I have to number them). She couldn't guarantee she'd leave the pub on time, and my other suggestion of a 6am start met with a vigorous shake of the head...

So I was on my own (again... sniff) and without a coat as well (hope my mum doesn't read this). You see, it would appear that some errant Eastern European had borrowed it... don't know why - it was held together with gaffa tape. I'd just have to hope it didn't rain...

I was at Brent Cross for midnight and within 15 minutes I had my first lift, with a Newcastle fan.

"I only picked you up 'cos I thought you were a Mackem!" he announced rather worryingly (I suspect he won't be the only person to be fooled by our new red and white shirts).

Anyway, he turned out to be a thoroughly decent sort with no violent tendencies, and he dropped me at Watford Gap.

Now, I've never had a wait of less than an hour at the Gap, and this was no exception. Indeed it was virtually on the stroke of my 60th minute that some podgy Scottish guy with hiccups in a Mini (the car variety, not a skirt, you sexual deviants!) drew up and beckoned me in. After listening to me whining on for five minutes about suffering as a Blade he said, "You think you've got problems? I'm a Hamilton Accies fan!"

We talked about 15 point deductions for a while, and then I cheered him up by reminding him of when they knocked Rangers out of the cup. He was on his way to Manchester, so at 4:30am he dropped me at Knutsford Services on the

M6. I'd always intended to make this my stop-off point, and I thought 4:30 was quite reasonable.

I wandered into the services and saw two drongos snoozing in Burger King, so I decided to sleep outside as I didn't want to be associated with them (I'm a high-class vagrant you know!). So I found a nice clump of trees and crawled into my sleeping bag... I slept soundly for 3 hours, but was rudely awakened at 7:30 by a torrential downpour, which was so heavy that not even the trees could protect me. I hastily packed my sleeping bag, and then stood under an extra-bushy tree until the rain eased off.

After an hour or so sat in Burger King waiting for the papers to arrive, I resumed my journey at around 9am, and after five minutes was delighted to get a lift with two Brummies (a father and son) who were on their way to see Rangers. They had season tickets for both Birmingham and Rangers (talk about mixing pleasure with pain!), which I did find a little hard to understand, and I was still trying to get my head round it when they dropped me off at the Preston turn-off of the M6. It started to rain again, and I began to wish I'd bought one of those trendy (!) raincoats I'd seen at Knutsford...

But fear not! Help was at hand... a car pulled into a lay-by, and the chappie offered me a lift to the ground. I'd just sent a text message to Musical asking where he was... "Come on, hurry up... I'm in Preston already! Greenwich." And it wasn't even 10 o'clock...

So, I got talking to this guy who was a PNE fan, and when he heard me say "London Blades" he asked if I contributed to "that SUISA site".

I owned up, admitting to being Greenwich Blade, and nearly fell out of the car when he said he'd worked with Soho Blade and had just sent an email to Musical telling him which pubs to go in at Deepdale.

So we stopped off at the ground and I sheltered from the rain in the club shop sporting my red and white stripes. Twice it was suggested that I buy a nice PNE anorak, and twice I told them not to be so cheeky.

Anyway, when Andy (the PNE fan) had bought his stuff, he gave me a lift into town and I purchased a Mac-In-A-Sac, and you guessed it - the rain ceased and we basked in glorious sunshine for the rest of the weekend!

I wandered around town and saw all it had to offer in about 10 minutes. Grim... I sent a text to Musical telling him and Woodford Green Blade to meet me in the customer lounge in the station where I would be attempting to grab some sleep.

And so 2 hours later Woodford Green and Musical entered the lounge, and I would have been raised from my slumbers to the strains of "Na na na na, he's a Blade and he's a Blade" if I hadn't already been awake. Sleeping in a room full of disgruntled Scots ain't easy...

We then got a taxi to the Sumners Pub where drinks and food were consumed with no unwanted interference from the locals.

At the ground we met Halfway Blade and Hanging On To Harry and in we went. I got in for £7 after establishing that students qualified for concessions, and Musical did the decent thing and relinquished his lofty seat in the stand to be with us proles below.

The match has been well documented elsewhere, but it really was a rare treat! I'd just got a text from a friend, Alex, after I'd told her we were 3-0 down. She said "Don't worry, things can only get better!" at which point Dev and Warnock both received their marching orders.

My response of, "No they won't! 1 player and 1 manager sent off!" apparently had her in tears she laughed so much.

At the end of the game I stood near the tunnel and told the ref and linesman how much I'd enjoyed their performance and then headed home.

Musical and Woodford Green had already run off to get the train, so I ran the gauntlet of laughs and taunts alone as I walked to the M6.

My first lift was with a Man Utd-supporting Dingle and his grandson, neither of whom I could understand.

One service station later I was in a car with a chap on his way to Stoke who got United and Wednesday mixed up and had no sense of direction. After one wrong turning too many, I erred on the side of caution and got out at Sandbach Services where I stood around until 8pm, growing ever-more irate at the amount of coaches full of Liverpool fans heading AWAY from Merseyside to places like Kent. Remember, they were the ManUre of the 80s...

Eventually an Everton supporting truck-driver picked me up and set me down at Corley Services. By now getting to London was out of the question, and I was hoping to make last orders at the Plough in Brackley instead. An almost instantaneous lift with a couple of Baggies fans revived this hope, especially as they dropped me at Rothersthorpe Services on the M1/A43 just 18 miles from said boozer just after 10pm.

The lift that brought me to the Plough was with a complete weirdo (rather worryingly). After asking me if I lived on my own and if I was married, I talked about the GIRLS I was meeting in the pub rather a lot, just to let him know where my persuasions lay. When he started to ask if it was only girls I was meeting in the pub, and did they have boyfriends, I realised that this freak was going to try and join me in the pub, thus totally cramping my style. So I told him that if it was anything like the old days "there'd be lots of blokes in there too..."

I got him to drop me off at a roundabout a mile from the pub just to stop him from following me in, and then had to leg it up the hill to get there for last orders! Amongst others, I was delighted to meet Princess Blade (Leah - not a Blade as such, but she did come to three London games with me last season) in the Plough...

So, I ended up staying for a very pleasant weekend in Brackley (unintentional visits are always the best!), before boarding a train in Banbury on Monday afternoon which took me all the way to Marylebone on a very special offer available only to members of the anarchists' society...

Top weekend, and a special thank-you to the Blades defence for doing such a good job of trying to ruin it... for 90 minutes, boys, you succeeded!

Chapter 2
Crates of Stella and Killer Phals...

Tuesday 22nd August 2000: Sheffield United 6-1 Lincoln City (Worthington Cup 1, first leg)

Missed this one. Typical really, we score 6 and I'm sat at home having to watch it on Ceefax, having only just finished my shift at Tesco. But don't worry folks - having studied United's fixture list, plans were already afoot to drop Tuesday evenings.

Saturday 26th August 2000: Sheffield United 2-0 Tranmere Rovers
Monday 28th August 2000: Watford 4-1 Sheffield United

Well, it would seem we could be onto something here, folks. Judging by the response I got from my Preston travelogue, it would seem most of you enjoyed my ramblings, and the thing is, me being me, I intend to get to the games by similar means throughout the season (although whether I'll be so happy to sleep rough in January remains to be seen). The other thing is, even when I do go to a match by conventional methods, things always seem to happen... Whatever, I was expecting an action-packed weekend, what with Tranmere at home on the Saturday and a London Blades outing at Watford on Bank Holiday Monday.

So, back to last Friday evening... Once more I found myself sitting at the checkout at Tesco until 10:30pm, but this time I planned to go to the pub with some of the female checkout staff when I'd finished. Trouble is, they'd moved on by the time I went looking for them, so I decided to just head for Brent Cross rather than forlornly wander around Liverpool Street looking like Billy No-Mates.

As I'd disappeared underground it was very humid, but on emerging at Brent Cross a fair old wind had whipped up, and what's more, lightning was illuminating the sky. I couldn't remember ever hitching in a thunderstorm before, and I didn't really want to start now. However, as I went under a foot-bridge, the rain started and boy, did it come down! At least my Mac-in-a-sac was getting used this time...

Once the rain stopped I ventured off again, but got caught once more so had to seek shelter under another bridge. If this carried on it was going to take me all night just to get to the M1. Anyway, it stopped and held off long enough for me to make it to the start of the motorway for bang on midnight.

My first lift was with an Italian guy whose English was not exactly brilliant, so I had to listen very carefully. I established that he liked football, but no team in particular, and he didn't have much of an opinion on Euro 2000 as he'd missed most matches due to working late as a chef. As he dropped me off near Luton Airport, he gave me his card and suggested I pop in for a feast sometime, but as I'm not much of a pizza man, I'll just give him a free plug on here...

"Eat nosh at Charlie's Pizza, 12 High Street, Hornsey, London N8, 0208 341 6257." There you go...

Next, it was just a short lift to Toddington Services where I found it a little unnerving to hitch right opposite the police station. It was now about 1:15am, and thankfully the law had better things to do than bother me, as one vanload of police and one car drove past whilst one copper sat in the window but didn't look at me once. Fine by me...

On the sign behind me someone had written, "Happy Birthday Q Mum!" You can be sure that it wasn't me... Anyway, one thing I found out whilst waiting here was that the lights in the ground illuminating the sign were brilliant for drying my wet rucksack. So, as I was stood there with steam pothering off my baggage, I noticed a figure running towards me across the petrol forecourt. The chap told me that they were only going as far as junction 16 but I was welcome to a lift. Never one to turn down a lift, and realising I could get to 15A, Rothersthorpe Services, I accepted. Trouble was the van had the words JESUS ARMY all over it. I feared the worst (I really wasn't up to a theological debate at that time in the morning), but all credit to them, they didn't once try to convert me, but rather they seemed quite happy to chat about football. I guess they just want to be nice to everyone...

At Rothersthorpe my sign saying SHEFFIELD emerged from the bag for the first time, and after a slow start (I had time to write "Greenwich Blade On Tour" and "Come On You Red and White Wizaaaards!" on the signpost) it paid off as two chaps from Swinton (the Rotherham version) pulled up in their little van and offered me a lift to the Sheffield Parkway.

"It's full in the back, but you should be able to find room," said the driver. It was a small Escort-sized van, and as he opened the back, I saw about fifty cases of beer, of which around thirty were Stella!

"Help yourself to a beer," he added kindly. I pointed out that I didn't drink but thanks anyway, and I wondered what the outcome would've been if he'd made the same offer to Musical...

The small space at the back was roughly Greenwich sized (me, not the place, you fool!), and there were a few blankets, so I settled down and had a lovely snooze. The next thing I know he was opening the back of the van and I was at the M1 end of the Sheffield Parkway at about 4 o'clock.

Ten minutes hitching here and I had a lift into Sheffield, or so I thought. I mean, I was quite happy with that, but as we chatted it became apparent that this chappie was i) a Blade and ii) lived on the same road as my mum and dad. Incredible...

And so by 4:30 I was pulling up outside my parents on Struan Road, and hoping that the caravan door was open. You see, I'd warned my mum I'd probably arrive at some unearthly hour, so I'd requested she leave the caravan door unlocked. She'd obliged, and a comfortable kip was to be had! Well, it beat Knutsford Services anyway...

What with breakfasts and beds and showers, the hardened traveller image was once more blown to pieces, but at least I regained some credibility by walking all the way to the Earl to meet those that travelled up on the train. A very pleasant hour-and-a-half was spent in the company of Radio, Alty, Soho (nice oven gloves!), Wimbledon, Woodford Green, Silent, Shiny, Rob and some bloke from Portsmouth (I told him he was two weeks late). It turned out he was on holiday in Matlock, and had decided to spend his afternoon watching the Blades. Good man! I also met justoutsidestokeblade for the first time.

Highlights of the match? Chicken Balti pies, Soho telling me I was "so Bourgeois" for sitting in the South Stand, the Bladettes, Dev running rings (literally) round the opposition (and receiving applause from sections of the crowd when he ventured near, like a cricket crowd applauds a wicket-taker as he goes to field on the boundary at the end of an over)...

We scored 2 but could have had 7, and this week's brawl only involved about 7 players as opposed to last week's free-for-all at Preston.

Afterwards I took the safe option of stopping over at my parents', and hitched back on Sunday afternoon. I cheated though, by getting my dad to give me a lift to Woodall Services. Woodall at 3:30pm, Swiss Cottage, London for 6:30pm! Pretty impressive hitch, eh? It was all one lift too, with a chap from Newcastle who'd recently won £250,000 as part of a lottery syndicate (and he had the newspaper cutting to prove it, with his photo). He'd invested his winnings in property, and is currently renting out 5 houses to students, at the same time as ignoring his ex-girlfriend's pleas for reconciliation! Class...

For Watford I employed more conventional modes of travel - the bus, the underground and the train. I mean, I could've hitched, but... well, for a start I had to meet the London Blades in the Fanfare and Firkin in Carnaby Street at midday.

And what a goodly gathering it was too! At one point I counted up 21 of us, but it could've been more. At some point two lovely young ladies (Sara and Beccy) whom I met at Stonehenge over Summer Solstice joined me. They were in London for the weekend, but sadly had 2 blokes with them. Ah well! I tried to get them to join us for the match, but they declined, and I guess you could say they were spared (but then what better introduction to life as a Blade than a 4-1 defeat away from home?).

And so we left the pub after a couple of hours and headed to Euston where we realised we had 3 minutes to board the train. Too late to buy tickets, but then the nice lady on the platform told us we could buy tickets on the train (well, some of us had travelcards, which would get us so far anyway...). Perhaps she told us to wait in the first carriage, but we must have misheard her as we all sat in first-class (as some of us have become accustomed) and no-one came. We thought our luck had run out however at the station, but we reckoned without an employee on the barrier who chose to look away as 20-odd London Blades passed through. We wanted to pay, but they just didn't give us the opportunity...

There was time for a swift one in some Weatherspoon's pub (recommended to us by some Watford fans we'd seen on the train on the first day of the season) before resuming our long march to the ground. Outside the ground I was delighted to find out that we didn't need to walk round the allotments anymore, and also we were being filmed by the Old Bill. Perhaps my tactic of pulling out "Football Hooligans; Knowing the Score" and reading it in front of them explained why we had the Plod sat behind us all throughout the game, and why they escorted us from the ground to the pub and then from the pub to the station afterwards. Thanks lads (and I hope the BBC didn't rip the town to shreds whilst the Law spent all their time shadowing us).

So, it was another show of defensive prowess from the Blades. I really thought when Quinny stuck that equaliser in (and what a beauty it was, eh folks?) that we were going to get something from this one. Ah well...

Entrance fee was justified not just by Quinny's goal, but by N6's rantings at the linesman about the offside rule.

During the walk from the betting booth to our seats we'd somehow got split into two factions, and after the game we failed miserably to get back together (well, some of us did, some of us didn't...), but one quick phone-call from Alty told us we needed to head back to that very same boozer as we'd been in before. Trouble is this time the bouncers refused to let me in with my Blades shirt on. I managed to wave to the rest of the boys inside, and Radio came to my rescue.

"Is it all reyt if he puts my jumper on, mate?" he asked. The bouncers nodded, and with jeers and cries of, "Let him keep his shirt on!" from passing Watford fans I put on said article of clothing. Upon entering the establishment I was subject to much ridicule.

Musical: "I never thought I'd see the day! Greenwich in designer gear..."

Apparently I was modelling Paul Smith... Upon leaving the pub I returned said article to Radio only to drop it, causing Radio much anguish and the Bobbies in the van much mirth...

Back at the station we (mostly) wussed it and bought real tickets (well, sort of), but we still rebelled by sitting in first class.

At Euston we stepped off the train and fell into the first pub we saw (the Royal George I believe). The vague plan was to watch the piggies on Sky and to have a curry, but we weren't sure in what order. Nothing ever got decided as every time someone suggested we move on, about five others had just bought another pint. The clincher was when we discovered the boozer didn't have Sky (even though they had a poster up advertising live football, one of the listed games being that evening's piggies v Blackburn game), so we upped and offed to the next pub down the road, the Prince Charles. However, the bar-lady said they weren't having it on because she didn't want loads of people coming in as she was on her own.

"You won't get loads of people! It's only Wednesday!" I pointed out helpfully, but to no avail. Then as we trooped off up the road Musical called us back saying he'd sweet-talked her into putting it on (still don't know what he promised her...).

An audible groan went up when we saw that the piggies were winning. Mind you, we cheered Blackburn on, and I'm sure they must have felt our support, thereby making their equaliser inevitable. I think the pub regulars were shocked by the cheer that went up when it hit the net, including the QPR bore that kept coming to bother me. ("Why don't you ask someone else that, as you've asked me the same question three times now?" snapped the only mature student amongst us.)

Sat in the pub with us were two Watford fans with their Blackburn supporting son. Forgetting the earlier result, I thanked them for Tony Currie, Stewart Scullion, Dave Bassett and Keith Eddy, but not Terry Garbett. Musical joined in, and we added David Holdsworth and Tony Agana to the "thanks for" list.

"Blimey! Have you got any more?" asked Musical.

Our final port of call was the Indian, except it was too far to walk, so we settled for a nearby Nepalese which looked good (it did Phal, so I was happy). By this time we were down to eight; myself, Musical, Ex-Wolves (now Hammersmith), Exiled Coal Astoner, Murdoch's Neighbour, Radio, Woodford Green and Windy (who'd spent all night saying she wasn't going to come for a curry with us - welcome to the London Blades Windy!). And yes, it's true, we did refuse to eat off blue and white plates!

Okay okay, so I was defeated by my Phal. I was determined to do it, but I was half way through and had already got through three glasses of Lassi, and it was proving expensive. I was told that if I gave up now they wouldn't think any less of me (most had tried it to see how hot it was) and so I admitted defeat. The waiter just laughed when we asked him if they ate that sort of thing themselves all the time. Alas, I fear it is just silly English people trying to prove a point...

And so it proved to be a twelve-hour binge. A toppermost day-out in top company. Shame about that bit in the middle with twenty-two blokes kicking a ball around on the grass...

Chapter 3
A Trucking Miracle

Tuesday 5th September 2000: Lincoln City 1-0 Sheffield United (Worthington Cup 1, 2nd leg) Sheffield United won 6-2 on aggregate.

Having been at the Oval on the Monday to witness England's heroic cricketers win back the Wisden Trophy from the West Indies, our first series win against them since 1969, I suddenly became a firm believer in miracles. Yes, I set off for Lincoln in the belief that if any club could squander a 5-goal lead, it was to be our brave boys in lilac and gold. Or if we did hang on, maybe an even bigger miracle would occur and we'd go on to win the prized Worthless Cup; or maybe we'd just settle for getting past the 3rd round this time...?

In line with every newspaper on Tuesday morning, I decided to have a quick look back to September 1969, specifically looking at how the Blades fared in that year's League Cup (as it was known then of course). You'll be glad to know that as Geoff Boycott and Ray Illingworth were relaxing after helping England beat the Windies, United were beating Newcastle 2-0 on Sept 2nd (goals from Woodward and Tudor). Following this on Sept 23rd we did Luton 3-0 (goals again from Woody - with two this time - and Tudor). That old familiar pattern soon emerged though, as on Oct 15th Leicester stuffed us 2-0... Have we ever done well in this competition? (Answer... NO!)

I set off with my dad's words ringing in my ears; "Yer daft! I'd give that one a miss if I were you..."

Due to one thing and another, I was later starting than I intended, arriving at the foot of the M1 at Brent Cross by about 1:25pm. I worried that I wasn't leaving much margin for error, as I was expecting it to take me at least 3 lifts to get there, and I was expecting hefty waits in-between. I needn't have worried, because within 20 seconds of setting my rucksack down and sticking my thumb out, a truck pulled up. This is a new record for me, and one that will take some beating!

Anyway, I explained to the driver that I was going to hitch up the M1 to Leicester and then go off up the A46 to Lincoln. The reason I'd not hitched up the A1 from the off was because I'd had bad experience of hitching on here before (see possible Greenwich Hitching Tale From the Archives if I have time - very funny, trust me!) and I figured it would be busier on the M1 anyway. The driver, who was heading for Castleford, just said, "Tell you what, I'll make your hitch a bit easier and we'll go up the A1, and I'll drop you at Newark."

A quick look on the map confirmed that this was only about 20 miles from

Lincoln, so with one very happy Greenwich, the driver re-routed himself round the M25 and up the A1.

There then followed a very entertaining and amusing lift as we swapped stories about hitching/ trucking etc, my favourite being one he told me about one of his mates in a lorry park near Peterborough:

A nice sunny day, trucker sitting outside his cab in just his shorts reading the 'paper and soaking up the sun. Old bloke approaches said trucker and the following conversation ensues...

Old Bloke: "Morning Driver!"
Trucker: "Morning!"
OB: "Lovely day!"
T: "Yes, lovely..."
OB: "This your truck then driver?"
T: "Yes."
OB: "Nice wagon!"
T: "Thanks!"
OB: "Do you want me to toss you off, driver?"
T: "No thanks..."
OB: "Okay... bye then, driver..."

All was reeled off in a matter of fact fashion with no break in the conversation apparently...

The driver had predicted that we would hit Newark at about 4pm, and he was pretty much spot on. With a shake of the hand we wished each other a safe and speedy continuation of our journeys, and I found myself wandering along to the A46 roundabout pondering what to do next. The sign said I was a mere 16 miles from Lincoln, and I was feeling a tad hungry. Up ahead I could see a Burger King, and I was just about to cross the road and enter when I noticed a car parked in a lay-by. The window was down and the driver was shouting something to me:

"Do you want a lift to the match?" he repeated on request.

I needed no further encouragement and hastily jumped in. It turned out he was a Blade who lived in Dinnington but was doing some work in Derby. He had friends in Lincoln (with whom he'd sat for the first leg), so he was visiting them first before going on to the game (and once again he was going to be sat in the Lincoln end). He'd spotted my Blades shirt, and whilst being a little surprised to see one by the A46 at four in the afternoon, felt the only thing to do was drive me into the city.

So, there I was; 4:30 and 3 hours to kill in Lincoln. I wandered into HMV and within seconds was accosted by an employee. It turned out he was an exiled

Blade and we had a good old chat. I began to wonder if I was going to meet any Lincoln fans in this place...

After that, I strolled to Burger King where the obligatory Double Whopper with Cheese satisfied my hunger. I then bought a postcard with a picture of a house on it. Underneath were the words "Margaret Thatcher's Birthplace". It was despatched forthwith to one of my Labour supporting friends back home, knowing I would make his day...

I then decided to take a stroll up the hill to the cathedral. You see, I'd visited this when I was about five-years old, and in a work-book at school we were asked what the tallest building we'd been in was. I put down Lincoln Cathedral, but then the next question was asking how many storeys it had. I'd put that it had just one, but worried (as only a kid can) that the teacher would never believe that it was therefore the tallest. I decided to go in again, 29 years later, just to satisfy myself that it really was as big as I remember it.

First though I had to negotiate the hill. Very steep, I can tell you, but the rewards were there, as I found the building absolutely breathtaking. It is hard to imagine how they built such things way back when, and it came as no surprise to read that in its present form it took 100 years to construct.

On the way out I picked up leaflets in different languages for all my foreign chums (i.e. Czech, German and Norwegian... thoughtful aren't I?).

By the time I came out it was well past 6 o'clock so I headed in a straight line for the ground. Somewhere at the bottom of the hill the team coach drove past, and I managed a brief smile in their direction (jumping up and down and waving my arms at my age just isn't on...).

Once in the ground (only £8 - those student concessions again folks!) I had a nice chat to the stewards who thought I was mad to hitch all the way from London (to add to this notion, one girl at work, the lovely Katrina, called me a "nutter", to which I replied that no, I was just an enthusiast...). Then as I settled in my seat, I was surprised to see how many other Blades were turning up. By kick-off it appeared that we outnumbered the home fans, but it was difficult to tell as they were spread round three sides. There were only 1,379 in total anyway, amongst which I met Hanging On To Harry (aka Nick), Halfway Blade, Halfway's son Aaron, and the wonderful Sandra.

We settled down to watch 90 minutes of thrilling entertainment. However what we got was... Well, their equivalent of the Bladettes (the Impettes?) were quite nice, although I guess they felt a bit silly performing to almost empty stands. And as for their mascot... the scariest I've ever seen. Unsettled me throughout, I can tell you. "It" is called the Poacher, and you have the chance to sponsor its kit. Unsurprisingly it had a full column of "availables" (matched only by the mysterious player, YTS), which is understandable if part of the deal is that your sponsored player visits you at work. It'd scare the life out of the office junior...

So, another memorable away performance. So much for turning up in the hope of seeing the Blades only away win of the season, eh Halfway? Still, I wouldn't have wanted to be anywhere else... nurse!!!!

Afterwards Nick, Halfway and entourage gave me a lift to the M1 via a pub (we went round the roundabout three times, once to establish there was a pub there, once to make sure it allowed kids in, and finally to find the way to drive in!). More than once they offered me a bed for the night, but I politely declined, saying I'd rather get a move on that night (although really it was my sense of adventure nagging at me - I think I really do need that nurse!).

After thirty minutes stood at junction 31, and with only four vehicles having gone by, I was beginning to regret my decision. Thankfully though, a van stopped and I got a lift to Woodall Services. It was now 1am, and I decided to bed down for the night rather than stand around hitching for hours with the risk of no result. As I sheltered from the rain in the petrol station I noticed someone had discarded his ticket for Leeds v Man City in the bin. £31:50 it cost him to watch his team lose (I'm assuming he was a Leeds fan). Ha!

Meanwhile the Oldham Athletic team coach drew up opposite. At the top of the windscreen was a large advert for Slumberland and a very cosy image of Oldham's players snoozing in the warmth of the coach came into my mind as I settled down behind a giant ad-board and crawled into my sleeping-bag inside my bivvy-bag. The Oldham bus eventually drove off, but in the wind and intermittent showers, this was one image that haunted my dreams throughout the night. Oh to be a pro footballer (even if it is only Oldham).

Dragging myself out of the bag at 8am (after a rather good kip bearing in mind the circumstances) was rather hard, but I managed it and was soon on my way.

After ten minutes waiting a German driver in a huge truck picked me up. It is quite un-nerving for us non-drivers sitting on the right in a cab, especially as when the traffic was going slow he insisted on doing his paperwork. He didn't speak much English either (like, he managed about four words; "London", "ferry", "back", and "Munich"). I worked out he was going round the M25, and he handed me a pen and a map. I interpreted this, correctly, as meaning I had to mark where I wanted to get off, so I put a big cross on Toddington Services...

Other than that I managed to communicate to him that I had "two German girlfriends!" It was too much to explain that one of them was an ex, and the other was a maybe-but-no-guarantee-and-she's-in-Germany-anyway... With appropriate sign language (use your imagination) I got across to him the fact that they were "nice girls!"

So, after the quietest two hours since I found myself with the then-girlfriend (the long-suffering Annie) standing on the Stretford End watching the Blades lose 2-0 to Man U ("If you think we've come all the way to Manchester just to go to the Arndale Centre, think again!"), I hopped out at Toddington and grabbed another Double-Whopper-With-Cheese...

One hour later I started again, and after fifteen minutes of waiting I jumped into yet another vehicle belonging to a German. Clutching my sign saying London, I'd just strapped myself in when the driver said, "But I'm not going into London, only round it, nein?" So I got out and carried on hitching...

Funf minuten later and I was settling into a cab in yet another truck. Considering that of late lifts in lorries have been few and far between, on this trip I'd had three out of five lifts with truckers. What's more, this was another top geezer who changed his route for me. He was supposed to be going round the M25, but said he may just as well go round the North Circular as it'd make "a nice change".

And so exactly 24 hours after starting out, I was back at Brent Cross and heading for the tube. What was the bigger miracle? United through to the 2nd round of the Worthington Cup? Lifts with truckers in broad daylight? Drivers re-routing their journeys? Kindly Blades picking up strays on the A46? Me giving 5p to a back-packing young-lady at the tube station? (Well, she was young, foreign and attractive.) The Blades losing away from home to lesser opposition?

Welcome to reality...

Chapter 4
Crisis? What Crisis?

Saturday 9th September 2001: Birmingham City 1-0 Sheffield United
Tuesday 12th September 2001: Wolverhampton Wanderers 0-0 Sheffield United

Two away matches in the Midlands so close together? For me personally, marvellous, but as the Blades somewhat disastrous away form was beginning to take on crisis proportions, it didn't look good. But no fear; I'd been happy about this long weekend since I'd first studied the fixtures whilst at Glastonbury. I was in the company of a young lady called Debbie, and she was complaining that I never came to visit her in Birmingham, whereas she'd headed London way on numerous occasions. So out came the hastily-removed-from-the-Mirror fixture list that was hiding in my wallet, and I was delighted to see we had these two fixtures in her area, and so early in the season too. I announced that I would be spending some time in Birmingham around the 9th September and for a "few days afterwards", and she seemed quite happy (maybe her senses were dulled?).

The downside was I had unpleasant memories of my last visit to St Andrews, back in 1996. I'd found myself at the wrong end of the ground and was crossing at a zebra with my lovely yellow away shirt slightly drawing attention to myself. At the other side of the crossing was a massive Brummie wearing a tent of a blue shirt and a scowl. Every time I tried to walk round him, he just moved his belly a little, and I kept walking into it.

"You're not f****** coming down here!" he politely intoned.

"So where can I go?" I asked, trying oh so hard not to sound clever.

"You're not f****** coming down here!" he repeated.

"Which way then?" I tried again.

His response? "You're not f****** coming down here!" this time accompanied with a finger pointing back up the road.

I thanked him for his help (I really did as well!), and headed away from the ground.

Walking up the hill a bloke with his young son said to me, "You're going the wrong way! The away end is back down here and up there..."

"Ah yes," I explained, "this big bloke just told me, er, not to go down there and er, I sort of thought I'd do as he suggested..."

"Follow us!" said the chap, and they smuggled me through to the away end. In the space of 5 minutes I'd come across the best and worst sort of fans...

Thoughts about this and other things went through my head as I sauntered up to Brent Cross at 9:50 am Saturday morning...

I'd intended to set off much earlier, like the night before for example, but a Mr Bungle gig at the Astoria put paid to this, mainly because I knew the friendly security there would not wave me through with my bigger-than-usual rucksack (they once forced me to take off my Blades woolly hat before they let me in). So there I was, not very early on Saturday morning, worrying that I may have left it a bit late. I needn't have worried...

Within 10 minutes I had a lift with a Kosovan guy and his delightful Romanian girlfriend (that purple top, the black bra-strap, her ample bosom... sigh!) The best thing was he was going all the way to Manchester, so I knew I was going to be in spitting distance of Birmingham. What I didn't expect was him to take me all the way into the city centre. It was before midday, and I was already in Birmingham. He got out of the car to get something to eat, so as I said goodbye I kissed his girlfriend on the hand (such a charmer), and she said I was "one of the nice people!"

She then asked me if I had any money, which, after my initial panic, was just her wanting to make sure I was all right for dosh. Aw, bless!

My early arrival meant I had time to find Debbie's house, dump my gear and then head back to the ground. Even so, thanks to my decision to walk (and eventually run) from the centre to the ground, I arrived with one minute to spare (shirt well covered up this time). Going through the turnstile in front of me was Puppet with Puppet jnr. It was nice to be recognised, but it took a while for me to register who he was thanks to the shades (sorry Puppet, but those Deathtrash gigs were a long time ago!).

I asked my usual question about concessions for students, and nearly had heart failure when I was told it was £1 for students. £1!!! Very happy...

Once in I met Radio and Stow with one of Stow's mates, and in the ground we were joined by justoutsidestokeblade and josb jnr. With my red and white stripes now revealed, I was ready...

After recent away atrocities, this was actually quite good. If Dev had been in the side we would surely have got something from it, and Benty was so close at the end. In the end we lost out to a dodgy penalty that went in off the post. Even Puppet was optimistic when I saw him at half-time...

The pain of an undeserved away defeat was tempered somewhat by the news that the piggies had lost 5-0 at home to Wimbledon. Oh dear, how sad!

My trip back to Debbie's was sad but not without optimism. After having a good old chat to a young lady called Stella from Cyprus (the last of the London Blades to feel the pull of Stella?), I was cheered up considerably.

So how to fill the rest of the weekend before the Wolves match? Easy... The Foundry (a rock pub - reminded me of the Wapentake), XLs (a night-club full of vampires, death-heads and fourteen year-old Slipknot fans), the Firkin, the Chinese, a stroll in the park, watching videos, playing with PCs at some uni in Brum with Stella...

By the time I boarded a tram to Wolverhampton from Birmingham Snowhill, the country was in the grip of the fuel crisis. Cars were queuing at every petrol station, and signs announcing lack of petrol were everywhere. Anarchy in the UK...

Still, there were more Blades than I anticipated there, and Shiny had made it up from deepest Gloucester, so mass panic hadn't set in just yet.

And what do you know? Another encouraging performance. A clean-sheet, and an away point, but really I was a touch disappointed, because I think we shaded it. Benty should really have buried that one-on-one, but then it was a good tackle (borne out by the highlights on Central Sports Special that evening). Mr Warnock tried to liven up proceedings with his rant at the officials (much clearer on tele by the way, the naughty boy!). At the time Shiny and I thought that NW was still serving a touchline ban, so we assumed it was Blackwell given his marching orders. This led to speculation about who was now in charge, so I sent a text to Musical saying that Captain Blade was calling the shots from the dugout...

The next morning I bid fond farewells to my charming hostesses Debbie and Stella, and set out on the trek home. Let me tell you something... Birmingham is impossible to escape from! I knew hitching from Spaghetti Junction was a non-starter, so I found a bus route (X80) that seemed to take me out towards a roundabout further down the M6. Fine, except that I waited an hour and a half for the thing and it never came. In desperation I went to an information office

("I want to escape!" I pleaded with the girl; her reply of "Why?" I may consider a classic in later years...), but they couldn't find a timetable.

Eventually a bloke behind a PC sorted me out in New Street Station, and you guessed it, there was one (yes ONE) X80 a day. And it had departed ten minutes after I'd left the bus-stop...Sigh.

So, plans were changed, and I decided to get a train to Birmingham International, walk to the M42, then aim for the M40. It worked a treat! Traffic was sparse thanks to the fuel shortage, but after a 10-minute wait, I had my first lift at 3:40pm. I was now grateful to the X80 bus for leading me a merry dance, as the small-business owner that picked me up (office interiors apparently) informed me that the M6 was "closed" due to a go-slow protest. As it was we sailed unimpeded down the M42 and M40.

He dropped me off at Cherwell Valley services, where after a call of nature, a Burger King and a quick marvel at the queue of traffic disappearing round the roundabout whilst waiting for petrol, I was mobilised again.

Thirty seconds later, and I had my lift to London. He was a mature student driving down to the Smoke to start the first year of his studies, and despite going into Oxford to pick up his South African friend, we still made very good time. We saw two "slow protests" coming up the A40 the other way, and numerous closed petrol stations, but our lane was clear. I was dropped off at Liverpool Street by 7 o'clock, even having time to pop into my Tesco for a sandwich, and there I saw the beautiful Katrina studiously serving away, looking stern but focussed (and lovely).

As I sat on the train to Stratford I looked out of the window and saw a huge fire at the premises of a scrap metal merchant. With thick black smoke and firemen everywhere, it just added to the feeling that I was in a country that was in the grip of anarchy. I guess I should be happy... Well, stranger things do happen... the Blades getting a point away from home for example.

Chapter 5
Served With Relish

Friday 15th September 2000: Sheffield United 2-0 Blackburn Rovers

I wasn't relishing this trip...

I sat at my PC staring out of the window of Lab 204 at the University of Greenwich, and just hoped it would stop raining. No chance...! It got to the stage where if I didn't leave soon I was never going to get a lift; and what's more, we all know (well I do!), it's much harder to get a lift in the rain...

I ran to the Docklands Light Railway (DLR) station at Cutty Sark, and hoped the rain would have eased off by the time I reached Brent Cross. And you know what? By the time I'd changed to the Northern Line and got out at said station, it was dry. However, upon exiting the newsagents laden with sweets (I'll never grow up) it had started again. Bad...

The result was a thorough soaking as I walked to the start of the M1 at Staples Corner, and no Mac-In-a-Sac was going to save me this time. The lorries rumbling by made it worse, and I had to keep moving to lessen the sprayings I was receiving. Altogether unpleasant, and after twenty minutes I'd take a lift with anyone, even a white-van man wearing a Man Utd shirt who was only going to junction 6 near the M25.

One of the rules of hitching is that you politely decline any lift that will drop you near the M25. It is far better to put that nasty motorway well behind you. But this time I scrambled eagerly in, just glad to be out of the downpour.

For a Man Utd fan he was okay, I suppose. He asked about the upcoming games against the piggies, and asked if I thought the Blades had a chance of the playoffs (me being the optimist I am said that of course we had). Terrible London accent, though... typical ManUre fan

Not long after I found myself at junction 6, and what a terrible junction it was. Not much traffic (not helped by the fuel crisis), and nowhere to pull in, apart from way up the slip road which was too far up really, and would only bring unwanted attention from the plod. As it was, the place I chose was still considered too far up; "Technically you are on the motorway, so you're going to have to move in front of the sign," said a friendly (and I mean that) copper. So forward I went, but still managed to write "Greenwich Blade On Tour" on the back of the afore-mentioned sign.

At least now it was only intermittent showers, but still thoroughly drenched, I didn't feel happy about getting a lift, and as time ticked away, I felt temptation.

"Get thee behind me, Satan," I said, but it was no good. You see, the day before I received an email off Maidenhead Blade saying that if he saw me on the way, he'd pick me up. He left me his mobile number, and so with trembling hands, I broke another unwritten law of hitching. I sent him a text message asking about the possibilities of a lift. If the grassy bank opposite had been full of spectators, they would undoubtedly have started to chant, "Cheat! Cheat! Cheat!" Sorry guys - it had to be done!

To my relief, Maidenhead phoned me back, and the arrangement was that if I was still there in an hour and a quarter, then he'd come by and pick me up. However, it would make life easier if I could get a lift a bit further north.

So I continued hitching, feeling a little more relaxed (but no less wet). I knew it was getting late when busloads of school kids went past. One thing I've noticed down the years - schoolboys will always laugh and point at hitchers, but schoolgirls always wave and giggle. Today was no different. However, before this trip Irish construction workers are something I've only come across once before, but they both asked me the same thing...

Today the Range Rover pulled up just off the roundabout (well, more of a long-a-bout actually), about 50 yards from me. He honked his horn and beckoned me over, and even though he was facing in a different direction, I figured he must have been offering me a lift. I gambolled eagerly up, only for him to say in his Irish tones;

"Would you be looking for some work?"

"No! I'm hitching!" I snapped.

"Where to?" he asked.

"Sheffield... for the football!" as if he was really bothered.

"What do you want to go to the football for?" he asked, but before waiting for my answer, he was off. Git! I was not happy!

At about the time I thought Maidenhead would be approaching, I got a lift. As I scrambled into the car, he phoned anyway, and we established that as the lift I was getting was only going as far as Luton, Maidenhead would pick me up from junction 9.

The lift to Luton was brief but interesting. The guy was Turkish but brought up in Norway. He was married to an English girl and was just selling up his Italian (yes, Italian) restaurant in Watford. Possibly more confusing than Brummies with season tickets for both Birmingham and Rangers...

And so the big cheat took place at junction 9. True to his word, Maidenhead and Maidenhead jnr (the famed Keith Edward, no less, mentioned on the web-talk page in one of last season's programmes) drew up and in I jumped. Identification was easy, as there was an abundance of red and white being worn...

The trip up to Sheffield was effortless. Very little traffic you see. The main topic of conversation was the Blades, naturally...

We arrived in Sheffield at 6pm, so with over an hour to spare, we retired to the Pump where food was ordered. I had steak pie, and I have to say, it was absolutely marvellous, especially smothered in Henderson's Relish. Twelve years away from Sheffield, and I really miss this stuff. I think I'll have a word with Tesco Bishopsgate.

Also in the Pump were Bradway (without sister... shame), Radford and Stafford. All are now claiming that their student days are over, but it didn't stop Stafford from wearing his lovely Stafford Uni anorak (sorry, should that be "bench-coat"?). Meanwhile, Radford was resplendent in his suit and tie. Lose a few more pounds, keep your hair and the Hartson-a-like jibes will be a thing of the past, son!

The walk to the ground was a chilly one, and I was most dismayed to find that paying extra for a South Stand season ticket doesn't mean they switch the heating on. Still, one glimpse of Blades Midas Gold, the new dancing girls, had me feeling much warmer. Very nice, but could it be just because the Sky cameras were present? I suspect that for Colchester on Tuesday, the Bladettes will return from exile, triumphant...

Now, before the game, most people (myself included) would have been happy with us getting a draw, so Alan Kelly's error and David Kelly's persistence had us leaping with glee. I couldn't bring myself to chant, "There's only one Alan Kelly!" though. And Dev's goal? One of the best I've seen at the Lane. Stunning...

We could have gone in at half-time better than two up, but let's not be greedy.

Whilst waiting for the second half to start, my mobile rang, and I was rather shocked to hear my ex, Annie, on the other end of the line. In Bassett's era she used to travel with me to all the games, and it was nice to hear her say, "You know, I never thought I'd say this, but I do actually miss all that."

After the call ended, I thought of her time as an honorary Blade. She started and finished with a 3-2 defeat; first, Norwich away in the Cup in 1989, and last, Chelsea away in 1994 for the last game of the season and our last in the Premier...

The second half we defended well, so we all left the ground glad of heart. I made the decision to head back with Maidenhead down the M1, and got dropped off at Toddington Services. Here it was bitterly cold and there was still rain in the air, so at 1am, I bedded down for the night under some stairs. My sleeping bag was warm, but I found it hard to get comfortable. Sleep of sorts was grabbed, but at 6am this cleaner guy woke me up saying I'd better move before management came. He was perfectly decent about it, so I was more than happy to roll up my bag, pack and move on.

Waiting for a lift was cold and miserable however, and well over an hour I had to wait before one came along. It was worth it, though, as the trucker went round the M25 clockwise and down the M11, dropping me off in East London at a DLR station. One problem, though; that section of the DLR was closed due to weekend engineering work, and I spent longer walking around in the cold trying to find the replacement buses than I had in my last lift! In the end, I saw a bus heading for Stratford, jumped on it and headed home.

I ended up spending most of the day asleep, waking up in time to hear that the piggies were losing 1-0 to Tranmere. The final score of 2-0 to Tranmere completed a perfect footballing weekend. Then a splendid evening and Sunday lunchtime spent in the company of some German girls I'd met on the DLR two days previously only improved it further. Being told my boots were the sort worn by soldiers who "jump out of aeroplanes with umbrellas" and that I was behaving "like a virgin" (we were in McDonalds at the time before you get any ideas) topped my weekend off brilliantly. Tanja, Melanie, Mirjam and Christina found themselves right up there with Dev and Murph this weekend. Ah yes, one to relish all right...

Chapter 6
Washed Out

Tuesday 19th September 2000: Sheffield United 3-0 Colchester United (Worthington Cup 2, 1st leg)

I stood in the queue in Boots (in boots) waiting to pick up my photos whilst the woman in front complained bitterly.

"Why is the colour so washed out?" she repeated again and again, with the odd, "The colour is so... washed out!" thrown in for variation. After listening to her desperate attempt at getting off paying for ten minutes, even I was starting to get impatient. I had a very important second round Worthington Cup match to get to, against Colchester no less. More than that, I wanted to get there before the rain started. Too bad...

As I emerged from Brent Cross tube, the heavy drizzle looked set. I popped into Tesco to grab food and a piece of cardboard (I'd forgot my trusty SHEFFIELD/ LONDON sign) and was surprised to see that once again panic was setting in at the petrol pumps. Some poor section managers were standing around in yellow coats trying to control the rumour-fed hoards, and I remembered exactly why it was that I'd stepped down from my lofty position as a section manager within that very organisation over two years ago now... One of them looked at me and said, "There's got to be something more important than queuing for petrol in the rain!"

"Aye... I've got to hitch to Sheffield in it. That's more important!" I replied. By the time I reached Staples Corner and the foot of the M1, I was already a little damp, but at least it was less of a downpour than my previous soaking on the way to the Blackburn match. The best thing of all, though, was that I only had to wait two minutes for a lift. 2:02pm and I was on my way. He was only able to drop me off at Toddington Services, but in the rain you take a lift anywhere, and at least this one was taking me beyond the M25.

He was a young chap who'd studied at an agricultural college, but ended up working as an engineer for a company that specialised in little plastic things printed by computers (or something). He drove all around the country from his base in Bedford and seemed happy with his life now he was settled with his girlfriend. Very sweet, but I'd still rather be in my position (honest).

Anyway, he'd heard the rumours about new oil blockades, so he decided to err on the side of caution by queuing for petrol at London Gateway. We sat there for fifteen minutes, but as we reached the pumps and the chap asked where to go for diesel, he was told that there was "no diesel for light vehicles, so could you move on please." Fifteen minutes wasted, then.

I remembered hearing on Radio Five-Live that the rain would spread north as the day progressed, so it was no surprise to find the deluge following us up the motorway. He dropped me at Toddington, and by now it was considerably heavier. Luckily I was waiting only another 2 minutes here before a business type stopped and told me he was heading up to Leeds, but he would pop into Sheffield on his way to pick up stuff he needed for his presentation the following day. Yes!!! (I wasn't there for long, but I did notice that the graffiti on the sign said 'God bless Q Mum', and was not wishing her a happy birthday as previously stated... sorry for this vitally unimportant mis-information.)

As we drove up, the conversation went from politics to the Internet to music (football was ruled out due to him being a rugby fan). He'd been a card-carrying Labour Party member all his life, having attended marches with his long-haired hippie friends in the 1970s (he owned up to possessing Yessongs, so I confessed too, but hey, I don't mind admitting that I love Yes!). To give me an idea of the sort of stuff he was buying now, he pulled a CD out. I looked at his balding, grey hair and said, "Well, I didn't have you down as a Rammstein fan!" Impressed I was... far too often I've been given lifts by similar types who listened to cutting edge stuff in the seventies (and I'm thinking more King Crimson and Henry Cow here), but now found Eric Clapton more to their liking.

This top fellow ended up driving me all the way into Sheffield, dropping me off just down from Lady's Bridge. Five o'clock and London to Sheffield in 3 hours. A new Greenwich record; shame about the rain...

I sought shelter in a phone box and phoned my mum.

"Get t'dinner on. I'm in Sheffield!" I announced, so my dad picked me up and I was able to tuck into some lovely home cooking.

My dad even gave me a lift to the Lane, but couldn't be persuaded to sit with me in the stand. Neither could many others, as just 3500 turned out, but then no one was surprised. The programme seller even asked me if I wanted to buy his whole bag for £2.

I met Halfway, NickBlade and Sandra (definitely NOT Halfway's nan!), and we settled in for a wet one. I don't think I've seen conditions that bad at the Lane, with football becoming more and more difficult as the game progressed, especially on the South Stand wing in the second half. Gus (Goooooose!) especially made a few big splashes, and once when coming to rest having surfed off the pitch, somewhat resembled a beached whale. The United bench manned the lifeboats, and Goose was winched back into play.

Without a doubt had Lua Lua been playing for Colchester, we would have struggled, but at the end, with 2 late goals and the rain still coming down, at least we could feel optimistic about the second leg. 3-0 though, a tad flattering...

Halfway dropped me off at the M1 end of the Parkway, and I hastily pulled on my old yellow away shirt to increase my visibility. It worked as I immediately got a lift with an old Blade driving back to Nottingham. He'd moved there from Sheffield in 1966, but still travelled almost everywhere to see the Blades, and in that time, one of his old work colleagues had sent him a Green 'Un every single week. When he'd become too ill to do this, the old colleague's wife had carried on. He'd just been to visit them and had told them that now, thanks to the Internet, they didn't need to go to all the trouble anymore. I suspect, though, that those Green 'Uns will still be landing on the mat. Blades fans, eh?

He dropped me off at Tibshelf Services, and here things got miserable. The rain seemed heavier, and there was very little traffic about. To cheer me up, I received a phone call from the lovely Clayre, and the silly girl confirmed that she would be coming to the return leg in Colchester with me

Whilst standing here, a car with three Leeds fans in it approached me without its headlights on. As they went past I noticed the window was slightly down, so I shouted, "Switch your lights on!" They stopped and duly did so, but as I approached thinking my kindness at alerting them to their imminent danger was about to be rewarded with a lift, they laughed and drove off. Scum! To leave a fellow football fan in the rain is bad enough, but one who'd just done them a favour... Sigh!

The next two lifts redressed the balance in Leeds' favour a little, as both were Leeds supporting truck drivers. One took me to Trowell Services, and the other took me to Heathrow. The latter was an ex-army Tory who'd met Mrs Thatcher ("timid" he said) and the Queen Mother ("such a sense of humour!"). Despite all this, we got on fine, even if I did fall asleep as we approached Heathrow.

Trouble was, by the time he set me down, the tubes had stopped running long since. How come I can hitch from London to Sheffield in three hours (and back in just 4, in the rain, at night!), and yet spend another three hours getting across from one side of the city to the other? London night buses, that's how! I wandered for far too long looking for a bus-stop for a start, and then spent even longer waiting for a bus to show.

At 5 o'clock in the morning I came through my front door, and by 5:30 I was collapsing into bed. Not so much washed out, just incredibly knackered!

Chapter 7
Storm the Palace

Saturday 23rd September 2000: Crystal Palace 0-1 Sheffield United

Most people probably realise that myself and Musical are not the biggest fans of the royal family (although let's not bring Zara Phillips into this!), so anyone with no knowledge of the beautiful game would automatically assume that we would be up to no good upon announcing we were planning a visit to the Palace. However, those of you in the know, which is all of you I presume, will be aware that Crystal Palace are a football team, and it was at their very horrible, featureless ground that our beloved Blades were playing last weekend. Besides, that has now enabled me to use the most frequently abused football pun of them all (with the possible exception of Blades Cut Down after a heavy defeat).

So folks, for those of you wondering how I was going to do this, I had no intention of hitching, although one or two did point out that it would probably be more of a challenge to hitch to Crystal Palace than it would be to Preston. Well, tough! It was a London Blades day out, and these are just as relatable as any silly hitching tales.

The plan was to meet in the Slug and Lettuce at Clapham Junction from midday onwards. I eventually arrived at 1pm and there was already a goodly gathering. Attending with me was a young lady by the name of Sara who was unfortunate enough (along with friend Beccy) to have her life intruded on by me when we all attended the Summer Solstice at Stonehenge last June. Obviously wanting to broaden her experience still further, she opted for a week-end in London, and the chance to see the Blades in action.

Well, plenty of action at the bar, as usual, but not so much towards the food. It all looked a bit posh to me, so I decided to have a pie when in the ground. Most people thought the same... if only we'd known.

Just before we left, I did a quick head count, and I reckon there were 24 of us, but I can't be sure. Anyway, it seemed we all left the pub together, but at the station we seemed to have lost a few. The train arrived, we jumped on, then as the doors were closing, more came running up the stairs. Musical held the doors, and kept holding them as even more London Blades appeared and attempted to board the train. Musical's antics held up the train for a good few minutes (and upset the station employees somewhat), but with Lords Blade and Woodford Green (it was you wasn't it?) still missing (plus one other?), the train pulled away. I believe the last to be squeezed on board was Shiny, complete with yellow shirt, who we needed badly as he seemed to be the only one who knew the way to the ground. That shirt is a beacon, Shiny!

At the ground I tried my usual; "Do students count for concessions?" trick. I expected the same answer I've had at every ground so far this season, but no, it was not to be.

"Nope! Only OAPs or juniors get concessions," came the shock reply.

Now, I had a choice. I could go for the nice approach and try to negotiate my reduction, knowing it may not work, or I could just go for the sharp-tongued retort, knowing I'd blow my chances, but I'd feel a lot happier. It was 5 minutes to kick-off, so I went for the latter.

Thrusting my twenty quid under the counter I said, "I'm so glad you got out of financial difficulty!"

He mumbled something about it not being his fault, and thrust my ticket at me.

I turned to Sara who was clutching her NUS card and said, "Put that away; it i'n't gonna do yer any good!"

By the season's end there will be a blacklist of clubs that aren't student friendly.

Sara decided upon entering the ground that she needed to pay a visit to the Ladies, so I had an agonising few minutes waiting as the game kicked off. Eventually we ran round to our seats with the rest of the London Blades, and a fine afternoon's entertainment followed. Lords and cohorts soon arrived, so we were set.

Well, by half time Sara was not sure that she'd become a football fan.

"What, you mean our attacking flair and the end to end nature of the game hasn't convinced you?" I asked. We could afford to be smug by this time though, as we were in the rare position of being a goal up, thanks to Bent and Kelly taking advantage of the worst defensive mix-up I've seen for many a year, Kelly the one latching onto the ball, and Benty being the one to stick it in when Kelly squared it. Did we laugh or what?

Almost as good as that had been Tracey's breathtaking save followed by Kelly's astounding goal-line clearance. I've never seen one like it; running back full tilt and meeting the ball which was travelling at some speed. What's more, he got the power and direction necessary on the header to send it out for a corner. He also knocked himself out on the stanchion at the back of the goal.

Somehow, we didn't expect it to be our veteran striker who'd made such a clearance, so we went through the whole team before we realised who it was...

Quote of half-time was from Musical upon seeing the bewhiskered programme seller; "Swap you a razor for a programme!"

And those pies! What were they heated with? They were described as Pie of the Day, but at that temperature we needed to come back next week when they may just have cooled off. I am not kidding when I say that fifteen minutes after starting to eat them they were still as hot as when we began.

There was also a selection of drinks advertised, so I asked for 7-Up.

"We only have coke," said the attendant.

"Okay, so I'll have pie of the day and drink of the day," I replied, showing my usual wit and charm...

No guesses as to what the highlight of the second half was. Ruddock's long march back to the tunnel, not waiting to be shown the red card, accompanied every step of the way by the Blades, to a man, chanting, "You fat b*****d!" It was so touching when he turned to wave to us before he disappeared.

An away win is a rare commodity these days, so there was only one way to celebrate; back to the Slug and Lettuce, with talk of a curry to follow.

By now Sara had contacted a chap that she met in London on her last visit, and the silly boy decided to come and join us. I'm sure he'll remember his brief liaison with the London Blades. The poor guy thought he was going to be wining and dining Sara on his own, but a certain LB intervened and suggested she'd be much safer coming with us. Thing is, they spent a long time discussing this...

In the end, this poor fellow had to make do with coming to the Indian with 20 or so merry London Blades. Not sure that he was too thrilled with this. Still, he was good enough to pay for Sara's meal.

No Phal for me this time, either, even though they did do lassi on request. I settled for Jal Frezi instead, and very nice it was too, although not everyone was enamoured with his or her meal. But was that an excuse to start a hot-towel throwing contest at the end? I think not! Having spoken to a number of people since, everyone claims to have started it (children, you're supposed to deny such infantile behaviour). All I do know is that wherever I was situated, the towels all came towards me. No problem when I was in my seat with no one next to me, but when I was at the other end of the table showing off my Blades socks... The guy with his girlfriend didn't look too happy when one sailed over my shoulder and hit his lady. Thing is, everyone else was too under the influence to notice, so it was left to me to give him a cheeky smile, say sorry and then slink back to my end of the table.

Once the bill was settled, we left in dribs and drabs, all very happy. A regular pattern emerging? Pub, match, pub, curry. Indeed, but this time the football bit was memorable... Oh, to be Blade away from home. I love it!

Chapter 8
Of Queues and Cures*

Wednesday 27th September 2000: Colchester United 0-1 Sheffield United (Worthington Cup 2, 2nd leg)

I knew the feeling. I woke up Tuesday morning with a sore throat and a raging headache. I also felt very weary indeed. Sure enough, it was a mild dose of 'flu (or maybe more of a heavy cold). Now, there is no real cure for the common cold or 'flu, but it is strongly recommended that you don't hitch to Colchester in the rain, then you may feel better. So I decided not to. I didn't feel much better by Wednesday morning, and most sensible people would have just stayed in full stop. But I knew that the London Blades were planning a trip up on the train, and that was going to be better than not going at all. Besides, it was fairly local, so I felt justified in cheating. If it had been in Carlisle, I would have hitched, all right?

The meeting place was the pub at Liverpool Street station (Hamilton Hall), directly opposite my place of work. Now, I'd negotiated a deal with Tesco which meant I didn't have to work, but I'm not sure everyone knew this. I think there could well have been a few staff members saying, "I'm sure I saw Adrian earlier wearing a red and white shirt." You see, I fairly unwisely decided to pop in to buy a sandwich. Never mind. The close proximity to Tesco meant that the London Blades there early enough got to meet Katrina, the new lady in my life, as she kindly joined us for a swift one prior to starting her shift.

Those present as we boarded the train at 4pm were Musical, Alty, Radio, Wimbledon, N6 and myself. I'm sure the commuters were delighted to see us sitting next to them, and we kept them entertained with our chatter throughout (especially as I was forced to give some unedited highlights of the Palace post-match frolics).

In Colchester we met Peter in the Kings Arms, and Alty's Palace supporting friend who we refused to wind up as he was such a decent chap. The sausage and mash from this establishment comes highly recommended!

In the rain we set off walking to the ground, but couldn't resist calling in to the Salisbury Hotel on the way. This little stop meant we were pushing it to arrive at the ground in time, not helped by the fact that we had to find Stow (sorry Stow, I missed you out in my match report as you weren't in the pub with us). ((That is, the match report I did for theBladesOnline.com - my first attempt at a real report, and one I was rather proud of actually.)

Things were made even worse when we saw a huge queue for tickets with just two minutes to go before kick-off. Apparently we should have bought ours before-hand, as "your club have had them for three weeks!"

"But we live in London!" came Musical's response.

"Then it wasn't a 300 mile trip, was it!" retorted the chief steward, blowing a huge hole in Musical's previous argument that this was the distance we'd had to travel to get there.

If I hadn't been so frustrated at not being able to see the start, I'd have found it all very funny. As it was, I did allow myself a little smirk as Musical was the only one who got searched on the way in. I'm sure the Prague police are happy in the knowledge that our Musical would have been over there right now if it wasn't for the Blades. As it was, we never found a McDonalds in Colchester (just a road called Butt Street... huh huh, hurr hurr, huh huh etc).

Normally the fun occurs before and after the game, but in this instance, so much fun was to be had during it, largely due to the close proximity of the pitch to the terrace. Yes, we were stood up, and yes, we were at the front.

Perhaps you'd better see my "serious" match report elsewhere, but suffice to say the referee was our good friend Mr Elleray. When he came close enough, Musical was able to ask, "Do I have permission to come and see you in ten minutes?" Sadly, the ref never came close to us again, otherwise we were going to start a chant of, "There's only one David Bassett".

As it was we satisfied ourselves with a fine slanging match that bounced back and forth between us and the Colchester fans. "Yorkshire! Yorkshire! Yorkshire!" sounds much better than, "Essex... Essex... Essex."

Other notables were references to white stilettos and enquiries as to the whereabouts of Lua Lua.

Over-exuberant clearances kept lodging in hawthorn trees prompting chants of, "Going bust, going bust, going bust!"

The hot dogs looked good, so despite the earlier sausage and mash, I felt the urge. Even better, you could queue and not miss any of the game. The guy in the hut was very very slow, so I spent the last 10 minutes of the first half waiting and waiting. He served everyone with a hot dog until he got to me.

"Hot dog please!" I requested eagerly.

"None left!" he replied, "no food at all in fact."

"Just a Bovril then," I sniffed.

"No Bovril either. Only got sweets left."

"Er... better give me a Twix then."

I queued 10 minutes for a Twix. Thanks Colchester...

The second half carried on much like the first, except we scored, thanks to Dev (with an assist from Goose).

Goose gave us the thumbs up as he was treated to the usual "Goooooose" chants, and he was thus rewarded with, "Na na na na, eeza Blade" etc.

We were close enough to hear Trace say to Jags, "Stay there Jags you daft..." as Jags ran off rather than wait for a short goal-kick.

"Leave him alone! He's only young!" said Musical.

"I'm only young too!" came Sime's witty reply. A 'keeper with a sense of humour? What next? (If Pressman hasn't got a sense of humour I suggest he develops one, and fast!)

Quote of the match though went to N6 when shouting back at some abusive 12 year-old Colchester fans. The ground went quiet just as N6 shouted, "Shut up, yer little tw*t!"

The abuse didn't stop there. As we were walking away from the ground after yet another away win to get our taxi, we copped some insults from (probably the same) 12 year-old Us fans. N6 and myself started to wind them up back, at which point one of them tripped over the kerb.

"Mind the kerb," I said, "You'll be crawling it one day."

Blank faces told me they didn't get it (good job, I guess).

"Don't worry about it. Ask yer dad!" I added helpfully (hope they don't).

"If yer know him." added Radio.

At this stage Wimbledon pointed out that we were the only Blades amongst a lot of Colchester fans, so we shut up (also a good job I think).

On the train we were sat with a truck-driving Blade who'd parked his wagon up at Witham to attend the game. He promised me a lift if ever he saw me hitching.

Most of us slept (somewhat lightly though) on the journey back to Liverpool Street, but even though we were back before last orders, nobody could face the pub, so we all went our separate ways.

Besides, what better way is there to cure your ills than to see back-to-back Blades' away wins?

*With apologies to National Health (the seventies prog band, that is).

Chapter 9
Soldering On

Saturday 30th September 2000: Sheffield United 1-1 Queens Park Rangers

Having made their debut at Colchester, I was in two minds whether to wear my new (but second-hand) German army boots again. You see, my feet were taking a bit of a battering, and as my old pair are so comfortable, snaking pleasantly around the contours of my feet, it was tempting to slip then on for one last time. Then I remembered the battering my reputation had received, so I decided that the best thing to run my boots in would be a brisk walk from Brent Cross tube to Staples Corner.

Once again I decided against the option of travelling through the night, as by the time I'd finished my shift at Tesco I was rather tired, and anyway I'd left all my survival gear at home (sleeping bag, bivvy bag, Blades woolly hat, yellow away shirt to enhance visibility in the dark). So home I went, bunged everything in the washing machine, then hung it all on the radiator to dry (red and white shirt essential for hitching in broad daylight you see). Whilst doing this, I settled down to watch the Olympics and was sorely tempted to stay up to watch the football final, Cameroon v Spain. I was intrigued to see how well Suffo coped with sitting on the bench, and also to see if he became the first Blade (presumably, anyone know of any others?) to gain a gold medal. Common sense prevailed, though, and I went to bed with the radio on, hearing the first minute of commentary (long enough to hear Spain go one up).

I'd set my alarm for 6 o'clock, and had every intention of making an early start. Well, I eventually dragged myself out of bed at 7am, and by the time I'd stuck my head under the shower and packed my bags, I was out the door by 8ish. The journey to Brent Cross then Staples Corner was uneventful apart from counting three abandoned cars with POLICE AWARE stickers along the way. I was worried that I'd left it a little late, and sent a text to Musical saying that if their train swept by (the line runs parallel to the M1) then they were to give me a wave. I also received a text from Alty challenging me to a race. I accepted, but really thought I had no chance. I figured I'd be happy just to make it for kick-off, never mind the Beer Engine meeting point at 1pm. I needn't have worried...

At 09:00 hours I was setting my bags down in glorious sunshine at the foot of the M1, and by 11:05 I was wandering towards Meadowhall Shopping Centre, Sheffield. How can this be possible? I'm still not sure myself. Look at the following facts:

When I lived in Brackley (about 80 miles closer to Sheffield than London), my record hitch was 1 hour 55 minutes. The train that the London Blades were on left St Pancras at 10:25 and arrived 2 hours 19 minutes later in Sheffield at 12:44. Most people when driving from London to Sheffield talk about having a 3-hour drive ahead of them.

All I know is, it happened and I feel that this may be one of those untouchable records...

At 9:02am a car screeched to a halt in front of me and I jumped in.

"Where you going?" asked the cockney-sounding geezer driving.

"Sheffield," I replied.

"Well, I'm going to Scotland, so your luck's in, mate!"

Indeed it was. He drove fast, very fast (the needle was forever hovering around the 100 mph mark), but at no point did I feel unsafe, even when the traffic density increased and the fog descended. And what a fascinating bloke he was. He was the same age as me and was currently the show manager for a very well known circus (I'd better not say, because several things, not least the excessive speeding, that I will mention could mean it is better to keep his identity secret). He was from a fairground family himself, the ones responsible for the only steam driven fair left in this country. At the age of 15 he had met the 30 year-old daughter of the circus owner, and they had been together ever since. They had spent almost every day in each other's company ever since, as they worked together, travelled together, lived together...

For many years they had provided the circus with their trapeze show, but when she retired, he'd given up himself.

"I couldn't do it with anybody else. It was ideal with her. Well, I mean, I couldn't drop her, could I?" he said.

So, he'd spent three years as a clown before becoming show manager.

He'd also spent a rather uneasy year facing a murder charge. He'd got caught up in it, but was innocent. However, he was getting done for it because he was refusing to say anything against his mate (the one who had done it). In the end he'd got done for five years for this perjury (or whatever they call it in these cases), but it was reduced to a year on appeal, most of which he'd spent on remand anyway. The reason he told me was that he thought I may remember it as the murder and court case took place in Sheffield. It was back in 1987, the year before I left Sheffield, but I couldn't recall it. (However, Crouch End could, as it happened near his parents' house.)

The chap got off because eventually his friend, a contract killer ("I don't agree with what he does..." a classic quote?), confessed (as all good mates would).

Never one to miss an opportunity (and never having had a lift with someone who'd been on a murder charge before) I asked, "So, what happened then?" Not sure if I'm happy I asked this...

It would seem (careful what I say here, even though it was 13 years ago) that the victim was allegedly of the type to interfere with young children, so one of his alleged former victims had allegedly hired a contract killer to gain revenge.

The (murder) victim was also a member of a very well known army regiment.

Allegedly, they'd spent two days in his house battering him and torturing him. This, allegedly, involved an unspeakable act with a soldering iron: "Showed the photos in court. The blister on his arse was as big as a balloon." Allegedly...

In amongst all this chat, it was hardly surprising that I didn't notice we were nearing Sheffield at a rapid rate of knots. Indeed, if we hadn't got stuck in traffic at the roadworks just before Woodall Services, it would have been under two hours (so I suppose that gives me something to aim for in the future).

We talked about the circus business in general, which he thinks is dying, and if it does, he will go abroad. I said I had memories of going to Billy Smart's Circus (I think) when I was about five in Firth Park (again I think), and how I remembered it to be huge and very packed.

"It ain't like that now," he moaned, and said that Billy Smart's had been a "bloody good show!". He was very scathing about the new Smart's Circus which has just started (apparently some very distant relative has started one up, having changed his name - allegedly - to Smart by deed poll).

And so this brilliant fellow set me down near Meadowhall at 11:05am. Two hours and five minutes to hitch from London to Sheffield! I'd shaved a mere fifty-five minutes off my previous best.

I was able to wander around Meadowhall for a while, get a tram into town, sit around reading Viz for half an hour and then meet the London Blades off the train (present were Alty, Wimbledon, Radio, Musical and Stow). We had a lift to the Beer Engine in the back of a transit full of ironing boards, during which journey I regaled all with the tale of the soldering iron. And then I repeated it for Radio who'd been too busy reading Viz.

Eventually we unloaded at the pub having gone out of our way to pick up a friend of Stow's. It was quite a gathering in the Beer Engine, what with Halfway, Crouch End (distributing our pre-ordered Blades Limited Edition Henderson's Relish... mmmmm!), Silent (who borrowed my pen again), Maidenhead and Maidenhead jnr, Rob, Robby Blade, Murdoch's Neighbour, Dorset, Peter (who'd met Ted Hemsley and Mick Jones outside the ground), and Stafford and Radford put in late guest appearances. I was also introduced to Luton Blade, a fellow prog rock fan...

The Beer Engine was pleasant enough, but the food was a little slow in arriving, and I'm afraid the sausage and mash wasn't a patch on the same dish I'd had at that pub in Colchester.

The match itself was a little disappointing. Three times the woodwork was hit, Dev's missed (twice) penalty, Benty's open goal, that stick-insect for QPR... all made it memorable (and need I say more about the lovely Bladettes?), but really we should have won. One thing we are learning - only shout "Goooooose!" after he's played the ball. This doesn't always work, mind you, as one of his interceptions in the first half led to me shouting, "Goooo... oh dear!" as I realised it was veering crazily out for a corner.

After the game Crouch End (with Murdoch's Neighbour in the back) gave me a lift to the M1 (they were both staying in Sheffield) and we had the pleasure of listening to Radio Sheffield's 'Praise or Grumble'.

The undoubted highlight for us was the following:

"It's a grumble against the Wednesday."

"Why?" (Silly question really).

"Paul Jewell just isn't picking the right team. He needs to give some of the youngsters more of a chance. Take young Alex Higgins for example. Now he just happens to be my grandson..." The rest of the ageing piggy's squealings were lost amongst hoots of derision from the occupants of the car...

Crouch End set me down at just gone 5pm and I knew I wasn't going to have much of a problem getting my first lift, as the traffic was very heavy on cars with red and white passengers. Mind you, so heavy was it that it was difficult for people to stop, as exemplified when I saw the very truck driver we'd met on the train after Colchester. He'd said he'd give me a lift if he saw me, and even though he was in his car, not his truck, he acknowledged me and tried to pull over. It soon become evident that if he did stop, he would cause a multi-vehicle pile up, and by the time he did manage to pull over way down the slip road, another Blade had stopped, so I gave him the thumbs up and off he drove. I shouldn't have been so hasty, as the Blade who'd stopped was going up the M18, so I turned down the lift and carried on waiting.

I wasn't waiting for long, as very soon after a Blade picked me up and dropped me at Woodall. Whilst waiting here I realised I had some kind of bladder problem, so I nipped behind a bush...

Not long after I picked up a lift with a Leeds fan, thus proving that they are not all scumbags... She was 35 years old, and married to an Arsenal fan. She lived in Heathrow, but was from up north originally, Sheffield in fact. Indeed, her first match had been to see the Blades against Stoke in the 70s. She couldn't remember much about it, but that it was in February. She was rather impressed when I told her the score had been 0-0. How did I remember this even though I'd not been? My brother was supposed to take me as a birthday present, but had ended up buying me a Yellow Pages Dinky toy bus instead. When he came home from the game he'd told me he'd done me a favour by getting me the bus as the match had been "rubbish". Funny how you remember these things...

A quick phone conversation with Alty had established that whilst I was going past the Mansfield turn-off, the London Blades' train was just approaching Derby. A later chat with Radio (via mobiles again) just as I was being dropped off at Heathrow Airport confirmed that I would meet the boys in an hour in the Harp near Charing Cross. It was now about 8:15pm, and really it had been another miracle hitch, but after the morning's success, this one was always going to pale into insignificance.

Whatever, I had more pressing matters at the airport as my bladder was playing up again. I have never felt relief like that I had upon finding the gents at Heathrow.

It got worse, however, as on the tube I developed stomach cramp, earache and sneezing fits. The (mild!) 'flu was obviously not out of my system, and most sane people would go straight home. Not me, though. I'd promised to meet the boys again, and besides, the pub toilet would come in handy as my bladder problem was resurfacing...

I don't think there can be many people whose hitching and pub attending in two different cities will have met with as much success as mine did that

Saturday. As I wandered into the pub at 9:30pm to be greeted with "Na na na na, Eeza Blade and Eeza Blade!" I felt like a real trooper. However, with my stomach cramp, Radio's final suggestion of a curry had me waving the white flag.

Greenwich rejecting a curry? Yep, I must've been ill.

Chapter 10
Nine Lives of Greenwich the Cat.

Saturday 14th October 2000: Sheffield United 1-0 Crewe Alexandra

As I struggled out of the door of our house on Friday evening, I had totally forgotten the significance of the date. Eva, the lovely Slovak girl who lives upstairs (and spends far too much time wearing just a towel around the house for my liking) reminded me.

"Are you going on one of your adventures?" she asked. When I replied in the affirmative, she said, "Well, good luck; you'll need it because it's Friday 13th and a full moon!" A quick glance out of the door proved she was right about the moon. Thing is, she owed me a quid, and as luck would have it, she had a pound coin on her.

"You see, it's my lucky day," I crowed, and with that I vanished into the moonlit night...

One hour later I found myself at Brent Cross tube, but I couldn't head straight for Staples Corner as I was meeting Gal, the cellist from Human Oddities, there. You see, they had a gig in Sheffield on the Sunday, so he was giving me some posters and I was going to drop them off at the Boardwalk sometime on Saturday.

Just before ten he showed up, just as I was receiving a phone call from the new love of my life, Katrina. To avoid embarrassment, I'll leave out the content of the call, but it had something to do with crying at funerals (as I always say, I've not been to a good one yet).

Gal kindly offered me a lift to the M1, but said he'd draw the line at taking me to Sheffield. The lift was welcome, but I was denied the chance to update the abandoned car count (I think I saw at least one as we sped past).

So, at exactly 10pm, I was positioned at the foot of the M1, and I knew straight away that there was going to be no record-breaking feat this time. The "vibe" was all wrong. I waited about twenty minutes for my first lift, and when it came, it wasn't stunning. They were two carpet fitters from Milton Keynes, the driver being an oldish chap, the other being no more than 20. The older one was a Sunderland fan, and yes, once again my red and white striped shirt had me mistaken for a Mackem. The younger lad was puffing on a roll-up, the smell of which left me in no doubt that it didn't exclusively contain tobacco. The resulting conversation confirmed this; the only responses I got off him were big smiles. However, even without weed, I doubt there was much activity between those ears. Nice chap though...

The bulk of the conversation was with the Sunderland fan. It turned out they were working nights at the Hilton in London, but Friday was their early finish, which as he pointed out, proved lucky for me. Or was it...?

After sixteen years of hitching, I still make mistakes. One rule is that you should always stick with your own intuition, even when the driver sounds convincing. I should have got out at Toddington Services, but the driver insisted that junction 13 would be my best bet due to all the trucks coming from the truck stop at Dunstable. Well, there were plenty of trucks; trouble is, most of them were ANC wagons, and they, along with Eddie Stobart, TNT and Tesco (grrrr) never stop.

One hour later I was still there, now starting to feel the chill. One thing I noticed throughout this journey, but especially here; more than the usual amount of jokers drove past giving me the thumbs up. The thing is about these people, I'm sure they all think they are the first person in the world to do it. You are not, you sad gits, and what is more, it is NOT funny!

Things got so bad even a lorry driver did it. They never normally stoop so low... anyway, I never show a reaction, as giving them the finger is exactly what they want (although my best friend Ian once did, and when the car pulled up, he went to see if he was going to give him a lift; all he did offer Ian was a fight which thankfully didn't quite materialise).

It was well past midnight when a vehicle finally stopped. I was somewhat wary though, as it was a taxi. The Asian driver asked me where I was going, and I told him Sheffield. As the pound signs came up in his eyes I quickly added that I'd be happy if he could take me to the next services.

"How much would you pay if I took you to Sheffield?" he asked.

"You ain't taking me to Sheffield," I protested. "I have no money!"

"But I'm a mini-cab driver," he stated, obviously suggesting that he only gave lifts for money.

"And I'm a hitchhiker. If I had the money to pay you to take me to Sheffield, I'd go back to bed and get the train up with my mates in the morning," I explained.

In the end, he agreed to take me to the next junction (14) for free, but he still tried. "How much could you pay me if I take you to Sheffield?" One final firm rebuff, and I was chucked out at 14. He just didn't get the concept of hitching.

"But how will you get to Sheffield?" he asked.

"By doing this!" I said, sticking my thumb out. He just sighed and shook his head. "Look, I do it every week, so I WILL make it!" I insisted.

I wasn't waiting long at this junction, as I soon had a lift with three Rwandan guys. They were going to Northampton, but couldn't remember which junction they wanted. If it was 15a or 16, I was laughing, as I could jump out at Rothersthorpe Services at 15a. If it was 15, I may struggle...

They told me they'd been in England for four years.

"So, you like it here?" I asked.

The one in the passenger seat turned to me and said, "We like English ladies!"

"Me too," I agreed, "but also Germans... and Czechs!"

"Ah yes, Czech girls; they are all beautiful..." he mused, trailing off as if recalling some distant memory of an au pair from Pinner.

It seemed I'd found a kindred spirit. Not that it did me any good. As they approached junction 15 they realised this was their turn-off, so once more I was turfed out just one junction up.

After a stupefyingly dull forty minutes here, I finally got a lift to Watford Gap. Not far admittedly, but now I felt I'd turned the corner. The guy was going up to Birmingham and described himself as "an armchair Blues fan." As he dropped me off at the Gap he noticed my Cardiacs bag. It turned out he was a fan himself, and so before I resumed my hitch we had a quick discussion about In A City Lining being the definitive Cardiacs song, A Little Man And A House And The Whole World Window being one of the best albums EVER and There's Too Many Irons In the Fire being a real catchy little number...

There then followed my shortest ever wait at Watford Gap - a mere twenty minutes. I got a lift with a trucker who was going up to Leeds. Initially conversation was hard work, but I persevered, and found out a lot about the guy. He'd been born in Bristol, brought up in Abingdon, married a Barnsley lass so had moved up there, then when they'd split up he'd moved to Dewsbury. He was full of praise for friendly northern folk, insisting he'd never move back south. It also transpired he knew the bloke who used to run Brackley Gunsmiths at the same time I'd been running Alldays in Brackley, which was right next door. Small world...

By the time he dropped me off at the top of the Sheffield Parkway it was 4am and it was raining. I was another half-hour here before yet another taxi pulled up, but this time I was prepared to pay to get home if needs be. I needn't have worried because not for the first time my luck was in at this spot. It turned out he had just finished work and was heading home... just off Carter Knowle Road. So once again I got a lift right up to my mum and dad's door, and at 5am I found myself falling in through the caravan door. I fell asleep almost immediately.

Four hours later I was up, as I needed to get my mum to sew up the split in my combats (pathetic, I know) and also needed to be at Sheffield Works Department Sports Ground for ten as I was going to turn out for the Blades

Internet VP team against the Crewe equivalent.

With the aid of a real paid-for taxi this time, I made it. Due to the damp conditions we ended up playing on the all-weather 5-a-side pitches, whilst what looked like a Blades girls' team slugged it out on the big pitch next to us. They were wearing last season's white away shirts, as was I, but I was talked out of trying to get a game with them.

We split into two teams and played two games (naturally). In an email to Colin, the organiser, I'd said that I'd once been a handy 'keeper, so no guesses as to where I ended up playing. Actually, I surprised myself as I seemed to stop the ball with every part of my anatomy (literally, and yes, it hurt). I swear that the shots were raining in on my goal on average one every 30 seconds, but by the end of the second game the exclamations of, "Well saved Greenwich!" from behind the goal were still sounding as surprised as they had done at the start of the first. The sad fact was that I let in as many as I saved, largely due to my inability to get back up to fend off the rebound after my initial save. Ah, the pain of getting old....

I'm not sure who it was that originally christened me "Greenwich the Cat". Robby? Greenhill Optimist? Webbo? Pommpey Blade? Whatever, I took it as a compliment, even if Katrina suggested in a text message that they'd called me The Cat because I was scared of the ball. Funny...

In the Pump afterwards as I regaled the London Blades (Radio, Musical, Soho, Blackheath and Wimbledon) with tales of my heroics, Robby perhaps summed it up best with, "He kept it down to 14!"

Actually, I think we lost the first 12-8 and the second 17-14! Meanwhile on the other pitch, our first-team had won one and drawn one, so sadly Crewe won overall.

It was different with the real thing, however. I'd love to be able to say the Blades outplayed the opposition, fully deserving their win, but anyone who was there will know we were a tad lucky. Santos bagging the winner with a header in the last minute was enough though, and we could all leave happy, especially Musical and Pommpey who were off to meet Mr. Warnock and the players afterwards. They'd managed to become guests after sucking up to the boss ("my mate Neil" as Musical referred to him all afternoon) following their trip to Trinidad and Tobago. (Only joking, lads, and yes, I was incredibly jealous!)

As there was the Human Oddities gig the following day, I stopped over at my parents, and it was a rare luxury to be able to buy the Green 'Un and purr with delight at the headline of "SIMPLY THE WORST". What could all that be about then? Why of course, the piggies had just equalled their worst ever run of seven straight league defeats. Can't wait till Tuesday... Come on Burnley!

So there I was grabbing forty winks on Sunday afternoon when my mobile rang. It was Gal telling me they were going to have to pull the gig as their keyboard had packed up. They'd spent 24 hours trying to get it working, and had tried to borrow one only to find it was not compatible, so that was that. Basically, lack of keyboards and samples has a rather disastrous effect on the sound, so they decided not to travel up from London. I was fairly despondent as I phoned Chris at the Boardwalk, but he was very understanding, and I quickly worked things to my advantage, making the decision to head back home that night.

So I did my usual cheat of getting my dad to drop me at Woodall Services. Here I broke a record by having a wait of zero seconds as the guy was waiting for me by the exit. He'd seen me walking across the garage forecourt and he knew from my rucksack what I was up to.

He used to be a trade-plater, so he knew what hitching was all about. He told me that once he was hitching behind a normal hitcher and a car had pulled up between the two. The trade-plater had asked him who he'd stopped for, and the driver replied, "The other guy, because aren't you waiting for the vehicle with that registration number?"

There are more people out there lacking in basic knowledge than we realise (and for those that don't know, the trade-plates that these guys have are their own personal ones which are attached to the new vehicles that they have just delivered somewhere, and they are now attempting to get back home... and if they are at a junction with you they will always get a lift first).

This chap (greying, late forties, divorced - fairly typical lift) dropped me off at Rothersthorpe Services, and within minutes I had a lift to Toddington Services with a youngster from Leeds. He was working in Fulham all week driving earthmovers, so he was travelling down to his caravan, which he had at Dartford.

After a bleak half-hour at Toddington, I accepted a lift with an Irish trucker who spent almost the entire lift winding up his mates via the CB that they'd missed the "quality bit of totty" that he'd just picked up from Toddington. I played along with this hilarious jape by pulling my woolly hat down over my eyes as we overtook one of them so he couldn't get a proper look at me. Laugh? I very nearly did, but instead got out at Enfield. He was going clockwise round the M25, so I decided to wander into town and look for a train station.

Here I had another stroke of luck, as taking a gamble by checking out Turkey Street station saved me forty-five minutes from if I'd gone on to Enfield, according to the timetable. So I avoided conversation with the drongo on the platform ("How big's your tent?" "I haven't got a tent, just a sleeping bag." "So, do you just put your tent up if you need to?" "I told you, I don't have a tent!") and snoozed all the way to Liverpool Street. I then catnapped the one stop to Stratford, arriving home by 11:30pm. Not bad...

If I had a fire, I would surely have slept in front of it, curled up cat-like, but as it is, I had to make do with bed.

They say cats have nine lives, and black cats are supposed to be lucky. Well, over this weekend, I suppose overall my luck (and United's) evened itself out. This season still has a long way to run.

Chapter 11
Knowing the Score

Tuesday 17th October 2000: Sheffield United 3-0 Huddersfield Town

I woke up on the morning of the Huddersfield home game feeling good! I felt confident that we could get 3 points, that I would have a trouble free hitch, and that at the Lane we would be kept up to date of the latest score from Burnley, where surely the piggies would break their record for the longest sequence of negative results. Eight in a row it had to be! Oh happy day...

My confidence was soon shattered... Twenty minutes waiting for a bus followed by the discovery that there was no Jubilee train for some reason. So I trailed upstairs only to discover that the Docklands Light Railway was only going as far as All Saints. So, back to the Jubilee, where at last a train arrived. It was standing room only though.

One stop later we were at West Ham, and a pre-recorded announcement said, "All change please! This train terminates here!" Lots of people got off, but not clever old me. I was justified in this as further confusion was thrown when the follow up announcement said, "This station is Willesden Green. This train terminates at Stanmore." A few got back on, but many remained on the platform wondering how they could be in both West Ham and Willesden Green at the same time. Without a word of apology or explanation from the driver the doors closed and the train left. I suspect a few complaints were received that day.

Meanwhile, I got off at North Greenwich, and once I'd negotiated the masses from Stevenage attending the Dome (and standing on the left on the escalator - a sure way to wind me up), I had to wait an age for a 188 bus.

By the time I arrived, twenty minutes late for my lecture, my confidence was shattered. United were going to lose (surely a victim of new-manager-syndrome after the departure of Mr. Bruce from Huddersfield just the day before), and the pigs were going to upset the odds at Burnley.

Things got worse when after my lecture I checked my email only to find that my piece on the Crewe game which I'd written on my new emailer phone and emailed to my university address had indeed sent, but missed out the last 4 or so paragraphs. Also, when I put it into Word it had green squiggles all over it, as it seemed to think that every new line was a new sentence. Before setting out on my latest hitch I had repair work to do so that my tale would be fit for you lovely people to read. I ended up leaving my seat of learning over an hour later than I intended. Not a good start...

When I left Brent Cross tube station, I noticed one of those dreaded trade-platers in front of me. I figured he would be walking to the same place as me, so I took advantage of the fact that he popped into Newsagent Tara (I'm sure it made her happy) and stole a march on him.

Despite my hasty dash to Staples Corner, I still managed to make a note of the abandoned car count; an impressive 5 (a new record), 3 of which still had their wheels, of which 1 was missing its registration plates. Nice area...

Despite it being well past 3 o'clock I was confident again, and within 5 minutes I had my first lift, with an Arsenal supporting lorry driver. As he drove me up to Toddington Services he told me many tales of his exploits, most of them to do with other teams rather than Arsenal. He now lived in Northampton, and he had mates that were Leeds fans, Man Utd fans, Blackpool fans, Northampton fans...

He told me how he'd hitched to Barcelona for Man Utd's Cup Winners Cup triumph and how he'd got in for free by helping some guys sell Barca t-shirts. All in all, the trip cost him about £4, whereas his chums had spent a small fortune (and he got there before them).

When he started to tell me stories about travelling to Hampden for the England vs. Scotland games in the eighties I began to doubt his denial that he was part of the Arsenal firm (he'd kept saying that he had mates who were part of the firm but he wasn't one himself). As I remember it, England fans wouldn't even dare go to the Wembley games, so it was only the real nutters who travelled to Hampden. He'd gone in 1986 and 1988, and in 1988 he was arrested for no reason other than he had an English accent in a Glasgow pub!

He described the scenes in the cell:

"There was 10 of us to a cell waiting to go into court, and I was with some right nutters. One Glaswegian guy had taken a Derby fan's eye out with a chain... This woman came in and started asking how much we all earned for 'research'. She became suspicious that we were giving such low amounts when we'd all travelled up from London, were stopping in hotels and were wearing designer gear. She tore up the sheet in front of us, saying it was a waste of time! We knew her game; it was a trick to try and find out how big a fine we could pay!"

He also told of one time when Glasgow police were thrown into confusion when a group of England fans started to fight amongst themselves. It turned out to be West Ham and Chelsea fans joining forces and fighting with Man Utd fans.

I told him that I'd just finished reading Football Hooligans: Knowing the Score and before I'd said too much he was already confirming that Chelsea fans had met up with the Owls Crime Squad (OCS) at England games and had plotted to "do" the Blades Business Crew (BBC, as if you didn't know) when all three were in town (United played Chelsea in the Cup, whilst the piggies played Arsenal in the league).

He then went on to tell me that he'd met up with the OCS when the piggies played in Europe in Kaiserslautern. By now I severely doubted that his meetings with these firms were all entirely coincidental! He just "happened" to find himself travelling across Europe with the OCS. Anyway, he described it thus:

"The lads told me that there were two coppers following them from South Yorkshire Police, dressed in plain clothes. When they confronted these two, the coppers denied it, saying they were just on a trip. The OCS told them it was b******s 'cos they knew who they were, so they told 'em to f*** off, and they went in different pubs. By the time they reached Germany the coppers reappeared and approached the OCS themselves. 'All right lads,' they asked, 'so how many of you are there?' The OCS told them there were only 15, so the coppers said, 'Only 15? That's nothing! If that's all there is, we're gonna f*** off and leave you to it!' They did, and we had a great time in Germany without any police interference!'

He told me that what made him stop mixing with the firms was when he met some of West Ham's 'top lads'.

"I'd met Arsenal's 'top lads', and they were all right, but when I met West Ham's, I realised it was time to mix elsewhere. Real dodgy geezers!"

He dropped me at Toddington and almost straight away I got a lift in a truck full of pet supplies. The driver was hard work though. Conversation was at a minimum, and every time I tried to start one up his response was nearly always just a smile or a laugh, rather like my carpet fitter friend from Milton Keynes on the last trip. However, I think this time it wasn't an illegal substance that prompted this reaction, but rather a distinct lack of activity between the ears. Still, a lift is a lift, but I did feel mightily relieved when he dropped me at Leicester Forest services.

Now my troubles really started! For one, the weather had taken a turn for the worse, getting somewhat cold. For another, I waited in this cold weather for over an hour. By the time I was picked up it was 6:15 and I new I'd be pushing it to get to the Lane on time if this lift wasn't all the way to Sheffield. My luck was in however, as indeed I was going to get dropped in the holy city itself. My SHEFFIELD sign does work...

The lift was a first for me, being with an Afro-Caribbean woman. She lived in Sheffield, and would be entering it from the Chesterfield end of town, which would be handy for the Lane. As I got in the car she said, "My husband would kill me if he knew I'd picked you up!"

We had a good chat about relationships, largely because when I was telling her about my plans to hitch to as many games as possible, she said, "Let me guess; you're not married, are you!"

She said she knew that she was going to marry her husband the first time she met him. Impressive... I said that all I thought when I first met girls was that I probably wouldn't end up marrying them.

She dropped me at a bus-stop on Chesterfield Road just as one was about to pull away (I think it was a 53), so I jumped on, subsequently arriving at the Lane 10 minutes before kick-off. The trouble was, I had to get a ticket for the Worthington Cup match against the piggies. There was a huge queue outside the ticket office, so I asked a steward where I could get one.

"They don't go on sale until tomorrow!" he said, so I pointed out that I had a season ticket and my ticket stub from Colchester away, so he went off to South Stand Reception to find out. He came back out saying that they'd sort me out in there.

They did, but it took a while. The poor woman who was supposed to be sorting it was fielding enquiries from all over. First off she was reading the teams out over the phone to someone, then she had people phoning about complimentary tickets. More freeloaders came in, some being guests of Blades, others of Huddersfield players. In between this she was trying to sort me as all these people in posh-frocks and what-have-you kept coming through, making me stand out like a sore thumb with my rucksack and still clutching my SHEFFIELD sign.

As I waited for my ticket, NickBlade (aka Hanging On To Harry) went up the stairs looking very smart. Apparently he was with the matchball sponsors.

After one cheque was destroyed (because they didn't do student discount - you'd have thought the Wendy would be trying to get everyone they could to go and see them) I got my precious ticket, and I'd only missed the first three minutes of the game.

I dashed into the stand and was able to locate Musical by hearing him bawling abuse at Di Canio's mate, that rather unstable referee Mr. Alcock. I settled down with him, Pommpey and Pommpey's nephew, young Oliver (who it transpired is dating my favourite Bladette - nice one son!), for the evening's entertainment, and what entertainment it was!

The joy of watching the Blades notch up three quality goals (especially Dev's screamer) was added to by knowing that the score at Burnley was going against the pigs. Also pleasurable was seeing the page in the programme that said, "Today's visiting team" and there was a picture of a very miserable looking Steve Bruce. If only they'd saved sacking him until after we'd beaten them 3-0.

I don't mind admitting that on the way home I cheated. I had coursework to do, so an early night was essential, and Musical was driving back to London. It made sense, but he insisted I stand in front of his BMW with my thumb out before I could get in. I was slightly worried, because last time I got in a BMW with a bloke whilst hitching, he propositioned me. Musical had no such things on his mind, however, with the only trauma occurring when he dropped me off at Baker Street tube, only for me to realise that I'd left my travelcard in his car. Thank heavens for mobile phones. At least I only cost Musical ten minutes in bed...

On the tube home I reflected on things... Here was a United side that was going to take some beating at home, and seemed incapable of even conceding a goal... And we had our porcine cousins from across the city on a record-breaking run.

The stark statistics did not lie on this occasion. I knew the scores all right; 3-0 and 1-0. More of the same please!

Chapter 12
Impaired View

Saturday 21st October 2000: Norwich City 4-2 Sheffield United

I should have known I was in for trouble when I bought the tickets for the Norwich game. Right across the centre of the ticket it said, "IMPAIRED VIEW". If ever there was an omen...

And perhaps I should have taken note of a lesson from history. Eight years ago I hitched to Norwich to go to a gig at the University of East Anglia. The gig was All About Eve (Musical would approve), but the object of my desire was actually the support band, The Sea Nymphs, a splinter group of Cardiacs.

It was quite a long and arduous hitch from Brackley to Norwich, and I was worried that I may be too late for the support (it was a Sunday, and all things tend to be a bit earlier on the Sabbath). I arrived at 9pm, dashed to the door to enquire as to whether I'd missed them or not, only to be told the gig was off. How often have I read, "Always check with the venue before travelling long distances," eh? Oh dear...

The hitch back was even worse, including a 7-mile walk round the Peterborough ring road at gone midnight. I was back home in bed by 7am, and slept all through my day off.

Well, at least this time I had female company for the first time in years (and for those wondering why Clayre never came to Colchester, it was because she realised she was working, so opted to go and see Cheese Cake Truck the following night; not that I hitched to Colchester anyway...).

Yes, for some strange reason Katrina decided she wanted to experience the joys of hitching as well as seeing the Blades away from home. To top it all, she'd decided she wanted to come and see the Hawkwind reunion all-nighter at the Brixton Academy that very same night. She drew the line at Cheese Cake Truck's gig in Sheffield, though. If we came through the Saturday, it had to be love.

The biggest problem I had was time. The day before I had coursework to hand in, and it had taken up most of the week (when I wasn't at Tesco), so I didn't have time to make any plans, like finding out the best place to start hitching for the M11. I knew from bitter experience that if sorted this could save me hours, and could even be the difference between getting there for kick-off or not. I thought to myself, no worries, you'll be okay.

I arranged to meet Katrina at 10:30 at Liverpool Street Station, but I was already worrying as she was about 10 minutes late. However, I figured I'd use the time wisely by checking a London A-Z in the nearby WH Smith only to find that the trusting swines had them all behind the counter.

When Katrina arrived we checked in a few newsagents but none of them had them on sale. In the end we decided to head off to Woodford on the Central Line and take it from there. We waved goodbye to Musical, NW3 and Wimbledon who were waiting for their train, and I rather optimistically said, "We'll see you in Norwich!"

We got off at Woodford, but were soon back on. At least we got to look at an A-Z, but couldn't buy it as we were both pretty skint. It wasn't very clear anyway, but it did seem that the walk to the M11 was a long one, so I made the decision. From my road atlas, Theydon Bois looked quite close to the M11 and M25, so we decided to get the tube there. Besides, I was certain there was a roundabout here as I had hitched on it myself once before. Except I hadn't. I was getting it mixed up with Harlow and oh dear, things weren't looking too good.

Precious minutes were ticking away as morning turned into afternoon and the drizzle started. Theydon Bois wasn't exactly overflowing with signs telling us where the M11 was either. Katrina suggested we ask someone, which was a good idea. Asking a confused old dear was not however, and after she'd worked out what planet we were all on, we went off in some direction. She was right to a certain degree, but failed to mention the rather important left turn which would have saved us 45 minutes. By the time we'd walked a long way past where we should have gone left, we were soaking wet and not happy. We passed under the M11, so I knew we were near, but how to find the junction?

My road atlas sorted it, and we headed back from whence we came, this time turning down a narrow lane leading to a bridge that was closed for repair work.

Up ahead I could see the M25 junction, but with two ways to get to it. One was along the hard shoulder of the M11 (or at the very least along the top of the embankment - both were illegal anyway), the other being across a field surrounded with a barbed wire fence. I knew it was private (the horses gave this away), but thought I could get away with it. So Katrina was treated to my display of how to get over a barbed wire fence, honed to perfection by many visits to Stonehenge for Summer Solstice (it has to be said that blankets over the top of the fence work better than coats, but you have to use what is available). Whilst I was doing this, from out of nowhere appeared two women to tend to the horses. They were a good hundred yards away or so, so I had no problem with carrying on, although I noticed them watching, more than likely aghast, as I helped Katrina over the fence.

One of the women then started coming towards us.

"She's coming Adrian, what shall we do?" asked Katrina.

"Just keep going! By the time she gets to us we'll be almost there!" I defiantly advised.

The woman realised this, so from 50 yards she shouted across the field, "This is private property you know!"

"Yeah, well, we're just trying to get to the M11 'cos the bridge is closed," I shouted back.

"But that's the M11 over there!" came her reply on the wind.

"I know, but it's illegal to walk on the hard shoulder." I argued.

"It's not a public right of way here you know!" she shrieked, almost getting hysterical.

"I know but... Right!!! Right!!!" (going into Basil Fawlty mode), "we'll go over here, but I really don't see that we were doing any harm going along the edge of the field!"

The two horsey women looked on probably not knowing what to do next as I helped Katrina over the fence before making the poor girl wade through brambles towards the M25/ M11. A brief but anxious walk along the hard shoulder and we were almost there, I thought.

"We'd better not be on Motorway Madness!" said Katrina. If we are, my Blades shirt will give me away.

We had to cross a rather busy intersection of motorways, and I began to doubt my perceived existence of the roundabout. So did Katrina. "So, where's this roundabout?" she asked. I hate difficult questions...

"It'll probably be just around this corner," I hoped. It wasn't...

So, there we were at gone 1 o'clock, stood on the intersection of the M25 and the M11, under a bridge and in a very illegal (not to mention dangerous) position. Basically we were on a hard-shoulder that continued in all directions and as far as both motorways stretched. We needed a lift, anywhere and quick. Forty-five minutes later it came, and it was a miracle that no police had been past in this time.

It was Katrina's first lift in a lorry, so at least that cheered her up. The driver was once again from Leeds (so, how many Leeds truckers has that been now?) and what a thoroughly decent bloke he was. He was heading up the M11, A14 and A1, so he dropped us off at a service station on the A14. On reflection, I'm not convinced that this was our best plan, but at least we were away from our M25/ M11 nightmare.

By now it was only 15 minutes until kick-off, and Norwich was still one hour away, but I was determined to see some of the match. I got Musical to text me the goals, and just after we'd walked from the petrol station to a lay-by half a mile away, the first one came through: "1-0! Kelly! Yes!".

"Wahey! We're winning!" I gleefully shouted, but then mused quietly, "wish I was there though."

Not long after we were two up, then it was 2-1, and I wondered what on earth was going on. Meanwhile there was no sign of a lift.

Two students finally picked us up, and as we got in, Musical sent me a text to say that Norwich had equalised on the stroke of half-time.

I continued for two reasons: I was determined to see some of the game as we had our tickets, and also I was certain that StowBlade and Radio had driven up in Stow's car, so there might at least be a lift back involved.

From here onwards, things got better. The students dropped us the right side of Cambridge, and straight away we got a lift with a rather strange guy who was going to Mildenhall. I'm sure he must have heard Katrina's hoarse whisper to me as we sat in the back; "This bloke's a bit of a weirdo!"

Weirdo or not, at least he went a bit out of his way to drop us in a good place.

By the time the next bloke picked us up, I knew that we'd only make it for injury time if we were lucky. I noticed that he had a green cross in the windscreen, above which were the words MEDICAL SUPPLIES. He also drove very fast! We had hope...

Once we'd negotiated where he would drop us in Norwich (for indeed he was going all the way) I asked about his sign. It turned out he was carrying a special lung machine. It provided oxygen to blood for people whose own lungs were incapable of creating it (or something like that). Every time someone's machine failed in East Anglia, he had to take out a replacement. "Erm, so is my request to be dropped off as near to Carrow Road as possible endangering anyone's life?" I asked.

It turned out it wasn't, as these patients always had a temporary machine that lasted for 10 hours, and he'd got the call around 3 o'clock.

As we neared Norwich, it was obvious that we weren't going to make it at all, not even for injury time, and I was very unhappy. We might have made it, if only it was all dual-carriageway, but slow single file traffic foiled us. One phone call to Musical established we were losing 4-2 and that Benty had just been given his marching orders. One call to Radio established that Stow and himself would meet us at Norwich railway station.

We actually arrived in town five minutes after the final whistle, and what a strange feeling it was to see all the fans coming away from the ground.

As we snuggled up in the warmth of Stow's car, I felt very mixed emotions.

I was gutted that I'd missed the match (especially having already bought the ticket!), and I was depressed that the Blades had lost, but what if we'd won and I'd missed it? But at least we'd have won, and that is the most important thing. In the end, it was my stubbornness that had led me to carry on. I was desperate to see something of the game, and even when I didn't, I felt I'd still achieved something by just getting to Norwich. I was still sad though, and Musical's text of "Top Blade!" made me feel much better.

At least the lift meant we got back in time for Hawkwind. This was something I'd waited for since discovering the Hawks at Sheffield City Hall in 1984, and having already purchased tickets for this, I wasn't going to miss them too.

On the tube to Brixton I met two Hawkwind/ Bury fans who were none too impressed with Mr. Warnock's previous tenure there. I said that I thought he was doing all right for us, and they said, "Well, he would! He used to wear his Sheffield United tie during games at Gigg Lane!"

Hawkwind passed off without incident (apart from one fan falling on us from a great height as we sat down before the start, thus rendering us in the same state as most others there), the biggest problem being Katrina having to sit through four hours of a band about whom she'd heard nothing. Well, so she thought. When they did Silver Machine at the end she announced that she knew this one. There were about 30 musicians onstage who rather surprisingly could still remember it too.

It went on all night, and by Sunday lunchtime, I was heading up to the holy city again, but no hitchhiking this time. I was travelling up with Cheese Cake Truck (for whom I work as Propaganda Director) as they were gigging at the Boardwalk in Sheffield that night.

Afterwards one of the chaps at the Boardwalk recognised me from previous gigs and conversations. He is a pig fan (albeit a nice one), and whilst he cleared away the debris that had resulted from a night of semi-naked Norwegians in tutus, he asked me if I had my ticket for the Worthington Cup match.

Indeed I had, and I felt another rush of excitement. Katrina had said it must be nice to be so passionate about so many different things. I had to agree, because there was always something to look forward to. Next on the list was Stockport at home, then Wimbledon away, then the piggy cup match.

Desperate excitement for all of them, but I am just going off to check my pig ticket. I'm sure the woman said something about restricted views at Hillsborough.

I won't be hitching to that one so impaired view or not, at least I will get to see some of the match...

Chapter 13
From Benfica to Frickley Athletic

After the horror that was the trip to Norwich, and the near miss on the way up for the Huddersfield match, I really needed a nice straightforward journey north for the Stockport home game. I decided to leave nothing to chance, and headed away from the University of Greenwich nice and early just after lunch. A relatively trouble-free journey across London via the Docklands Light Railway and the tube, and all was going nicely.

My first disappointment came on the walk to Staples Corner when I realised that the abandoned car count, having peaked at 5, was now down to a big fat zero. I'm sure they'll be back, though. This is Brent Cross after all. Indeed, I thought I could see one as I came over the footbridge. It was parked nicely on the slip road, right where I usually stand to beg for a lift. Perhaps it was someone who'd seen me approaching and had decided to give me a lift? I jumped the fence and headed for the car, only to find it was full of Japanese tourists looking at a map. When they saw me peering through the window, they panicked and sped off.

I wasn't too worried, and five minutes later a white van pulled in. The driver was Portuguese, and when I asked him where he was going, he said St Albans. Now, as you may have gathered, even after 16 years of hitching I'm still prone to mistakes, and this was no exception. For some reason I thought of Dunstable, so I asked the driver if this was after Toddington Services. His reply was positive, so in I got.

It turned out he was a Benfica fan, and I won his instant respect by uttering the words Jimmy Hagan.

"Ah, Hagan!" he drooled. "Champions three times!"

Having checked the map, and now realising that we were going nowhere near Toddington, I thought this might be the way to get him to go a bit out of his way.

"Hagan was my dad's favourite!" I ventured. "He is still revered at Bramall Lane."

"Good manager!" said my Portuguese friend.

I moved things on a little further by mentioning Brian Deane.

"Ah yes! Big and black! Good striker!" he said.

He had the man! "One of my heroes! Wish we'd never sold him!" came my reply. I decided to miss out the bit about the delay in the arrival of the money, but perhaps my failure to mention Dean Saunders was the reason why he still dropped me off on the M25/ M1 interchange? Or maybe me neglecting to mention Souness was what saved me from being dumped on the hard shoulder? Whatever, I found myself at junction 6, the exact same place I'd got stuck on the way up for the Blackburn game. At least this time it wasn't raining, and I wasn't quite so late. I wouldn't have to send out a "come and get me" plea to Maidenhead just yet...

I just had time to add to my "Greenwich Blade On Tour" graffiti from my last visit (something like "Greenwich Blade Again! 24/10/2000") when a very flash sporty car stopped. It was not the usual type of vehicle to get a lift in, but I was not about to complain.

In the past I have had many people tell me that I remind them of Mr Bean/Edmund Blackadder. I respond by telling them that if they think I look like him, they should see my brother. Meanwhile, my poor big brother (who works for the British Transport Police and will kill me for this, but he once had an entire carriage of football fans singing the Blackadder theme at him) has never been able to point to anyone else who bears an even more striking resemblance. Until now...

So, big bro, next time someone pokes fun at your Blackadder features, you can say, "Well, if you think I look like him, there was this bloke who once picked up my little brother who looked so much like him..."

This guy had the lot. He was Blackadder II personified. He even had the goatee...

Top bloke though. He was one year younger than I was, and was the MD of a successful cleaning business. Perhaps I did it all wrong after leaving school by going to work for GT News (after a year on the dole...)?

He told me how he'd been up in Sheffield a couple of weeks ago and had walked through the Mayfield Valley. This got me all nostalgic, leading to reminiscences about many a family picnic at Forge Dam when I was 5 years old, and watching the remote-controlled model-boats on Wire Mill Dam (do people still do that?).

He was going on to Birmingham, so I was brought back to earth and the present day as I got out at Watford Gap. It had just started raining again, so I dumped my bags under the bush by the slip road and was just contemplating adding to the two lots of "Greenwich Blade On Tour" graffiti already present when a 24-seater mini-coach pulled up. Now this was luxury...

I was the only person on it, so I had the whole thing to myself. So nice to be able to spread myself out across the seats. Why, I even had room to get my A4 pad out and take notes.

The driver had seen my sign saying SHEFFIELD and said he could take me to Woodall Services as he was going up to Frickley. When I told him I was going up to see the Blades, he picked up his mug and said, "That's the only team for me!" It was a Frickley Athletic mug, and immediately I felt respect coming on. Basically we think we have it hard as Blades, but such devotion for a non-league side demands admiration.

He was a vice president at the club and his story was as follows:

He had been working for the family coach business, and they used to provide the travel for the team. When the pit in Frickley closed, the club struggled financially and ended up owing money to the coach firm.

"Me and my brother, being fans, decided not to push it too much, but became vice presidents so's we could keep an eye on the financial situation... We still haven't got all our money, and I don't think we will, unless we have a good cup run..."

It turned out that they were playing Hyde United in the FA Cup 4th Qualifying Round that Saturday. He said a win in that, then some friendly draws "enabling us to get to the 3rd Round, then get drawn against United at Bramall Lane... that'd do us nicely!"

I told him I'd keep an eye out for the result (as it happens they won 1-0, and now face Northampton away in the First Round proper).

He went on to tell me tales of previous FA Cup exploits, including a dodgy ref who played 10 minutes of injury time against Rotherham, allowing the Millers to equalise. "We got stuffed 3-0 in the replay... they just didn't want us to win. You get some terrible refs at our level..."

He also told me that the club was struggling in the league. Over the summer one manager had left, and then early in the season so had the newly hired one. In the meantime they lost 12-0 to Worksop Town. The senior players had ended up picking the side whilst the board sifted through applicants. They were delighted to receive an application from a certain David Hirst who they subsequently interviewed. He obviously made an impression as they offered him the post. However, at this point Hirsty bottled it saying that he wanted to get into management but thought this was too big a challenge to start with. Big fat neshing piggy git!

I got out of the coach at Woodall (just to bring you up to date, the chap now had his own business, as he felt he wanted a change, so his family bought his shares allowing him to set up on his own), and as it was early (not even 6pm) and as I'd got stuck at Woodall before, I decided to get the bus. If you cross over to the Southbound carriageway, go through a gap in the hedge, walk across a field and down a muddy lane, you find yourself in Woodall itself and by a bus stop. Buses go regularly into Sheffield, or at least to Crystal Peaks. However, I was stood here for just long enough (about 45 minutes) to feel uncomfortable, so I ended up getting the first bus that came along, which took me into Killamarsh. The driver advised me which bus to get from there to get to Crystal Peaks, so whilst I waited I had the pleasure of observing some of Killamarsh's social problems first hand. Thirteen year-old girls drinking vodka whilst their male counterparts threw fireworks at each other. Such little charmers... I hope the Social Security offices will be big enough in three years time...

Eventually my bus arrived, and before long I was travelling in style once more, this time courtesy of the Supertram in the company of fellow Blades.

In the end, I arrived in good time (over half an hour before kick-off) so I was able to collect my two inflatable pigs from Halfway Blade and NickBlade. One was free due to me "being a legend" (awww, shucks... all shy!), and the other was for Alty. As these two magnificent salesmen intensified their efforts, Halfway was heard to use the following sales pitch:

"Get yer inflatable pig here! Gerald Sibon in a box! As used by Adam Burley." And sure enough, there could be seen going into the shop where Bri and Irene's used to be, Mr Burley and an amused-looking Andy "Smudger" Smith...

We were soon joined by Musical who seemed put off by the fact that the pig had a hole in its rear-end...

And that, dear reader, was the adventure almost over for the day. The game wasn't the best, although I did suffer a minor trauma at half-time when I discovered the Balti pies had run out. Not good enough, Mr Stock Controller - do you by any chance work at my Tesco?

Murph secured the points from a corner, and I secured a lift home with Musical by standing in front of his BMW with my sign held out.

"London, mate? You're in luck!"

I couldn't even liven things up by losing my travelcard. All in all, a pretty stress free trip, but after Norwich, it was exactly what I needed...

Chapter 14
A Pig of a Week

Saturday 28th October 2000: Wimbledon 0-0 Sheffield United
Wednesday 1st November 2000: Sheffield Wednesday 2-1 Sheffield United (aet) (Worthington Cup 3)

It all started so positively. Despite the terrible weather (just how many trashed umbrellas can be seen discarded around the streets of London this autumn?) the next seven days were going to make me happy happy happy, I was sure of it. It was the Thursday before the Wimbledon away game and my student loan cheque had arrived (late). This meant I could indulge myself (although I didn't quite expect to do this by buying a gramophone player, but there you go) and not worry too much about living it up a little with the London Blades at Selhurst Park on the Saturday, and then at Hillsborough for the Worthington Cup game the following Wednesday. One other thing - there was going to be no hitching involved this time. Just relax... everything would be okay!

After the success of our last visit to Selhurst just over a month earlier, Sara had obviously been lured into a false sense of security so she decided to risk it again... And it really was a risk as it involved travelling up from Salisbury on the train. Dangerous, with the whole rail network plunged into chaos what with engineers spending the weekend repairing track with Polyfilla and Superglue. Happily though, the trip on Saturday lunchtime to Clapham Junction was trouble-free, and by the time we arrived at the Slug and Lettuce, the London Blades had already formed an impressive gathering.

By the time we left, we were about 30 strong, swelled by the arrival of Copenhagen Blade. Now this was far more impressive than Greenwich hitching to a game (although Copes, I'd have been even more in awe if you had hitched rather than flown in).

Copenhagen's arrival was my cue to introduce everyone to my inflatable pig, as he had been so keen to see it. The little porker was still in its box, but Copes soon had it out and inflation began.

As we walked to the ground (with a nasty wind whipping up) there was much discussion as to how we were going to decorate our grunter. There was talk of blue marker pens and tippex, but then one inspired moment from Copenhagen sealed it. He popped into an electrical shop and came out clutching two rolls of insulating tape, one blue and one white. So now it was a race against time. We had to get to the ground in time for kick-off, but had to dress up our squealer along the way. With the help of Cope's mate Pete, strips were torn off and I carefully stuck them on. Impressively Cope's didn't spill much of his Stella whilst helping with this.

Finally as we reached the ground my pig was ready, and with two fingers inserted in the conveniently-placed hole in its rear, I waved it in the air. The group of Blades milling around the ticket window started up the chant; "I never felt more like swinging a pig...!" Surely my proudest moment!

In the end my pig was the star of the show as there was little on the pitch to keep people entertained. By now the rain was swirling around making me glad we weren't at Fulham on their open terrace, and really not much else was happening out there, so I swung my pig for almost the whole 90 minutes. It didn't go unnoticed. As I queued for a pie (sold out, incidentally) at half-time, I got chatting to Puppet and he said, "I presume the pig's yours...?" (I'd left the porker grazing with the London Blades).

At the end, with the score on the pitch finishing 0-0, the score in the stand became 15-0 to Greenwich. As most of the LBs raced off to the station, an enthusiastic Blade came running over to ask me where I'd got the pig. I was trying to explain how Halfway and NickBlade had been selling them, but he started talking about buying mine from me.

"Oh, I could never sell it!"

"We're talking big money here..."

"No, really, I couldn't..."

"Fifteen quid!"

Short pause, then, "Aye, all reyt then!"

By the time I'd caught up with everyone and we were huddled on the stairs at the station sheltering from the incredible downpour, word had already spread of my windfall. Those that didn't know soon did as I paraded the notes around like the FA Cup. The thing is, I'd got one pig for free, and I'd got another one waiting in my bag. Accusations were rife about me being a fat-cat capitalist.

Despite the weather, our ardour was not dampened and we returned to the pub, followed by a visit to the curry house. Tradition you see...

It was a rather busy curry house as well. We had to wait rather a long time for a seat, but the North London Blade kept everyone amused by telling the kids in there that he was Thierry Henry.

"Hey, show some respect! I won the world cup, you know! I'm going to order my food and then I'm going to bring in the European Championship trophy!"

The terrible weather continued over the next few days, and the country was brought to its knees by both rail problems and flooding. I wasn't risking anything for the match on Wednesday though. Yes, it was the long-awaited Worthington Cup match against the piggies, and this time I was getting a lift up with Alty at the wheel and in the company of Musical and Wimbledon.

I woke up Wednesday morning and felt a wave of excitement wash over me. Then I remembered that I'd felt like that on the morning of Boxing Day in 1979, so I tried to ignore my feelings. (For those that don't know, the pigs stuffed us 4-0 on that occasion.) En-route to meeting the boys at Kilburn Station I picked up some more blue and white rolls of tape, as well as a Chupa Chup for that added authenticity.

As we drove up, I regaled them with the full story of my hitch to and from the Leeds game, Boxing Day 1989 (don't worry, that one's coming up!).

We arrived at Swillsborough by 4:30, parked the car and headed back into town on the Tram. For the other three it was their first journey on the Supertram, and didn't they get excited! We ended up in the Bankers Draft and met Hightower, Attila and Rob amongst others (Stow had made the journey up but Camden was laid low with flu). The food was nice (especially the sausages), and cheap it was too (London has its pitfalls).

As more people gathered, the anticipation grew, and it all made for a rather nice trip to the ground...

The tram we were on was 99% Blades, and the atmosphere was electric. It reminded me very much of the train journey to Old Trafford for the cup semi in 1998, but this time it was ALL Blades. Swinging a Pig, The Greasy Chip Butty Song, No Pig Fans In Town and more (order now for Christmas).

Once inside the ground I had to separate myself from the rest as I was in a totally different part of the stand. Still, left to my own devices it meant I had 25 minutes to get on with decorating pig mark II.

By the time the teams ran out, the grunter was ready, and if anything it was even better than my previous effort. The Chupa Chups wrapper was the icing on the cake I thought, so I waved the porcine one with extra vigour!

So wound up was I that within five minutes of the start I was threatened with ejection from the ground by a steward for gesturing at the Wednesday fans. I tried to explain that it was the pig that was doing it, and I had no control over it, but it didn't wash, so I calmed down.

The pig in the end had a sad demise. It survived a battering when the piggies went 1-0 up, and just avoided being launched pitchwards when Browny equalised. It was not so lucky late in the second half when Browny shot just wide, and it developed a split trotter. The fatal blow was applied, though, when Benty slammed that one against the bar in the last minute. A huge gash appeared in its snout, and there was no doubt, this was one pig that was going down, and fast!

When Ekoku scrambled the winner in extra time the largely deflated pig was sent over the edge onto the Blades below in the lower tier. At that moment I knew it was all up; in fact I think I knew when Marcus missed his sitter.

The journey home was very quiet, not to mention cold (but then I suppose Alty staying awake was necessary). Thanks to extra time I'd missed the last tube, so had to suffer the Night Bus From Hell which did nothing for my mood.

When I woke up the next morning with that dull, despairing ache, I thought about what Katrina had said about how nice it must be to be passionate about things. Well, this was one time when I would have happily given anything for the result to mean nothing to me. Defeat is always bad, but to the piggies? Unbearable...

That evening I saw a number of West Ham fans at Tesco, and all were told to "stuff the Wednesday out of sight for us in the next round!" It couldn't change the result, but it made me feel a little better...

What with the trains, the weather and most of all the football, it really had been a snorter of a week. I really hate "the day in the middle of the week" you know.

Chapter 15
Have Faith - Will Travel

Saturday 4th November 2000: Sheffield United 1-2 Gillingham

About seven years ago now, in the summer of 1993 I believe, I was returning to Brackley from a gig in London late at night. I'd been to see The Sea Nymphs at the Islington Powerhaus and I was making the return journey from Brent Cross tube to Staples Corner (at least I only had to hitch to junction 15a back in those days). On the very same night that The Nymphs had been entertaining a tightly packed but enthusiastic audience in the small venue, U2 had been playing to a somewhat larger crowd at Wembley. A certain Mr Salman Rushdie had been guest of honour and had made a rare public appearance onstage with the band. Well, Rushdie or not, I knew where I'd rather be, preferring the delicate tinkling and eccentricity of the Sea Nymphs to the drudgery of U2 any day...

So anyway, there I was, wandering past the Holiday Inn rapidly approaching the M1 when I noticed two big posh cars (I think one was a BMW) pull up in the bus-stop next to me. Straight away these very big, mean looking blokes in suits got out and I thought, "Dodgy!" I was expecting to see some drugs deal go down, or a revenge shooting, but instead out of one car got Salman Rushdie. I was passing within 15 yards and he looked across at me. So did all his bodyguards, and I thought to myself that if I stopped, put down my rucksack and started fumbling around inside it, I'd probably be dead within seconds. Instead, I just smiled at our Salman as he got into the other car and watched them speed off. Not someone you see every day...

Every time I walk past that spot (and as you will have gathered by now, it is frequently) I think back to that rare sighting. Today was to be no exception, but with the Gillingham home game still 160 miles up the M1, I was soon concentrating on other things, and it was much later that day that Mr Rushdie would re-enter my thoughts once more...

But I'm getting ahead of myself...

I'd set off early in order to ensure my safe arrival, waking at 6:15 and arriving at the foot of the M1 two hours later.

The editor of one of our wonderful fanzines had sent me an email saying that one of his misgivings about these collected writings coming out as a book was that it may become a bit samey. I emailed him back to say I'd already thought about that and that I had considered varying my route a little in the future. I'm still contemplating that one, but had no intention of changing things this day. I had arrived at Staples Corner quite early (8.30am) but just wanted to get up to Sheffield as early as possible because hitching on a Saturday can be most unpredictable sometimes. However, circumstances beyond my control meant that my route ended up quite a bizarre one.

Once again I had a very short wait at the foot of the M1, and within 5 minutes I had my first lift, this one with a white-van man. He said he was heading to York but had to go up via a place called Melbourn near Royston from where he had to collect some gear. Now, this chap was a shopfitter from Wales (a Wrexham fan no less) who constantly worked away from home, therefore spending much time on the road. You would expect the one essential item for his van would be a map. However, all he had were some difficult to understand directions scribbled down on a scrap of paper, so in the end he had to rely on the tiny map in the back of my University of Greenwich diary. We located Melbourn just below a scribbled message, "Holly used to live here!" and thereby deduced we would leave the M1 at junction 10 and head to Hitchin on the A505. (Once whilst hitching to Reading Festival in 1986 the driver that stopped asked me where I was going. I followed up my reply of Reading by asking him where he was going. "Hitchin" he responded. "Yes I am, but where are you going?" "Hitchin!" he tried again. "Yes, but..." This carried on for several minutes before the penny dropped. I'd love to say this hadn't happened, but much to my embarrassment...)

The traffic in Hitchin was a nightmare due to extensive roadworks and poor diversion signs, but eventually we negotiated it and sped on towards Baldock and Royston. As I seemed to have become chief navigator, I spent my time working out how we would get things back on course. He was planning on going back the way we had come to rejoin the M1, which would have been fine for me as he had originally told me the way he goes to York is straight up the M1 to Leeds rather than come off at the M18. However, I shot myself in the foot by telling him he was daft to do that as it'd be much quicker to head back to the A1 and go North that way. Thus I threw away the chance of a nice lift to Meadowhall followed by a stress free trip into town on the Supertram. Instead I was looking at getting turfed out at Clumber Park and hitching into Sheffield that way. It could be tricky, but I had confidence in my ability and I had plenty of time, so what the hell!

Meanwhile we were now in Melbourn, a place that seemed to consist of an industrial estate and not much else. The collection was made and we continued on our way towards the A1, passing very close to the scene of mine and Katrina's disaster on the way to Norwich. As we zoomed through Cambridgeshire we got to see a number of lakes with telegraph poles sticking up in the middle. Those pesky floods - why, I almost expected to see John Prescott or Tony Blair paddling their way to the scene to comfort the distressed...

The chat mostly centred on music - we shared a mutual respect for Moby, both claiming we were into him before he made it big as we both had

Everything Is Wrong and Animal Rights well before Play came out.

Eventually we reached Clumber Park and I got out at the junction of the A1 and the A57. I was waiting about 10 minutes when the driver of a truck that was parked in the nearby lay-by whistled me over. As I got nearer to the snack-hut he was feeding at, I realised it was called Piggy's! The woman congratulated me on my Blades shirt, so I commented on the Piggy's name. After the result earlier in the week, that cheered me up no end.

The driver was from Hyde and was driving to Manchester. He said he was on overtime so he could take as long as he liked, therefore giving me a free choice of where I wanted to be dropped off. So, half an hour later at 12.30 he was dropping me off outside Sheffield Midland Railway Station. Hope he appreciated the extra money...

On the way, as he was from Hyde, the conversation naturally turned to Dr Death, Harold Shipman. "Everyone knows someone with a relative who he did!" he said cheerily.

After a trip to Burger King and the club shop I found myself in the R&R, a new pub for pre-match shenanigans. In there I met Musical, Champagne and Crouch End (who'd all suffered a torturously long journey up in standard class thanks to Railtrack - bit of a comedown, eh chaps?) (late correction, they tell me they upgraded to first class in the end - posh gits!) as well as Attila, Rob, Born On Shoreham Street, Robby, Stow, Putney, Radford, Stafford, Maidenhead, Maidenhead jnr and Lepps. Lepps is a bit of a legend as she had come all the way over from Australia for a month of Blades games. Her devotion to the Blades comes from her admiration of Def Leppard, in particular Joe Elliott. She was envious when Musical told her that they'd been sat in front of our Joe for the piggy cup match, but she was none too happy when Musical questioned his singing ability having heard Joe attempting the Greasy Chip Butty Song.

Lepps had the pleasure of sitting with us in the South (sorry, Laver) Stand, so we all tried to be on our best behaviour. However, the language turned somewhat blue when Gillingham's second goal went in, suspiciously offside as it looked. I'm not sure how we lost the game, actually. The post, the bar... sigh! Jaffa's masterful header gave us hope, but it was not to be. Our first home defeat, and on sober reflection this was just as disappointing as the defeat to the grunters, if not more so.

So, full of despair and gloom, I traipsed out of the ground and headed to Granville Road to get the Supertram. You see, there was nobody around to give me a lift to the M1, so I decided to head to Woodall Services. After the length of the journey on this occasion, I think next time I'll just walk to the Parkway.

One tram journey later I was at Crystal Peaks, and as I waited (and waited) for a bus, I got talking to two young teenage chaps. One was a Blade, the other a piggy, and give credit to the grunter, he didn't gloat over the cup result, or the ending of our unbeaten home record. Instead the two of them were most impressed by the fact that I hitched everywhere.

Eventually my bus arrived, and the long slow journey carried on. By the time I got off in Woodall, it was cold, wet and very dark. It was also two hours after the final whistle and there were many firework displays lighting up the sky. However there was not enough light for me to spot that I was entering my usual field (across which lay the services) in the wrong place. When I disappeared up to my knees in mud I sussed it and turned back. Once the correct path had been found, I was there. Just one thing was needed to add the final touch. Woodall's exit is not the most brightly lit, so I pulled my last-season's lime-green fluorescent away shirt out of my rucksack (complete with Bob Booker's signature) and put it on over my many layers, including my coat. I may have looked like I had the figure of Michelin Man, but at least I was visible. Mind you, I began to doubt this as I waited for over half an hour...

In the end, not for the first time this season, a Leeds fan rescued me. What's more, he was another top geezer. My old prejudices about Leeds fans are starting to disappear...

He was now living in Coventry, but was a season ticket holder for Leeds and had been up for their incredible 4-3 win that morning over Liverpool, with Viduka scoring all four of the Leeds goals (I'd seen the last two on Sky whilst purchasing my new woolly hat - Katrina didn't like my old red one - from the club shop). He'd gone to a relative's house to grab some sleep and then headed home, which I guess was lucky for me.

He'd spotted my shirt with "Blades" on it, and felt as a Christian and a football fan that he should pick me up. At this point I was worried because as a Mormon I usually find myself arguing with people who try to ram their faith down my throat (about 6 months ago a lift to London with a born-again resulted in a lively exchange of views as he insisted that we weren't Christians and I insisted that surely if we believed in Christ we most certainly were - one section of the debate went something like this: Greenwich, in between constant interruptions from our born-again chum - "The word Christian is derived from the word Christ, so surely if you believe..." [another interruption]... Greenwich loses cool: "Look, will you shut up for a minute and let me finish!" He apologised and let me end my sentence.)

Thankfully this guy was nothing like that at all; as a football fan, music lover and Internet addict we had plenty of other things to talk about.

He said that Leeds liked Sheffield United, but couldn't understand why we didn't like them. He then took a call on his mobile and I never got round to explaining to him. So Dave, if you read this think Mick Jones, Tony Currie, Gary Hamson, Alex Sabella, Keith Edwards, Brian Deane... then sit down to watch Leeds - sorry, Yorkshire - TV and Look Leeds - oops, there I go again - Look North. Still don't understand? Well, get in a time machine and visit

Greystones School playground in 1976. There you'll see a young Greenwich and a few other Blades supporters, but you'll also see a whole host of Leeds fans who didn't even know where it was on the map. So, nothing against Leeds fans in particular (especially ones that give me a lift), but some wounds take a long time to heal...

When it came to music, I was interested to find out that he was just about to open a record shop in Coventry, and that they'd be selling copies of Radiohead's latest opus Kid A for just £9.99. What's more, he'd got a box of them in the boot, and as I'd not got round to buying it, when we got to my drop-off point of Leicester Forest East I relieved him of a copy in exchange for a tenner. He also chucked in a can of deodorant, of which he also had a job lot in the boot. A thoroughly decent bloke...

He offered me a lift to Coventry station, and was prepared to give me half the train fare to London, but I turned it down on the pretext that it was cheating (cue Attila), and said I'd prefer the adventure.

One hour later, still standing at Leicester Forest (and having forgot my gloves), I was beginning to regret rejecting his kind offer. However, I saw a car coming out of the petrol station with no headlights on. As he went past I shouted, "Switch yer lights on!" and he stopped. Getting bored with the firework display in the neighbouring field, it was the natural thing for me to get in.

"Your lights ain't on!" I said as I got in. He was grateful and put them on, unlike those Leeds fans after the Colchester game...

He was going into London which was rather handy, and what's more, I'd be back in time to get the tube home.

He was quite an interesting bloke. He actually lived in Sheffield, having been brought up in Stoke. His father was Jamaican and his mother was Algerian, and the whole family had embraced Islam. He told me that as a kid his best friend had been Dalian Atkinson, and in Sheffield he'd been great friends with Paul Williams (the ex-porker, not the goal machine that scuffed shots for the Blades in 1988) and Carlton Palmer. I told him that it was interesting, but as a Blade I failed to be impressed. He then told me his best friend in Sheffield was Prince Naseem. Now I was impressed with that, purely because if I wasn't, he might send Naz round my house to sort me out. I asked him if Naz was serious about buying that local pork butchers round Swillsborough-way (I may not have worded it quite like this at the time) and he said that he was.

"None of us thought he was serious at first, but he is," he said.

I told him to give some advice to Naz, and that was that a merger was NOT a good idea.

Round about Watford Gap he started to tell me about Islam, and from then until he dropped me at Hounslow West tube I hardly got a word in edgeways. Those that know me will find this hard to believe, but it is true.

I didn't know much about Islam, but now I know many of its philosophies. Try this lot...

"Woman was made from the rib of man... a rib is curved, so what happens if you try to straighten it? It breaks! Don't ever try to straighten or change your woman, or you will break her."

"Woman is like a diamond. If you polish a diamond, it gives you more and if you keep on polishing it, it will give you even more! Polish your woman - treat her good and she will give you more, and she will treat you good!" Katrina had a great week after this...

And so to our friend Salman Rushdie who opened this tale:

"Salman Rushdie tried to change Islam, and that was not good. I think the Fatwa was taking things a bit far, but he shouldn't have tried to change it."

For the second time I thought about my close encounter with Salman all those years ago and I would have told him about it, but he was already telling me how to combat stress (it involved a visit to an Islamic bookshop on Mayfair and treating Katrina good if you must know).

At West Hounslow my head was spinning, but I felt I'd increased my general knowledge a little (he'd also told me all about the prophet Mohammed and the Qoran). It gave me plenty to think about on the long tube journey home.

Once home I discovered there was a party at our house, and about 50 Eastern Europeans had overrun it. My room is on the ground floor right next door to the party, so sleep was a non-starter. I ended up chatting to the only other English guy there, an Arsenal supporting death-metal fan. I then remembered that my best friend, who lives on the top floor, was currently on holiday in Slovakia so I retired to his room and got a reasonably good night's kip.

The next morning I was talking to Mr. Patel, the proprietor of the local newsagents.

"How are you?" he asked.

"Bit grim! My team lost again yesterday," I replied.

"The trouble with footballers is they lose because they spend too much time chasing women and not concentrating on the football," he philosophised.

"Bit hard to believe with our ugly bunch," I shrugged, "but you might have a point!"

"Have faith," he said, "and they'll get better again!"

Have faith, eh? After 29 years in this particular cult of the Blades I have the utmost faith, especially with the board. Yep, I can trust them to sell our star players and yet tell us they are still ambitious for a start. Ah yes, we can still reach the Premiership... just don't tell Sam Hashimi (or Samantha Kane for that matter).

Chapter 16
Bagpuss

Saturday 11th November 2000: Burnley 2-0 Sheffield United

The killer 'flu got me, and when I say killer, I mean killer! I was confined to bed for three days, so had to rely on Stafford's text messages to keep me informed. As full-time approached I got, "PENALTY TO THE BLADES!"
One minute later: "JAFFA'S MISSED IT!" Ah well.
I raised myself off my sick bed that night to go and see Cardiacs at the LA2, but I wasn't my usual self, not even venturing into the moshpit. I only started to feel better afterwards as I sat by a huge outdoor heater underneath a big tarpaulin round the back of the Garlic and Shots in Soho, chatting to members of Miranda Sex Garden and Dark Star, amongst others...

Saturday 18th November 2000: Sheffield United 3-2 Grimsby Town

Considering my age, I have played in relatively few competitive football matches. At High Storrs School (1978-1984) I never got a sniff of the first team (or second) in any year, although I did turn out fairly regularly for the house team, first Herring and then Stephenson (my proudest moment was scoring the 3rd goal in a 3-1 victory over Carey House in a 3rd and 4th place play-off - I was hovering on the edge of the area at a corner, the ball was partially cleared, but only as far as me and I carefully placed my shot into the corner: my teammates finally caught up with me somewhere near the tennis courts as I went on my victory charge).
My only real competitive games as a 'keeper were in a 6 a-side competition in Garforth in Leeds (1983). It was the Crusader tournament (we were Sheffield West - Crusaders was a non-denominational Christian youth club... I went because I fancied most of the girls there) and we were up against three other teams. I'm proud to say I kept three clean sheets as we won 1-0 and 4-0, drawing the other game 0-0 against the hot favourites Garforth. In the end we won the tournament on goal difference. I was a hero and Garforth were very, very upset.
But we have to go back to Greystones Middle School (1974-1978) for my most regular appearances. I don't remember all the games (I remember being most upset at being left out of a game against Hunters Bar), but a 4-0 defeat away to Dobcroft springs to mind. My dad turned up to watch, and I was on the left wing. As I am totally right footed, it wasn't easy. I remember the Dobcroft fans chanting "Two four, soap and water, who are we about to slaughter?

Greystones!" We decided they were all namby-pamby poofs (sorry Crouch End!) but, er, they slaughtered us. When I was in year M3 (aged 11) most of our games were against Ecclesall C of E School up at Maud Maxfields (a somewhat bleak spot), and we always got murdered. One game will always stay in my memory. It was blowing a tremendous gale and there was torrential rain. We were kicking with the wind in the first half, but by half-time we were 6-0 down. I was playing left back (that's how desperate we were) with Guy Thompson (a fellow Blade) in goal. At half-time as we stood shivering, we had the most inspirational team-talk ever. Mr. David Taylor said, "If they can score six goals in one half, so can we..."

I remember thinking, "What a load of crap!" and sure enough in the second half, kicking into the wind, we never once got out of our own half. Ecclesall went into second gear, knocking in another 4, running out eventual 10-0 winners. I remember seeing our subs playing 3-And-In on an adjacent pitch, and I felt envious. They were having fun and I most surely wasn't...

To a certain extent we gained revenge in M4 when a lot of those Ecclesall players were playing for High Storrs First Years and we took them on. My brother confidently predicted we'd get hammered, but we ran out 5-1 winners, which was as big a surprise to us as anyone else. I played the first half on the right side of midfield, but was told before-hand that I'd be substituted at half-time. I remember feeling slightly guilty as I watched one of my best friends (Michael Spooner) limping off injured after only 20 minutes and I felt happy. That meant I was going to get a full game you see...

I'm not sure if N6 was playing for High Storrs in that game, but I know for sure that he was playing for Ecclesall in the 10-0 hammering. And sure enough as I strolled onto the platform at Bank Station on Friday night thinking about those past matches and my up-coming game the next morning against the internet Grimsby team, there indeed was N6 himself!

It's nice to know that I had another witness, just in case any of you think I make all this up. There I was struggling along the platform with my larger rucksack (including full kit you see), complete with card saying SHEFFIELD. As we travelled north on the Northern Line we spoke about all things Blades and hitching. I told him if I was in Sheffield for midnight, I'd be very happy.

And so after my enforced absence from the Burnley away game (Killer Flu!) I was back where I belonged - on the road, and at the bottom of the M1 at Staples Corner by 7.45pm. The obligatory 2 minutes later I had my first and only lift that night, with an oldish chap smoking a pipe. He lived in Bury (he'd been to Gigg Lane once, the same as me), but said he could just as well go up the M1 and across the M62 as head up the M6. This was fine by me, as it meant I'd be dropped off at Meadowhall well before the Supertram stopped running.

Mind you, it was fairly hard work, as conversation did not flow naturally. I found out that for most of his life he'd worked as a model maker, but was now working for a company who installed sprinkler systems. He was currently working all week in an under-construction retail outlet on Oxford Street, driving home at the weekends.

I tried to get the conversation going by bringing up all my usual subjects (football, cricket, Tesco - I left out the music as I doubted he'd appreciate the intricacies of Cardiacs' total recorded output), but it never really got going properly. I resorted a lot of the time to pointing out traffic jams way up ahead (and there were plenty that night, I can tell you - no-one on the trains you see), a skill learned from 16 years of hitching.

I also spent much of the journey trying to phone my mum and dad as I thought I'd better let them know I was coming... There was no answer at home or on the mobile, so I was contemplating an attempted break-in on the caravan. As I walked across Meadowhall at 10.30 I was still trying, finally managing contact as the Supertram was sweeping into the city centre. They'd just got in from Leeds, and ironically had left the M1 about the same time I'd been arriving at Meadowhall. "We could have picked you up, but yer mother had the blummin' thing (the mobile) switched off in her bag!" said my dad. To make up for it I walked to the station and he picked me up from there.

So, a very trouble-free journey. Call me weird, but I'm looking forward to the snow in January and February...

Unlike my last appearance between the sticks for the Internet Blades (Crewe, remember), this time I had a decent amount of sleep before the game. My dad gave me a lift to Heeley Bank Road and as I walked into the dressing room, several voices said, "It's the Cat!" Meersbrook Blade presented me with a pair of gloves, and I felt ready! On emerging from the dressing room, we discovered Lepps was in the crowd, and that the Blades Under 14s girls' team were playing on the adjacent field again.

We had enough between us for two sides of nine, with the Blades having several subs, of which I was one (I shared goalkeeping duties with a young chap called Liam... maybe we should call him the Kitten?).

Stafford and Radford turned up to add youthful exuberance (and in one case weight) to the team. Stafford won quote of the day with, "I don't know about the Cat - more like bloody Bagpuss!" And this was during the warm up, the cheeky young whippersnapper.

Well, I'm not sure about Bagpuss, but I certainly dropped a few Clangers (arf arf!).

With about 5 minutes of the first half to go we were losing 1-0 and I came on as an outfield sub. One beautiful move ended with the ball being played to me on the edge of the area. With only the 'keeper to beat I launched my shot very high and very wide. Thank goodness for that rather high fence around the pitch that saved me from a very long trek to retrieve the ball.

In the second half it was my turn to don the gloves. Let us just for one minute look at the statistics. When I came on we were losing 1-0, and by the time the ref. blew the final whistle we had won 4-1. A clean sheet for the Cat then. But of course, stats don't always tell the whole story.

One Grimsby free-kick was hit from somewhere over near Crookes (somewhere on the horizon, for those with no geographical knowledge of Sheffield). By the time it reached me it bounced and had lost what little pace it had. An easy catch, but somehow I palmed it onto the bar. Don't ask me how... I was just mighty relieved to see it bouncing back towards me off the woodwork.

I was saved by the woodwork again minutes later. An attempted clearance (a kick from hands) hit the legs of the Grimsby player stood in front of me. He didn't know much about it, but the ball cannoned off him and flew past me towards the goal. In an almost perfect re-enactment of David Kelly's goal for the Blades against Alan Kelly and Blackburn, I found myself scrambling helplessly back to save my embarrassment. I had no chance, so I couldn't believe my luck when the ball struck the inside of the post and rebounded into my arms. I tore my knee to shreds trying to get that one. We scored from the resulting clearance - an assist for the Cat...

It can safely be said that I did not inspire my team-mates with confidence (although if you read the report of the game, I seem to have had quite a good one - cheers Colin!). Some of my clearances shall we say, erm, lacked direction too.

Strange isn't it that the two games against Crewe when I let in about 18 earned me the nickname the Cat, and yet a clean sheet earned me another name? Bagpuss may have started as a joke, but by the end, I felt I'd earned it...

The real stars of the show though were young Nathan whose penalty made it 1-1 (he may be about a third the age of most of us, but the name on the back of his shirt said DEVLIN and you can rest assured, Paul, that this young chap can give you lessons on how to take a spot-kick), Webbo (who is a shield for the Cat... didn't stop him from sending me an email telling me to "now behave" the other week though), Stafford, Radford... well, everyone really - it's a team game (this should not be seen as a reaction to criticism of my self-indulgent postings on SUISA post-match).

Afterwards whilst Stafford went home for a shower, myself, Radford and Lepps negotiated the bus to go to the R&R wherein there was the usual gathering (Rob, Attila amongst others, and this week's London Blades - Musical, Wimbledon and Hammersmith).

We all said the same result as the Internet game would be nice - well, we got the same amount of goals. Who else but United could make you feel uneasy when you are 3-1 up at home with the opposition down to 10 men? Grimsby played much better after the sending off, and after their second goal, we felt we were hanging on a little. But a win is a win, and Lepps looked relieved as we had started to say she was a jinx.

For me, the star billing went to Big Georges Santos. His cheeky back-heel flick for our first had a touch of Dennis Law about it, and that thunderous shot that smacked the bar (I think it's still shaking now) brought back happy memories of one Tri Dellas. It was also nice to see Benty get back on the scoresheet with a brace (but...).

So, my plan to delay kick-off by 9 hours by tying up the Bladettes so that Suffo's ban would have expired leaving him free to play was not necessary. Still like to try it though...

Another thing not needed was my thumb, or my sign for that matter as Musical forgot to make me stand in front of the car with it. I just got in and off we went, me in the front and Wimbledon and Hammersmith in the back.

After the obligatory Praise or Grumble, we were entertained by 606, especially a Norwegian Arsenal fan called Per who wanted Wenger sacked and Keegan to replace him. Richard Littlejohn quote: "The trouble with going out on the Internet is not only do we get our own nutters phoning up, but we get all the nutters from other countries phoning in too!" There were large guffaws from the occupants of the car throughout this exchange.

I got home in time to watch Match of the Day, after which I was ready to nod off. It could have been a trick of the light, but my gramophone player by the side of my bed really did start to look like a mechanical mouse organ as I drifted off to sleep...

Chapter 17
Tooth Hurty Kick-off

Tuesday 21st November 2000: Sheffield United 1-1 Fulham

Nearly six years ago now I had a lot of dental problems. In the end the staff at Tesco could no longer bear my whingeing and I was driven forcibly to the local dental surgery in Brackley by Liz from the kiosk. Much suffering ensued via a series of appointments, the pain only eased by the attractiveness of my young female dentist. One root filling and an extraction later we were nearly there, apart from one broken tooth that was proving too difficult to get at. I was told that I would have to wait for the monthly visit of the "extraction expert". I didn't like the sound of this, but did I have any choice?

Eventually the day came, and I recall being almost strapped into the chair. Our expert injected my gum and then placed what resembled a small Hoover into my mouth to suck away all the gunge. When she felt the anaesthetic should have taken effect she produced a giant pair of pliers, but before she started she said, "If it hurts, tell me."

It hurt, oh how it hurt! I tried to tell her, but I had a Hoover and a pair of pliers in my mouth. I gripped the arm rests tightly, and eventually the tears streaming down my cheek made her realise that my grunts were not an indication of pleasure, but sheer agony. "Does it hurt?" she asked.

"Thyeth!" I spluttered, so I was subject to another giant needle...

Eventually, after much pushing, probing and pulling (in my imagination I always remember it that she had to put her foot on my head to get it out) the extraction was complete. I have never been to the dentist since, and will take some persuading. Mind you, the time is getting close, as three broken teeth and severe bouts of killer toothache are taking their toll. Just before setting off for the Fulham game, having finished off some coursework (on Private Eye) in agony, I paid a visit to the chemist and came away with some toothache tincture. I applied it liberally whilst travelling on the Docklands Light Railway, noticing that the pain subsided a little, but more worryingly all feeling in my lip disappeared.

As I approached Staples Corner I checked my watch, as always, to record my start time. It was 2.30pm and I thought, "Ha ha, what time do you go to the dentist? Tooth Hurty!" Mind you, I figured that that would be far too corny to use as a title...

Two minutes later I had a lift with a trucker who was going to Northampton. His son was a Man City fan who'd only missed about three games in six years. Not bad, I thought...

He was a very chatty fellow, and we exchanged stories about run-ins with bosses, him in a factory building JCBs, me mainly from my nightmare stint as a night manager for Tesco. The frequent sight of me with a cotton bud in my mouth didn't seem to disturb him...

He dropped me off at Rothersthorpe Services, Northampton, and here I was in for a shock. Since this season started I have not come across one single rival hitchhiker, which proves that I am part of a dying breed. Five years ago at places like Staples Corner, you could always guarantee there would be at least one other hitcher there, even at 3 in the morning. On one memorable occasion in 1993 there were about 8 of us all queued up on the slip road at approx. 10am. A police car pulled in at the bottom and the plod beckoned us all down. "Now, this is not a public footpath - you are all technically on the motorway therefore breaking the law. If we come back in fifteen minutes and you are still here, we'll nick the lot of you!" And with that they drove up onto the M1.

A hitchers' union meeting led to me suggesting that whoever was at the front of the queue should keep an eye on the other slip road, the southbound exit, and if they saw the police, shout to the rest and we would all leg it. Sure enough, I was now at the front and I saw the jam-sandwich coming onto the roundabout. A frantic shout of "PIGS!" and the four or so hitchers that were left scrambled down the slip road and we all vaulted the fence and then hid under the footbridge. We were peering through the railings and could see the police in their car looking for us as they waited at the traffic lights. The fact that they must have seen us as they came off at the other side made their puzzlement even funnier to us as they drove past where a few seconds earlier we had all been standing.

Anyway, there I was at Rothersthorpe, and for the first time this season, there was another hitchhiker. What's more she was a young lady, and she was going to Sheffield. Mind you, she was accompanied by a dog on a string, and the prospect of sharing a hitch did not appeal. On top of that, hitching separately would be tricky too as she was stood in a very difficult place. Mind you, I was reminded of the last time I'd seen a girl hitching. This was about six years ago, and once again I was at Rothersthorpe. It was getting quite late in the evening, and as I hitched I saw a young girl approaching me. She was wearing a very short skirt and her only possessions appeared to be in a Tesco carrier bag. Despite being obviously very young, she was very pleasing on the eye and I was quite surprised when she came up to me and asked, "Are you going anywhere nice?"

"Well, Sheffield," I replied, "and you?"

It turned out she was 15 years old and was hitching from London to Leicester. She'd run away from home in Leicester six months earlier, and had spent her time in London "working" (I didn't ask, but I had an inkling...). She'd decided to return home and so had contacted her mum by phone, for the first time since running away, that morning and they'd both been in tears over the phone. So now she was heading home, and I felt that I had no choice but to make sure she got there safely. I couldn't believe she was out there on her own, so I suggested we hitch together. We had a lift in no time, and we got a lift with a young couple who lived in Leicester who said they'd take her to her parents' front door, so I could get out at Leicester safe in the knowledge that she would get home safely. Mind you, for me the fun was just beginning! I ended up walking along the top of the embankment from the Leicester turn-off to Leicester Forest East Services, which resulted in another brush with the law. It also resulted in my first (and only) hitch in a police car...

So, back to my current predicament. I told the girl that I would go to the shop and when I came back in fifteen minutes, hopefully she would be gone. Thankfully, when I did come back she was no longer there, and what's more, she had taken her dog with her.

Ten minutes later I myself had a lift in a lorry cab (that is, just the cab bit), driven by a trade-plater from Scotland. He said he very rarely hitched after he'd delivered his vehicles, preferring to sleep on the train. Sensible chap...

He was a Ross County fan, but as he now lived in Livingston he had a season ticket for them instead. Hmmm, can't see me ever rushing out to get a season ticket for West Ham, Charlton or Leyton Orient...

He was delivering his cab to Doncaster, so he dropped me off at Woodall Services. As I was there for 5.30, I still figured I could go to Burger King, get the bus and arrive at the pub in time to meet Musical well before kick-off. Ah well!

As I picked up my rucksack and wandered across the car-park, I saw a Fulham fan having a quick ciggie outside his coach.

So i) What Greenwich would like to have happened:

He runs across to me, grabs me and says, "Are you that Blade that hitches to all the games?"

ii) What you lot probably think happened:

I approach him, grab him round the neck and scream, "Do you know who I am? I hitch to all the games you know! Just say you know me, and I'll let you go!"

iii) What really happened:

I go over to the guy and say that I don't want to wish them luck for tonight as I'm a Blade. I then point out that I've just hitched up from where they've come from. He asks, "Are you that Blade who hitches everywhere?" Cool! It turned out he'd read my story about the murder charge guy in that compilation magazine. I voiced my displeasure at how badly edited it was, but added that I was pleased with the publicity.

After a casual stroll through Burger King and a slippery one through the usual field, followed by a wet jog along Dowcar Lane in Woodall, I had an even wetter wait for a bus. By the time I caught one to Killamarsh, it was looking bad for the pub. The driver was helpful though, and also very chatty. He told me all about his adventures hitching when he was in the RAF, including one night on his birthday when he was completely ratted, tried to hitch back to the barracks (or whatever the RAF call them), fell asleep in the car and when he was woken by the driver he was ten miles in the wrong direction.

Via a second bus, I was now at Crystal Peaks waiting for a tram. I could have had fifteen minutes in the pub too if they were anything like efficient. Three went in the opposite direction, but I had to wait half an hour for one to take me to the Lane. As it was, I arrived just in time for kick-off, but at least I was kept occupied by admiring the girl in the nice leather trousers sitting opposite. However, her mate did have hair disturbingly like Kozzie's before he found his clippers (and if Koz develops lady bumps like hers, he will definitely be off for a "random" drug test...).

As I walked to the ground my dad phoned. I told him I was at the Lane (bless him, he's still waiting for me to miss a home match so he can have my season ticket), and then I asked him if he was coming down.

"No," he said, "I've just had a broken tooth taken out today, so I'm a bit groggy!" As if I needed reminding. More tincture applied! (As I write this, I can feel it raging again - talk about psychosomatic.)

I ended up meeting Musical and Attila in the ground, and as we watched the Bladettes getting wet, I was thankful that I was cheating by getting a lift home with Musical.

Maybe the wet conditions were the reason why United didn't touch the ball in the first five minutes? 1-0 down, we were prepared for a cricket score, but miraculously we got back into it when Jaffa netted after hitting the bar followed by a scramble.

All in all, it was top entertainment, and a draw was a good result against the team who are apparently going to walk this division. But how big an idiot was that ref?

Wimbledon joined Musical and I for the journey back to London (he'd come up on the coach). I was quite noisy on the way back, (high on tincture I think) relating many hitching tales to keep those two awake (ho-hum).

Once home, I struggled to get to sleep. It was probably the pain, but thinking about how on earth Jaffa's goal had squeezed in didn't help me. Thoughts of girls hitching with dogs, leather trousers on the tram, Kozzie with boobs and Bladettes in the rain were all in there somewhere too. Maybe I don't need a dentist after all, just a therapist.

Chapter 18
Progressive Nonsense

Saturday 25th November 2000: Sheffield United 1-0 Bolton Wanderers

Two things have always vied for top spot in my life - music and football. Luckily there have been very few times when I have had to make a choice of one over the other, but I have certainly put myself to a lot of trouble trying to squeeze both in. Immediate examples that spring to mind are a League Cup game at home to Blackpool in 1993 and the FA Cup 3rd round tie with Bury in 1998.

In the Blackpool case we were 3-0 down from the first leg at Bloomfield Road (and yes, I had hitched to that one too), and I decided that I needed to add my voice to the crowd to try and get us back into it for the home leg, so I hitched up from Brackley. My decision to attend was aided by the fact that Fish, the former Marillion singer, was doing a gig at the Leadmill that night, so I reckoned I could fit both in.

Well, United won on the night 2-0 and we were only denied extra time by the post when Mitch Ward (or was it Dane Whitehouse?) hit it in the last minute. Angered by the aggregate defeat I stomped off to the Leadmill and was slightly cheered up when I realised I knew the woman promoting the gig, which meant that after the gig not only did I get a lift to the M1, I got to meet Fish too. Ten years before, Marillion had been my band of the moment (I was one of what Sounds described as the "fresh-faced young hippies" there to see them at Glastonbury in 1983), but now it didn't mean quite as much to me - however, I was still chuffed!

The best thing was when Fish saw my Cardiacs t-shirt and we had a good old natter about that band of bands (Fish is one of Cardiacs' celebrity fans, along with Damon Albarn, all of Faith No More - especially Mike Patton-, Charlie Harper of the UK Subs and Marina Mowatt, the Queen's second cousin). What's more, Fish put me on the guest list for his gig later on that week in Aylesbury.

The trouble was, after all this frantic ligging it was very late. Even though my promoter friend gave me a lift to Trowell Services, I knew I was going to have problems, especially as I was due at work for 8.30 the next morning. Progress was slow, and by 2.30am I'd only got as far as junction 23a. Five hours later I was still there and I was getting desperate. This remains my record longest unbroken wait, and by this time I knew I was going to have trouble with work. I was almost on my knees begging traffic to stop, and at about 7.35 some bloke eventually took pity on me. Thankfully he was able to drop me off at junction 15a, meaning I was only twenty miles from work, which lay west along the A43. The trouble was it was already 8.30 and I had a rival hitchhiker. He was an old chap in a dirty mac who was bordering on the hobo...

After five minutes this young guy rescued us both, with the old guy getting in the front. I held a conversation with the driver whilst the tramp fell asleep (or passed out) in the front, his head sliding alarmingly down towards the driver. Sitting in the back I carried on the conversation whilst frequently moving the dirty-mac guy's head back upright whilst the driver kept turning to me and going :-{ (that's the best I can do!).

I rolled into work at 8.55, casually did the shift change-over by cashing up the tills, then nipped home, returning to work with my sleeping bag. I went up into the stockroom to sleep leaving the instruction with the staff that they were only to disturb if it was "a director or higher - if it's the area manager, fob him off!" Unsurprisingly, two weeks later I gave my notice...

(And if you want to know what happened with the Bury match, read my 1998 FA Cup article in Flashing Blade - it's on my web site at http://www.gre.ac.uk/~ba024)

So here I was on the eve of the Bolton game again squeezing both music and football into my life once more. Cheese Cake Truck were gigging in Norwich on that Friday night, and in my role as Dr TragIcall I was duty-bound to attend, especially as my gramophone player was making its debut (you'll just have to come to a gig to find out more). At least this time I made sure I got to Norwich by travelling with the band. I slept most of the journey so I avoided the trauma of seeing the places associated with my disastrous trip there a few weeks before.

The gig was a resounding success with moshing aplenty, and we even had our first crowd surfers and stage divers. I was kept busy behind my desk selling twelve CDs and three t-shirts whilst taking names for the mailing list.

The venue doubled as a night-club, so we stayed until the early hours with much ligging taking place. Unlike the Fish gig, though, this time it was myself and the Cheese Cake Truck boys loving all the attention (hi Spiky Em and Kirsty!).

By the time we'd left, got something to eat, driven to London, unloaded the van and dropped everyone off, I was crawling into bed at 6am. My alarm went off one hour later, and one hour after that I was leaving the house, propping my eyelids open with Red Bull.

Just after 9am I was at Staples Corner (no abandoned cars for ages!) and within five minutes my Blades shirt got me a lift. The chap was a Luton fan called Wayne who was living in London. They were playing Port Vale away that day so he was going to pick up his mates in Dunstable before continuing his journey. He told me about how through work he had a trip to Spain sorted, part of the deal being that they got to see Real Madrid. The problem he had was that same weekend Luton had Darlington away in the cup "and I've never been to their ground before, so I really want to go there." He still hadn't made his mind up what to do. Darlington or Real Madrid...? I like to think he made the trip to Feethams...

Anyway, he dropped me at junction 11 in Luton which was not the best of places. There was nowhere really for the cars to pull in on the slip road and I foresaw a long wait, putting my pre-match arrival at the pub in jeopardy. After about twenty minutes though, I was delighted to see a car come round the roundabout being driven by a chap wearing a red and white shirt. He pulled over and in I got. It turned out to be SUISA contributor Luton Blade who was also giving a lift to a Chelsea fan mate of his who obviously fancied some culture Blades-style.

A few years ago now, whenever my music-loving friends and I were heading from Brackley to London for a gig, as we entered Bedfordshire we always had a snigger at the sign: "BEDFORDSHIRE - A PROGRESSIVE COUNTY". The joke was always that Bedfordshire must be full of Marillion fans. Ho ho...

Well, now I know it's true as our Luton Blade was indeed a lover of progressive rock of all ages, including Marillion, so once again our Fishy friend entered the story. The conversation headed down the route of sinister jesters and the legend of Grendel, as well as reminiscing about many a gig in the 80s at Sheffield University that it turned out we'd both attended (Solstice with Haze as support, anyone? I bootlegged that one myself).

We were in Sheffield in good time, although the teeming rain had us all worrying about a possible postponement. Anyway, I had time to get food in the Beer

Engine and then move on to the R&R to meet the usual crew. Musical had driven up with Radio and Camden, meaning there'd be room for me on the way back if I wanted...

The main topic of conversation was the sale of Marcus Bent. The general opinion was that we could do without him, but we were all very angry with the deal that had been done. A player whose value had been touted as £3 million who'd said he only wanted to go to a Premier League side, so we sell him to promotion rivals for £1.35 million, with the deal possibly being worth £2.1 million depending on appearances and promotion for Blackburn... should be fun if we get them in the play-offs. Anyway, what a great deal! Well done the Board. Progressive as ever... if only it hadn't happened before (and of course, it will never happen again... *sigh*).

There were a few rumbles of discontent about the quality of the game, but for me the biggest disappointment was the absence of the Bladettes. Surely they weren't part of the Bent deal? Or perhaps they were on strike knowing that they'd be ousted in favour of Blades Midas Gold (who were rather nice) when we take on the piggies in front of the Sky cameras? Or maybe they just didn't feel safe after hearing of my kidnap plan before the Grimsby match? Whatever, I know I wasn't the only one disappointed, as one Blade was looking forward to the game after I'd informed him that his favourite was actually 17 (to avoid Hightower's embarrassment I won't mention his name...).

But anyway, I actually enjoyed the game (maybe I'm just easily pleased?) especially the perfect minute when as the Blades prepared to take a corner the scoreboard told us the pigs were losing 1-0 at Crewe. And what happened from the corner? Super-sub Sandy headed the winner! It doesn't get much better than that...

After my toothache-tincture-inspired high of the last journey home, this time the trip was a peaceful one for the London Blades as I snoozed happily in the back. I woke up at the services, though, to see a guy pumping petrol all over his foot rather than in his tank. In the queue inside he reeked of fuel - silly boy...

Once back in London as I waited for the Tube at Baker Street one posh-sounding chap spotted my United hat and so engaged me in conversation. It turned out he'd worked with that sport's psychologist that came to the Lane when we were bottom of the old first division in 1990/91. He felt that they had played a huge part in United's recovery and wanted to do it again.

By the time I'd munched my way through a Chinese and watched Match of the Day, I was ready for bed, so to help me drift off into a past world I put on an old Marillion album. Great memories, the only trouble being whenever I hear "Chelsea Monday" I am reminded of the way I felt returning to work one Monday morning after a rather horrendous Saturday at Stamford Bridge in May 1994. Scarred for life, I'm afraid...

Chapter 19
Top Cat and Dibble

Wednesday 29th November 2000: Nottingham Forest 2-0 Sheffield United

A verbal agreement with Tesco about my Christmas floating day wasn't enough to get me to this match. I made the big mistake of phoning up in the morning to check that I was still allowed to have the evening off, only to be told that lots of staff had called in sick, and as I was contracted I should turn up or risk disciplinary action. What really got me was that I'd never been to Forest's ground, and what made me even angrier was when I got to work, I found out that Katrina had been one of those to phone in sick! Thanks a lot everybody...

Once more I had to rely on Stafford's texts, this time having to sneakily hide my mobile behind the till. It didn't sound like I missed much, anyway...

Saturday 2nd December 2000: Stockport County 0-2 Sheffield United

People often ask me why I hitch, and my responses are quite numerous. Firstly I do actually enjoy it, and the misery of standing around in the rain for hours on end sometimes is easily(ish) out-weighed by the feeling of euphoria one gets on completing a particularly tricky hitch. The other thing is the money aspect. I know recently I've played the impoverished student card, but what about when I was earning a decent wage as manager of a convenience store or as a Tesco night manager? Yes, the truth is I'm a tight-fisted git, or more to the point, I like to have as much dosh as possible available for the purchase of CDs.

Another reason is that I don't have too much confidence in public transport. For example, on two consecutive Saturdays sometime around 1996 or 1997, United were at home and I tried to travel up from Banbury on the train. On both occasions delays were experienced at Birmingham New Street, and the delay meant I would miss most, or all, of the game, so I turned round and went home - both times! And on both occasions I claimed a full refund (the only moment to brighten up these two dismal days was an announcement over the PA at New Street as I sat in the waiting room: "Would Mr Eric Shunn contact the station master's office, Mr Eric Shunn...").

But one near miss in particular was responsible for an increase in hitching activity in the early 90s. In September 1991, the Blades were away to Oldham and I travelled up on the train. I don't remember the exact details, but I do know that I ended up having to change at Stockport. As kick-off neared, I was still stuck there on the platform with my train to Oldham nowhere to be seen. No British Rail employee I asked could help, so I got angrier and angrier. I was with my then-girlfriend Annie, and she did her best to calm me down, but I was not happy. We ended up having to get a taxi when we arrived at the station in Oldham, and just as we came through the turnstile, Oldham went 1-0 up. As we settled in our places Oldham went two up, and by half-time United were down to nine men, having had both Paul Beesley and Charlie Hartfield sent off - and in my view, solely to blame? British Rail!

These memories were brought to mind by a nightmare tube journey to Brent Cross on the night of Friday 1st December. All was running smoothly until I got on the Northern Line and I boarded a train at Bank that was terminating at Hampstead for some reason. Well, it was heading in the right direction, so on I got. The next one that came along was terminating at Edgware, which was fine for me as that is after Brent Cross. However, it got as far as the next stop Golders Green and the announcement was made that it would terminate there for some reason. So with grumblings and mutterings arising from the disgruntled passengers, we all got off and waited for another one... As I waited for this to arrive I got a phone call from Katrina. Now, the day before we'd decided to call a halt to our relationship, mutually and amicably. She sounded a bit fed up and asked me if I was going up to Sheffield. When I replied in the affirmative, she expressed regret that she hadn't known as she was bored and was travelling up to Leicester to see a friend, and we could have travelled up together. Heaven forbid, she may even have chosen to come to watch the Blades instead. If only... anyway, I suggested that we'd had more important things to talk about the day before, but I spent the rest of the weekend thinking that this would have been the ideal weekend to make her a Blade for life.

And so eventually my tube train arrived, and everyone boarded it. However, London Underground still had a few tricks up their sleeve. The train waited and waited, and then another one appeared on the next platform heading in the same direction, and that waited too. Which one was going to go first? I said out loud, "Okay, do we risk running across to that train, or do we wait here?" I followed this a few seconds later with, "Right, I'm going for it!" and legged it across to the other train. After I led the way, quite a few followed, but even on the other train, still we waited. I wouldn't have minded but I only wanted to go one stop...

And then it happened... after a wait in total of a good twenty minutes, the announcement was heard from the other train (are you following this?), "This train is ready to depart..." and every occupant of the train I was on spilled onto the platform and made for the other. An unseemly struggle took place as we all battled for places, but then the doors closed and we were off. A few stragglers were left on the platform, and I was reminded of one similar incident at Harrow-On-The-Hill when some poor unfortunate decided to swap trains and just as he got to the door of his new one, they closed and it pulled off. Then as he turned and rushed back to his original train, those doors also closed, and that one pulled out too- natural comedy... you just can't beat it.

Finally I arrived at Brent Cross, half an hour later than I'd hoped (it was now 8.30ish), but as ever I didn't have long to wait. My fluorescent yellow away shirt from last season soon got me spotted, and I got myself a lift with a typical Friday-nighter; a youngish chap travelling home having spent all week at work. The trouble was he was only going as far as Luton, and he was able to take me as far as junction 10a. His description of this made it sound like a bad one to me, but I soon had reason to take this lift as far as I possibly could...

It turned out he worked for the BBC, working on interactive TV. When I told him I was hitching to as many Blades games as possible and writing about it, he immediately became interested. He said he had a friend who worked on a sports programme, and he was on the look out for "oddball sports stories". Hmmm...me, oddball? Well, I wasn't about to argue, as a little bit of media exposure was, I felt, just what the doctor ordered. So, as I gave him my email details and various web addresses at junction 10a we nearly caused a pile up, and I looked around to see that yes, this was indeed a bad junction.

The trouble with this place was that hitching here you could either be going north or south (look it up on the map, I can't be bothered to explain), so I hastily had to add "M1 NORTH" to my folding cardboard sign. Whilst doing this, two cars stopped for me, both of which were going back to London. After that most people just ignored me, and it was getting cold and windy. In the end, I spotted a truck coming round the roundabout with the word "CORBY" on the side of it. I knew this to be north of Luton, and so I held my sign right up so it was almost at his eye-level. I knew such drastic actions would force him to stop, and he did. Obviously, he couldn't take me too far, but he was able to drop me at Rothersthorpe Services, thus getting me back on track (give me services over junctions any time). The lift was long enough to establish that his record collection was bigger than mine, but it seemed that he just collected them for the sake of it and (going into musical snob mode) his tastes obviously weren't as specialised as mine, as the names Van Der Graaf Generator and Henry Cow meant nothing to him. However, we did have a good chat about Sparky's Magic Piano...

Rothersthorpe is probably the best services of all to hitch from, because not only do you get the service station traffic, you also get everything coming off the A43, and providing it isn't heading up the M6, an awful lot of it is going in a Sheffield direction. Thus I feel confident that the SHEFFIELD part of my sign can be unfurled (you have to hitch tactically, you know - it is not advisable for example to have a sign saying SHEFFIELD when stood at Brent Cross - when there all you are interested in is getting beyond the M25). It soon paid dividends on this occasion as within minutes I was in a car heading north with a chap from Bradford who was going home. He had a broad West Yorkshire accent, and it was soon apparent that we had a lot in common. He was a curry fiend for a start, and he'd done a lot of hitching, so we swapped tales from the road. His longest wait had been the best part of a whole day outside Dover when he was hitching with his 19-year-old niece. The reason he'd got stuck had been because she was out of view, curled up fast asleep whilst he did all the hard work - now me, if I have a member of the opposite sex hitching with me I believe in making them work (and look where that got me on the way to Norwich).

His most famous benefactor had been when he got a lift in a Rolls Royce driven by Norman Wisdom (who bought him lunch at a services - how sweet!). I was jealous on two counts; firstly the best car I've had a lift in is a Merc, as well as a couple of Jags (although the soft top MG was rather cool on the way to Reading Festival in 1986); and secondly because the most famous people to give me a lift have been a chap who played for Notts County reserves as understudy to Tommy Lawton, and the former bass-player from Picketywitch.

Best of all though, this chap seemed to share (in part anyway) my " specialised" tastes in music, in that he was a big fan of the likes of Pink Floyd and Yes, as well as Porcupine Tree and Marillion. For the second week running, jesters were a major topic of conversation on the journey. It turned out he'd been at Stonehenge in 1984, and he'd seen Marillion at Nostell Priory near Wakefield when I'd also seen them, again in 1984 (back then, as we walked into the centre of Wakefield through the night, one of my mates decided it would be a good idea to keep warm by dismantling a road-side fence and setting fire to it - as we all sat around keeping warm, we were disturbed by three van-loads of police who ticked us off, but luckily they had a more pressing engagement with the Peace Convoy back at the site, so they told us to put the fire out and go away, and then they moved on to give the Convoy a taste of what was to come in June 1985 at the Battle of the Beanfield, but don't get me started on that...)

Anyway, it was one of those splendid lifts where the conversation never faltered, and what's more, he dropped me at Meadowhall just before midnight where my dad was waiting to give me a lift home...

The next morning I was up early in order to get ready for the first big game of the day, the Internet Blades against QPR's equivalent. You see, QPR were playing the piggies that afternoon, but the QPR internet team didn't want to play the grunters' 'net side as they considered them to be "a bunch of thugs" (they said it, not me), and so they lined up to play the gentlemen of SUISA and Blades United instead. All those that played were promised a lift to Stockport in the afternoon, and as that is the currency I deal in my name was first on the teamsheet.

After my Bagpuss miracle-clean-sheet nightmare, most people were a bit more cautious about lavishing the nickname The Cat on me this time. Besides, my youthful fellow 'keeper Liam (who I'd suggested we should call the Kitten - well it turns out his nickname has always been Mouse... The Cat and Mouse - it actually gets better and better!) was set to play the first half in goal again. As we were short of players this meant I had to play outfield for the first half, so the crowd (Lepps, Gleadless Valley Blade and a couple more) were treated to my woeful distribution, and finishing that saw all my attempts on goal either clear the fence (we were playing 9-a-side on the all-weather pitch again) or smash into said fence. I think they were glad to wedge me between the posts in the second half. Sadly at half-time we were already trailing 2-0, but I felt I prevented it from being more in the second period with a much-improved performance compared to last time (no near comedy goals this time), my favourite save being one when a cross went to the edge of my area where a rather large QPR bloke with long hair was lurking. I dashed out to meet him and as he lashed his shot goalwards I stuck up my left arm and deflected it over the top. Just in case it wasn't clear, I pointed out to ref Colin (who would also be writing the report) that I had indeed got a hand to it...

I believe we pulled one back in the second half (I should get up to date with this writing), but it wasn't enough. From my point of view, I was quite happy as my efforts (combined with Webbo's unorthodox but effective methods in defence) meant another clean sheet for the Cat!

As promised, I got a lift to the match in Stockport with Gleadless Valley (otherwise known as Debbie) along with her son, the afore-mentioned Mouse. We went the scenic route, passing such delights as Speedwell Cavern and some very big hills, the type of which you forget exist when you live in London. The sights of Stockport were not so pleasant, although the existence of Nobbin Restaurant made us all chuckle...

Thanks to Stockport's antiquated ground we were afforded the pleasure of standing behind the goal, a rare opportunity these days. It seemed to have brought the Blades out in force, as there was a goodly gathering of us on the terraces, including Andy from the Internet Blades team (formerly known as Scallywag, apparently), Dorset Blade (along with Mrs. Dorset), Stafford and Radford. Despite spilling my first pie everywhere (including on Mrs. Dorset), as half-time approached I decided I needed another, so I ventured to the pie-stall once more. It was one of those stalls where it was possible to queue and watch the game, and it was from here that I gleefully watched Kozzie's magnificent through-ball and Dev's run and finish from an angle on the stroke of half-time. My celebrations were cut short upon reaching the front of the queue when I was told they were out of pies...

Thanks to Andy Dibble in the Stockport goal, the second half was one of the most enjoyable ever. The Blades close proximity meant he could hear everything that was said, and he didn't like it. At first he kept turning round and shaking his head, then it was rumoured that he made a gesture behind his back and tossed something in our direction. A chant went up from those in front of us of "Na na, Dibble is sh*t, Dibble is sh*t!" which he didn't seem to like, and his constant fiddling in his shorts led to one witty Blade singing (to the tune of "Chirpy Chirpy Cheep Cheep"), "Dibble's got the crabs, Dibble's got the crabs!" (modesty prevents me from saying who this was.)

And then we got Dibble's coup de grace... a long back-pass was heading to the edge of Dibble's area, and as he'd looked a bit suspect before, Jaffa chased it resulting in Dibble hitting his clearance against him. All of a sudden Jaffa was clear in the area, and was just shaping to roll the ball into the unguarded net when Dibble hauled him down in a style more appropriate to Twickenham. A more obvious sending off you will never see. As the ref reached for his pocket we all knew what was coming. Given the red card he threw his gloves to Tod who, in the absence of a sub keeper, was given the job of going in goal. As the stewards were escorting Dibble off the pitch someone obviously pointed out that Tod would need his shirt too. We realised what was about to happen... all afternoon the Blades had referred to Dibble as over-weight and illegitimate, and now we were going to see evidence of at least the former. He had the indignity of standing in the middle of the 6-yard area minus his shirt whilst the Blades chanted loud and clear, "You fat b*****d!". Tod's shirt did seem rather tight on Dibble too, so with the chanting continuing and as the stewards carried on their escort service, Dibble turned to the Blades and shouted, "F*** off!" Justice has never been so poetic. Bye-bye Dibble, you miserable git!

To cap it all, Quinny stuck the penalty away, and we were home and dry at 2-0...

Return journeys are always brightened by an away win, and this season these have been few and far between. Debbie was able to drop me off at Woodall, and here my trusty yellow away-shirt was put on over my coat. However, I was stuck for about 40 minutes before I got a lift with a Southampton fan driving a mini-bus. He'd just dropped off his youth-group who were taking part in a roller-hockey tournament in Sheffield, and was travelling to a relative's in Leicester for the night. As I'd waited, and at various points in the lift, I tried to phone Radio Five-Live's 606 programme, but it was constantly engaged as I'd left it too late. Ah well, maybe next week.

I was dropped off at Leicester Forest where I stuffed myself with a Burger King Double-Whopper-with-Cheese before continuing the hitch. By now it was getting late, and I feared I wasn't going to be back in London in time to attend the party to which I'd been invited. It was being held by a group of art-student girls from Goldsmith's College in New Cross, and believe you me, I wanted to attend. As I waited and waited, it suddenly occurred to me that Katrina was but a few miles away in Leicester, so I sent her a text message. She phoned me back, and she said I could crash at her friend's house if I got stuck. This also appealed to me, as I was already missing the girl (ahhh, you big soppy git!), and by 10.30pm I was seriously considering it (I'd been waiting one-and-a-half hours), but then as all seemed lost, the party was back on! Just as Katrina phoned me again a car stopped and two chaps gave me a lift.

"Have you been to see United?" asked the passenger.

"Aye... at Stockport!" I replied. This sent them into a state of confusion, as it turned out they were Man Utd fans, and of course, they all think they are the only United...

They gave me a lift because they thought I was a Man Utd fan, the two-inches-wide of red, white and black scarf round my neck being what confused them, having managed to miss the several square feet of yellow shirt with BLADES emblazoned across it...

As Man Utd fans they were, of course, heading to their home, in Hemel Hempstead... But let's not be too hasty to judge. They were originally northerners, the driver being from Macclesfield (okay, maybe I'll let him off), but the other was from Bradford, and a former Bradford supporter - indeed he'd been part of the Bradford crew. Guilty as charged! Mind you, as a former member of a crew, I kept these opinions to myself... Instead he told me some rather scary stories about encounters with the BBC and OCS in the eighties.

They dropped me off at Toddington Services at 11.30, and I realised that if I was to get to London in time to get a tube to this party I was going to need a lift straight away. It didn't happen, so in the end after an hour I abandoned the hitch and after buying some grub from the garage, I headed into the services.

At Toddington they have PCs available to surf the 'net, but I've still not sussed them yet. I tried again this night (without success), and whilst fiddling about, a drongo sat next to me said, "You trying to hitch as well?"

"I was, but I've given up for the night," I replied.

"I've been waiting for someone to pick me up since 2.30," he announced. This suggested to me that he was doing something very wrong...

"Well, I'm going to sleep round the corner," I explained.

"You won't be able to sleep round there," he advised.

"I've done it before and I'll do it again," I said and left him to it. He was still sitting there when I got up in the morning...

The corner I slept in was the same as after the Blackburn match, just by the stairs leading to the restaurant. Despite the hard floor, my sleeping bag and woolly hat made it slightly more comfortable. I slept by the Rupert-the-Bear kiddie ride, and at one point my sleep was interrupted by the sound of a child crying as he went up the stairs. I hoped it wasn't because of me, but I had a horrible thought going through my head that there was a parent saying, "No Johnny, you can't go on the Rupert the Bear ride... there's a weirdo sleeping by it..."

Other than this, my sleep was only interrupted by the awful Granada Services radio that blares out all night playing inoffensive (to most of the population) hits of the eighties... "Young at heart; Young at heart." Ughh!

At 7am I was woken from my slumbers by an employee who told me I shouldn't really be sleeping there, so it was time to move on. By 7.30 I was on the road again, but some quick advice for Granada; as well as dispensing with your woeful radio station, please fit locks on your toilet that actually work. Only my rucksack up against the door prevented me from being joined in my cubicle by what could well have been an elderly gent who'd spent previous hours loitering round a truck-stop near Peterborough...

I waited another hour in the freezing-cold early-morning, until at 8.30 a truck stopped. His wagon (unarticulated, if you know what I mean) was towing a huge film-location caravan, which was fine going down the M1, but caused a few problems trundling round the streets of Hackney. Yes indeed, this was one of those rare lifts that took me into my part of London. He was a Glaswegian who was on his third trip of the weekend with such a caravan. I asked him what was being filmed...

"I have no idea," he shrugged, "I just pick these things up from Liverpool and then bring them back to their depot in Hackney."

No problems anyway, as he was able to drop me at Hackney Central station for 10am, and I was soon on a Silverlink train journeying the three stops to Stratford... It wasn't long before I was tucked up in bed catching up on sleep, dreaming of two heroic goalkeepers - Top Cat and Dibble indeed...

Chapter 20
Radio Blade
(with apologies to, er, the real Radio Blade... sorry Lee!)

Saturday 9th December 2000: Barnsley 0-0 Sheffield United

As well as being asked why I hitch everywhere, another question I am frequently asked is why, at the age of 33 (18 months ago) I decided to ditch my "promising" career with Tesco and head into further education. I suspect that anyone who has worked as a night manager for Tesco will understand why. Okay, so it wasn't an immediate decision. Indeed, after escaping from that night job at Tesco in Brackley, I spent a very enjoyable, stress free 9 months working at Tesco in Pinner Green surrounded by friendly (and attractive) female staff, in a store that was frequented by Czech and Slovak au-pair girls. Oh yes, very therapeutic, but as I'd voluntarily stepped down to general assistant, staying there was hardly a good career move. So I decided to retrain if you like, and head off to Uni. But the key to my original step-down is that word stress...

Two occasions spring to mind from my time at Brackley. You see, the General Manager there was most definitely the worst man-manager it has ever been my displeasure to work with. On one Friday night (our busiest night) I had both my back-door man and my fruit-and-veg man phone in sick. I ended up delegating the management of the rest of the shopfloor out to a senior member of staff, and then set about doing the work of three people in one night. I worked right through my lunch hour, as well as the second break of half an hour later on, only stopping for the last 5 minutes of both breaks in order to have a Mars Bar and down a couple of ProPlus tablets with a Red Bull. Oh, and to make sure the rest of the staff came back on time...

That night I took in every delivery myself, cleared the shopfloor and put out all the fruit and veg. Meanwhile the rest of the staff finished everything apart from a little bit of can-tidying on aisle 7. I was very pleased with my performance, but guess what...? The General Manager came in and played merry hell with me because of the little bit of untidiness on aisle 7. After a nose-to-nose argument in the office I went home but couldn't sleep, so I went back to the store at midday, and we had another row in the office. Happy days...

By the time my German girlfriend dumped me one month later in April 1998, I was sick of the bloke, and after a few violent mood swings (smashing that glass cabinet hurt) I trotted off to the doctors, and he signed me off with stress and tension. The wonderful thing was, the Blades had two away matches that week which would decide our play-off fate, so I headed off to Birkenhead to see us draw 3-3 with Tranmere. A cure for stress this was not, and neither was the game two days later when we lost 2-1 at Crewe. Just prior to hitching up for this one, the second incident occurred. I was summoned to Tesco and sat in the office with the General Manager and Trading Manager pleading with me to work "just tonight and this weekend, then you can have as much time off as you like..."

I steadfastly refused, and the looks on their faces said it all. "Have you got anything else to say?" asked the GM.

"Yes, I hope when I come back that you won't hold this against me," I replied.

"Why should we?" he asked.

"Because I've seen you do it to others," I said, thus ensuring that I WOULD suffer on my return (sometimes saying things like that gets you nowhere, but you feel SO much better).

The fact that I was wearing my white away shirt all the way through the interview probably annoyed them even more, and straight after leaving the office, I was hitching to Crewe...

Upon my return to work, they refused to transfer me to days as I requested, so my decision was made; London and a general assistant's job there please...

In my last week, I had two parting shots. First of all they sent a security man round to see how easy it was to get in the store on my shift. He succeeded, finding a trainee manager first. The trainee proved that he would go far in the company by denying all responsibility and sending him to find me stuck down aisle 10, wading through cardboard and putting biscuits out.

"Hello," he announced with a stern look, "I'm (insert whatever his name was here), the head of security for the area. I've been in your store undetected for twenty minutes now. What have you got to say to that?"

"Well done!" came my sharp reply.

"I've got to write a report on this that will be seen by the regional director..." he continued.

"Write away, and don't forget to write that it is a greater security risk to have a night manager who is working his notice in-store with no other management..." I encouraged.

When the GM read the report in the morning, he was not happy.

"The Regional Director will read that!" he bellowed.

"Ah well," I replied, and wandered off, perfectly happy...

And on our last morning together I wrote a rather barbed comment in the duty-manager's handover book.

"Listen you," said my pal, "I don't need you writing sarcastic comments in my duty-manager's book!"

"It's not sarcastic, it's the truth!" I defended.

He then read it out. Maybe he had a point...

"Well, it's the sort of sh*t I've had to put up with for the last four years, and to be perfectly honest, I ain't gonna miss it..." I said (you must understand, I was very bitter).

"Could you please get out of my chair," was the only retort he could muster. Why, I'd almost forgotten that all this had been delivered whilst I swivelled in his comfy chair and he stood up...

As I did a spot of shopping on the way out, he bumped into me.

"I'm sorry we couldn't have ended on a better note, but thanks for all your hard work," he said.

"I didn't expect you to hug me and give me flowers," I smiled, and so I got out whilst the going was relatively good.

On the night of Friday December 8th 2000 as I hitched towards Sheffield in preparation for Barnsley away the following day, these stories were trotted out for the benefit of the giver of my first lift. He took me from Staples Corner to Leicester Forest, so we had plenty of time to chat. It has to be said that I have told those stories on many hitching occasions, but with this guy they were even more appropriate than usual. Despite him being considerably older than me (in his fifties I would say) we had a lot in common. He'd worked as a professor at a university, but had eventually left it after having a nervous breakdown (I don't think I was far off myself) brought on by an unsympathetic boss. He'd worked 60-odd hours a week, and was always getting it in the neck from those above. Thanks to a supportive wife, he'd come through it and was now working on the technical side of a company that made lenses for the most expensive television cameras money could buy... He'd also lived in London in the early seventies, including a stint in New Cross and Deptford. Wish I'd made it to that art-student girls' party...

I waited about 20 minutes at Leicester Forest before I got a lift with a young chap who was heading up to Leeds. He'd been a student there so was off to stop with old friends. He was living in Oxford, but only temporarily; "I'm flitting from friend to friend at the moment. I have no fixed abode right now. Saves on rent..." Respect.

In order to get up to Leeds (where he was hoping to patch things up with his ex) he'd developed an elaborate hoax to get the time off work. This involved getting a female friend to phone up work pretending to be his mum or something, and included a car breakdown story. I lost the plot, so I can only assume his boss was equally confused and just said, "Oh, okay..."

He was able to drop me off at Meadowhall, and as it was before the cut-off time of midnight, I was able to get my dad to come and pick me up... Another night in the caravan avoided...

Barnsley being a very cheap hop, skip and a jump away on the train, I opted for Railtrack the following morning, and whilst purchasing my ticket, I met Rob and Attila. We travelled together on a very crowded train, and a very interesting chat developed with some Spurs fans on the way to Bradford, with odd interjections from a nearby Barnsley fan.

We disembarked at Barnsley station, and Rob assured me that his mate who was accompanying us worked in Barnsley, so he knew what pubs were safe. Well, I wasn't convinced by the Court House right opposite the station, and kept my coat zipped right up round my head to hide my Blades shirt.

We were surrounded by Dingles shirts and eighties Bon Jovi hairstyles, whilst the lads sporting no colours right next to us made me feel even more nervous. I expressed my concerns to Rob, but then in walked Billy Whitehurst, and all of a sudden I felt a whole lot safer! He went up to the guys next to us, and if they were mates of Big Billy Tightshirt, then they were obviously Blades and the sort of guys who nobody would mess with.

By the time Lords joined us, I was almost confident enough to reveal my Blades shirt, but instead we headed for a quieter pub. I didn't like this one much either, especially as the barmaid (not a looker, that I can tell you) was heard to say, "Dee dar, dee dar!" after she'd served us. Me brother's me dad, as they say in these parts...

In the end we retired to the pub in the shopping centre which appeared to be taken over by Blades. Within minutes of our arrival, the Greasy Chip Butty song burst forth, and from then it was a repeat of the tram journey to Swillsborough. At times like this, I love being a Blade...

Just as the police filed through the pub, someone started to sing, "Who let the pigs out?" and Lords, not realising the law were around added, "Oink oink, oink oink!"

A copper grabbed Lords and said, "Listen, we don't want to ruin your day, so don't you ruin ours..."

Lords nodded his head looking most bewildered, so I butted in; "Okay, but can I just say that we were referring to Sheffield Wednesday fans, not yourselves!"

The until-now stern copper then broke into a huge smile and said, "Oh, that's all right then!"

There was a match that afternoon. It was not good. I seem to remember we wore white shirts which to us signalled the demise of the lilac-and-gold ones. Fordy hit the bar with a cross/shot and... well, there was a lot of us there (over 3000 Blades). I missed the highlight though, whilst queuing for a pie at half-time. Apparently it came over the tannoy, wishing somebody called Chris (?) Dingle a happy birthday. Arf arf... 0-0 away from home - okay I suppose.

After the game I said farewell to Lords at the station (he was going up to Bradford) and jumped on a train bound for Meadowhall, leaving Blades and Dingles scrapping of a heap on the platform.

Yes, Meadowhall! I was going to shun the chance of a comfortable night in Sheffield at my parents and hitch back to London that night. I had a plan you see, and timing was all important. At 5.50pm I was scurrying across the car-park at Meadowhall heading for Tinsley Viaduct and the M1. I chose this time to phone 606, 15 minutes before they went on air, knowing that I'd probably get through. I did!

"Hello 606... what would you like to talk about tonight?" asked the nice girl.

"Well, I'm reporting from the road. I'm a Sheffield United supporter living in London, and I'm trying to hitch to as many games as possible this season..."

"Really?" she said, and I knew I had her interest. She then asked me lots of questions about how many games I'd hitched to this season, and when I'd started etc etc. She wound up by saying, "Okay, the producer most likely will call you soon after we go on air." Yessss!

As I scrambled across the roundabout and over fences to get to the junction, I missed the call. As I stood hitching on the slip road, I felt gutted. Had I missed my chance? Luckily, 10 minutes later the phone rang again, and it was 606. They told me that Richard Littlejohn would talk to me in about 5 minutes, so then I listened to the other callers before it was my turn. I felt a little nervous at first, and didn't think I came across too well as I explained why, when and wherefore. But then Mr Littlejohn set me up for another chance...

"Listen Adrian, what we're going to do is try and sort you out with a lift tonight, and then we'll call you back and see how you are getting on. Where are you again?"

Greenwich: "Junction 34 of the M1, Tinsley Viaduct."

RJ: "And what are you wearing?"

G: "An old bright yellow Sheffield United away shirt - you can't miss me!"

And sure enough, two minutes after going off air, a car pulled up, and the driver said to me, "I can't take you to London, but..."

The chap was called Mark, and he ran for Sheffield Athletics Club (despite being from Wakefield). He was on his way to Birmingham to see his girlfriend, so we established he could drop me off at Trowell Services.

As promised, 606 phoned me back, and after a quick chat to the producer, I was on air again. All relevant information was passed on to Mr Littlejohn and the good listeners of Radio Five-Live.

RJ: "So what time do you expect to arrive at Trowell?"

G: "Erm... ETA in about 15 minutes."

RJ: "Okay, so if there's anyone there, look out for Adrian in about 15 minutes. He's wearing a yellow Sheffield United away shirt..."

G: "... with Bob Booker's signature on it..."

RJ: (laughs) "With Bob Booker's signature on it?"

I had a feeling I was going to get a lift easily here.

As we drove into the car-park at Trowell, I noticed some young Reading fans waiting outside a coach, and after I'd given my email address and web addresses to Mark they accosted me as I got out of the car.

"We're here to help!" one of them said.

They were on their way back from a cup match in York, and as there weren't many of them on the coach, they had plenty of space.

"We asked the guy in charge, and he says it's okay to give you a lift!" he continued.

They weren't leaving for about 20 minutes, so I had time to go to the cash point to get some dosh, and to phone Katrina and tell her to tune in. Whilst doing this I was approached by Spurs fans who asked me if I was the hitcher. When I told them yes, but I already had a lift, they said, "Well, we would be pushing it for space anyway."

I was then offered a lift by some Luton fans, and again I had to tell them that I was already sorted thanks. To have people fighting over you for a lift... every hitchhiker's dream!

And so when 606 phoned again I was sat on the Young Royals' (as they are known) coach, waiting for it to depart. If I'd felt more relaxed the last time, this time I was supremely confident, sitting there with my feet up. I told Littlejohn that they would drop me at Toddington Services, and he said, "There, we've done you a huge favour tonight!"

Cheeky Greenwich: "Yes, I think we should do this every week!"

RJ: (sounding exasperated but amused) "We're not doing it every week. This is a one off!"

We then got into a discussion about what I did and my age.

G: "I'm a mature student... if there is such a thing."

RJ: "So how old are you?"

G: "That's a very rude question... but I'm 34!"

Tesco somehow got brought up.

RJ: "No greater love does a man have than to give up his job with Tesco..."

G: "It was an easy decision, I can tell you... but I still love 'em!"

He said they'd come back to me one more time before going off the air, so then as the journey started again, I had a great chat to the guys from the Young Royals. Can I just say if you read this boys, you are all top geezers, and I was genuinely upset for you when York fluked the replay at the Madejski.

My final call from Radio Five-Live came as we trundled down the M1 towards Milton Keynes. RJ wanted to know what time I was expecting to arrive at Toddington. I said it was tricky as we had to pull off at Milton Keynes to drop some people off, so it could be a while. It turned out that some chap was waiting at Toddington.

RJ: "Should we tell him to go? He's on a promise in London you see."

G: "Well, if he's on a promise, he should go... I would!"

RJ: "There's a chicken tikka massala with his name on it in central London..."

G: "Tikka massala? That's for wusses! He wants to go for a Phal! The London Blades swear by Phal..."

At this point RJ seemed most amused.

Then the email woman came on saying that someone had emailed asking if I was Greenwich Blade. I owned up, and she said he read my stuff on the Internet, and then asked if I had anything to say about the "jailbird stockbroker and the gypsy". I later realised that this was a reference to my soldering iron story, but at the time I was flummoxed, so I said, "The Jailbird Stockbroker and the Gypsy? Sounds like an album by Van Der Graaf Generator..." For some reason Mr Littlejohn almost expired with laughter at this... maybe he has a copy of H to He Who Am the Only One lurking somewhere...

And with this, it was ended:

RJ: "Listen, Adrian - it's been great fun having you on the show tonight. Please phone us back next week and let us know how you got on for the rest of your journey!"

Heh heh! A license to phone up again...

So 606 was off air, but my adventure was not through yet.

The coach pulled off into Milton Keynes, and as the few disembarked there, the guy in charge shouted up the coach, "Adrian, we've got a lift for you!"

Slightly dumfounded I got off the coach after saying cheerio to the Young Royals and got into a car with a Luton fan.

He lived in Staines but was travelling back from Darlington with his Arsenal fan chum, so he was able to drop me in North London.

They'd tracked my hitch south. They'd had a look at Tinsley Viaduct, but I'd already gone, but then they saw the Young Royals' coach not long after

Early technique displayed on the way to
Stonehenge in 1985. This was very early one
morning at Tinsley Viaduct. Nice hair...

Fuel crisis. See chapter 4.

With some lovely German girls in Regents Park. See chapter 5.

Held responsible..
mum and dad

Text message from
Katrina? Greenwich
cheating on the train
from Colchester.
See chapter 8.

Before the hot towel fight. London Blades
curry (clockwise from left: N6, Warminster, Architect,
Mrs. Architect (hidden), Lords, Radio, Windy, not sure,
Murdoch's neighbour, Musical, Exiled Coal Astoner,
Wimbledon, Sara.

Katrina - she's a shy lass
you know...

Norwich ticket, sadly intact and unused

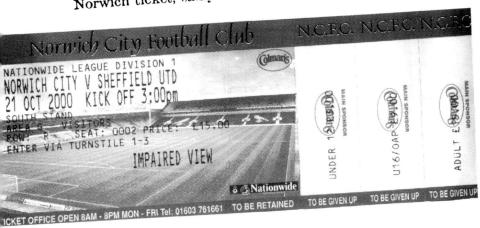

Tim Smith of Cardiacs, probably playing a real catchy little number... see chapter 16

Sir Bob Booker and Greenwich with ink not yet dry on that signed shirt. See chapter 20.

Not above a little name-dropping... My famous niece, Angellica, CBBC presenter. See chapter 24.

Michaela on the Serpentine, just prior to causing New Year mayhem... see chapter 25.

Clayre - the original Checkout Chick. I
sent her delirious, poor lass...
see chapter 29.

Cheese Cake Truck - lovely lads really...
see chapter 29 and lots more.

Musical, Alty and Copes (actually in a
bar in Munich, which should be in the
sequel, but as there might not be one...

The long-suffering Annie. An honorary Blade, she started and finished with 3-2 defeats. Crabs have proved more reliable than the Blades.

Spiky Em and Kirsty, keeping me feeling young. (Don't make me go to the Electric Ballroom again, girls - I've knackered my knee). See chapters 29 and 41 amongst others.

THE LB's flag before someone got green paint on it. From left: Musical, Murdoch's Neighbour, Soho, North London Blade, Woodford Green, Camden. See chapter 43.

What shall we do with a drunken sailor? Camden, WGB (with sword), Soho, Capt. Blade, Blackheath (kneeling), NLB, Alty. See chapter 43.

Greenwich trying to scramble up to the party in the box. Settled for bugging Warnock in the end... see chapter 43.

My hitching post at Watford Gap - being constantly updated...

Agent and client after
the ritual signing of the
contract at Stonehenge...

Internet Blades. Back l-r: Jason, Mouse, not sure, Tom McKaig, Webbo, Stafford, Bagpuss, Radford, Stafford's mate. Front: not sure, Nathan, Andy Elliot, Meersbrook, Donny.

Trowell. They weren't sure if it was the right one, but figured if it came off at Milton Keynes, it must be. So, they followed it into town, and asked if I was on board when the doors opened.

This I was enjoying! They were able to drop me at Arnos Grove tube, and I rang Katrina before getting the train. She greeted me with, "My little star!" The fact that she'd heard me made me feel all glowy inside...

I relaxed on the tube journey home and reflected on what was definitely my proudest moment. I reckon I must be the only hitchhiker to have his hitch tracked live on national radio. What's more, it meant I was home in time for Match of the Day. A stress and tension-free hitch, with my fifteen minutes of fame included... now that I could get used to!

Chapter 21
Hog Tied

Saturday 16th December 2000: Sheffield United 1-1 Sheffield Wednesday

Our year tutor has told us on more than one occasion that it is not a good idea to try and finish your coursework on deadline day, and despite frequent mishaps and panics on that dreaded day, there is usually one thing that is a common sight in the lab on those days. There, in amongst the scrimmage that takes place, you will find Greenwich Blade scrapping for the CD burner or printer with the rest of the idlers/ procrastinators.

You see, I'd spent the best part of two weeks slaving away on my latest coursework project, a rather ambitious interactive CD-ROM of my desert island discs (this course enables me to tailor most of our coursework to my own self-indulgent desires, hence essays on Private Eye, United [that docu-soap], and Blades pages - not to mention music and my Fave Chicks - on my website, which can, of course be found at http://www.gre.ac.uk/~ba024). So, there I was on deadline day with what I described to my colleagues in Cheese Cake Truck as "just an hours work" left to do on it, so I could hand it in before lunch, then join them in their van as we drove up to Oxford for their latest gig. Easy...

The trouble was, everything that could go wrong did. First of all Cool Edit was malfunctioning, so that all-important extract from The Gates of Delerium by Yes could only be added after I'd bugged the life out of the poor university lab-technicians. I was soon back when my video clip of Cardiacs playing Is This The Life at Salisbury Arts Centre in 1990 appeared then disappeared and wouldn't come back. Once again, Technician Stuart saved the day, and (not for the first time on this course), I was beginning to think that if I get this degree, I should really award it to him.

And then I decided to tinker with a few of the effects, despite my better judgement telling me, "Don't tinker, you fool!" Nothing went wrong, but it did add on another hour. By this time I'd phoned Cheese Cake Truck and told them to go without me. "I'll hitch up when I've finished here, lads," I said confidently.

Now everything was working beautifully, so all that needed to be done was the burning to CD. Guess what? The CD burner decided to throw a wobbler. "Stuart...!"

With an hour to go before registry closed, it was finally ready. The only problem was, I also had to finish off and print out a small amount of work for Business Skills in Multimedia, and when I went in that lab, it was heaving. Fights were (literally) breaking out in the queue for the printer as bits of paper flew everywhere. The only good thing about this panic was that whilst queuing I got to stand next to the nice blonde girl who is in the first year...

With fifteen minutes to spare I was charging from one end of the campus to the other, two courseworks in hand. This was made even harder by the fact that I had my rucksack attached to my back. As I queued to hand them in, I picked up a voicemail message from Carly Bassett at SkySports (and yes, she is related!) saying, "Sorry we can't do anything this time Adrian - we are just so short of reporters. But we will keep your number with a view to a feature in the future." 606 has a lot to answer for, eh?

By the time all was safely handed in it was gone 5pm, and all of a sudden hitching to Oxford didn't seem like such a good idea, so I ventured into London and got on the Oxford Tube (a bus service that runs from London to Oxford all day and all night). My biggest problem was that I didn't have a clue where the venue was, only knowing it was above a pub called the Wheatsheaf, somewhere in Oxford. I phoned up Rog the driver of Cheese Cake Truck's van, and he gave me vague directions, but as I jumped off the coach in the centre of Oxford I hoped for a miracle... and it happened. Just as I picked up my bags from the pavement, I turned round to see Endre, CCT's guitarist, walking towards me. Things like that can give you a good vibe for any ensuing hitches, you know.

So, it was a good gig, although I was a little dismayed that those two lovely female Sisters of Mercy fans didn't want a CCT tee-shirt because "it's not black!" (tsk, Goths!), but they did go on the mailing list.

After all the gear was packed away, we all piled in the van and I was dropped off on the way out of Oxford at the (relatively) new services between junctions 8 and 8a on the M40. It was 1am, my Bob-Booker-signed shirt was acting like a beacon, and it was very, very cold! If I thought my appearance on 606 would mean that drivers would be fighting over me to give me a lift, I was soon brought back down to earth. I was only waiting 40 minutes, but in those temperatures, and at that time of night it felt like an eternity. I also had in the back of my mind that there wasn't much margin for error, as it was an 11am kick-off. Mind you, a little cheating on SUISA the day before had ensured that one or two Blades driving north early in the morning would be coming up via the A34 and M40. (Oh, and it's not really cheating, it's showing initiative.) I also had one or two mobile numbers stashed away in my memory ready to get used if necessary (I'd also happily dished out my number on SUISA for all the world to see, deciding that the risk of being stalked was worth it just to get a lift to the pig match).

I was rescued from my icy tomb by an Asian taxi driver, and as usual we went through the motions of him trying to get me to part with cash and me trying to cadge a freebie lift. And as usual, I triumphed, but (as usual) the lift wasn't that far, although by then any lift was worth it. He dropped me off at Cherwell Valley Services just south of Banbury (but a few miles from where I spent ten happy years in Brackley), which was actually pretty useful. Before I started hitching I went to the shop to get a top-up card for my mobile (just in case) and then took up my position at the junction.

I got out my many cards plotting my various routes to Sheffield (M40/ M42/ M1/ SHEFFIELD and all combinations thereof) and waited, and it was still rather cold. Ten minutes later I had my lift, and as I clambered in to the truck's cab I did that time-honoured hitching thing of casting a quick glance at the side of the lorry to see where I might end up. To my delight I saw it had a York address, and I knew I was on my way!

The driver was a rarity for a trucker in that she was a middle-aged woman, and it turned out she was indeed going my way. She was heading for the M18 via the M1, so I figured I'd be dropped off at Woodall services, which to my mind was pretty good. It is very rare that one gets a lift cross-country like that all in one go.

As we trundled along the various motorways we chatted happily, her about her slightly dysfunctional family, and me about all my usual stuff (a bit of football, some music, Tesco horror stories...), stopping off for a quick bite to eat at Donington services on the M1. As we approached Woodall she said that she might as well go up one junction to drop me off at the end of the Sheffield Parkway before driving back to the M18, an arrangement I was more than happy to concur with.

So there I was, well before 5am, and already hitching into Sheffield. I soon had a lift with a tip-up truck that was heading over to Lansdowne Road (those who don't know their geography of Sheffield may like to know that this is in enemy territory, and nowhere near where I wanted to be), but once again a trucker came up trumps and went out of his way to drop me off at Hunter's Bar. From there it was a short-ish walk to my mum and dad's (all uphill though), and then into the caravan. As I set about the flask of soup that had been left in there for me, my mobile rang (it was about 6am now), and it was Shinjuku (a SUISA Blade now based in Japan). He'd stopped in a hotel in Oxford that night, and we'd traded numbers and emails just in case I got stuck. I gleefully informed him that I'd just had one of my most fortuitous hitches ever, and was about to go to bed. Cheers anyway, Shin...

With mobile switched off, I got about three hours sleep in a very cold caravan, before it was time to venture indoors and have breakfast. As my dad was giving me a lift to the Lane a little later I got a phone-call from a photographer who wanted to snap away at me in full hitching get-up. I told him what time I'd be there, that I'd be in the car-park and that he'd be able to recognise me by dint of the rucksack.

Before he arrived I was able to rendezvous with the London Blades, and what a happy (but slightly anxious) gathering we were! When the photographer turned up it was much to the delight of the London Blades (not in that they were happy for me, you understand) and as the photographer and I walked away to a part of the car-park where they wouldn't be able to put me off, a voice that sounded something like Musical's called out, "Media Whore!" If only I was getting paid...

As I stood there with my SHEFFIELD sign, Matthew Bell (no relation), editor of Flashing Blade, came up and introduced himself, and one or two others pointed (and laughed). The photographer kept saying, "Big smile!" and I kept thinking, "This is as big as it'll go mate!" but still he wanted more. If the photos had actually got published I may well have been embarrassed (I'm more into ironic smiles - take note editors!).

Meanwhile, back with the London Blades my dad was providing entertainment whilst looking after the photographer's gear. Apparently he was heard to mutter, "I've got a family of idiots!" thus making Crouch End's day.

Upon my return, we realised that the photographer had gone off without his stuff, leaving Old Man Greenwich holding the baby. Now, my dad was most dis-chuffed that he hadn't been able to get a ticket, so perhaps he saw a way in (if anyone could do it, it would be him - I once watched Yorkshire against New Zealand at Scarborough from the members' enclosure after my dad traded stories about Hutton with the gateman). However, his idiot son located our photographer chum, called him out of the crowd going into the ground and got him to lock all his expensive gear in his car. I suspect my dad drove home shaking his head saying once more, "I've got a family of idiots!"

As we entered the ground I tut-tutted at how absent minded the photographer had been, and then someone asked to look at my programme. Oh dear... I'd given it to him to look after whilst he clicked away, and had then entirely forgotten about it. Ah well, I'd get it back afterwards as he said he'd meet me again for a few more shots...

I can't say that I enjoyed the match. I was way too tense, and I think I speak for the majority of the London Blades present. To add to the tension it did seem a bit like "Hooli Central" where we were; lots of Stone Island gear in evidence (and not just on Musical). A few chants of "We'll see you all outside!" left us in little doubt that we were close to the BBC...

Bobby Ford's penalty was the undoubted highlight, but if anything this made us all feel worse. The pressure was really on now, and when the pigs got that lucky deflected equaliser... *sigh*. The only good thing about this was when Tracey legged over that stupid pig-fan that ran on the pitch.

Dev hit the post, Fordy the bar - we should have won, but... How I hate those grunters...

Afterwards I turned down a lift home in the London Blades' mini-bus, instead opting to pose for more photos, and to get my programme back. I waited, and waited... I watched Sky winching their gear down from above, observed the helicopter hovering around London Road (and deduced that indeed they must have "seen you all outside"), bought another programme just in case, watched Curtis making a bee-line for the pub, Fordy carrying his boots around, Sandy looking as miserable as I felt. Yep, this was one drawn game that felt like a defeat.

In the end, after about an hour and when it started to rain, I gave up waiting and headed to Woodall via the Supertram and the bus. The photos never got used in the end anyway, although a piece in the Daily Star (replicated pretty much in London's Evening Standard) described me as "Football nut Adrian Bell..." going on to claim that I'd hitched 100,000 miles to follow my beloved Blades. Well, maybe if you took every hitch I've ever done for any reason, I may just get close to that figure... Far better was the bit in the Sheffield Star from the previous W*******y where I had almost a whole page to myself, and there was a cartoon of me hitching, complete with Bob Booker shirt.

I was about 30 minutes at Woodall before I had a lift, by which time darkness was already coming down. After a bad afternoon though, things picked up. The West Indian chap who gave me a lift was driving to Ilford in East London, meaning I had a lift almost all the way to my front door. It doesn't happen too often like that you know...

The chap had lived twenty-odd years in London, but had decided that it was not the place to bring up his four young kids, so he'd moved to Sheffield to send them to school there. Wise chap. Meanwhile, he was still working as a mini-cab driver in Ilford, meaning a drive down once a week.

On the way we pulled into Watford Gap services to enable me to speak to Richard Littlejohn on 606 again. I had to let the nation know how my journey had ended the previous week, and then I said I didn't need any help this week as I had a lift almost all the way home. FiveLive weren't going to give it anyway ("It was a one-off!" said Mr. Littlejohn). I finished off by giving my views on the game, saying that W*******y were lucky (I didn't use the word "pigs") and that at the end the W*******y fans were smiling "and I don't like that!" And that was that...

I was hardly smiling myself as I waited for the bus in Ilford for longer than I'd had to wait for a lift at any time that weekend. By the time I was home via the Chinese take-away and the obligatory chat with a Manchester United-supporting Irish guy in there about Paul Devlin (this keeps happening to me), I had cheered up a little, but not much. I was totally knackered anyway, so I went straight to bed and thought to myself, when is a draw not really a draw? Answer - when it's Hog Tied. Damn piggies! Roast pork sadly not on the take-away menu...

Chapter 22
Up Pompey (Then Back Down Again)

Saturday 23rd December 2000: Portsmouth 0-0 Sheffield United

I know this is really sad, but at home I have a map of the UK stuck on my bedroom door. On said map there are red dots where I've seen the Blades and green dots where I've seen Cardiacs (the Cardiacs book will complete my trilogy after the Stonehenge book!) So this means that if I've seen United in the same city at two different grounds, then on that city there are two dots (e.g. Sheffield, Bramall Lane and Swillsborough). However, there are a few grounds that have been bugging me for years because I've been there, but not to see United. One is Maine Road where I saw Pink Floyd in 1988, and another is Walsall's Bescot Stadium, to where I hitched from Banbury to see England B against Switzerland (I think) somewhere in the early 1990s just because Deano was playing...

Another was Fratton Park. You see my Uncle Billy, who lived on Hayling Island, was a Pompey season ticket holder, and as our family have always been keen on doing things as economically as possible, we spent a few holidays down that way, including the summer of 1975. That of course was the start of one of the Blades' worst ever seasons (we were relegated from the old first division by Christmas), but we missed that start because we were on our hols. Indeed, I remember we set off on the opening day of the season, the day that United opened the new South Stand whilst taking on reigning champions Derby County as well as unveiling our new record signing, Chris Guthrie (thanks to my dad, he soon became known as "Carthorse").

My brother was livid with my mum for arranging our holiday thus (I think it actually had something to do with Sheffield Works' shutdown fortnight), but he saw a chink of light when on the Friday night before, his little brother, a then-9-year-old Greenwich Blade, became violently ill (I reckon he poisoned my cornflake supper). I was up all night vomiting, but the following morning I was miraculously cured. The family rejoiced, apart from Julian who I think wanted me admitted to hospital just to be sure.

So we drove down to Hayling Island with ears glued to Radio 2, and learned that the Blades drew 1-1, Jim Brown saved a penalty, and Guthrie hit the post...

One week later United were tonked 5-1 at Old Trafford, but whilst this was happening, we were watching Portsmouth play Forest (back in Cloughie's early days) with my Uncle Billy. I'm not sure of the score, although I'm certain some-one can look it up for me (I would myself, but our server's down) - I know that Portsmouth didn't win though. The thing I remember most is how strange the ground looked to me just because it wasn't the Lane, and also that Forest missed a penalty, leading my dad to say that Cloughie had "a face like thunder!"

That night we all sat down around my Uncle Billy and Auntie Wendy's tele and watched United getting murdered by Man Utd on Match of the Day. Not pretty...

In 1980 another holiday on Hayling Island provided another visit to Fratton Park. Accompanying us this time (for a pre-season friendly against Spurs) was a German family who were also staying at my Uncle Billy and Auntie Wendy's (their teenage daughter Anja could be seen as the genesis of my interest in German girls). Rolf, the head of the family, was highly delighted when the Spurs fans started laying into the Pompey faithful: "Ze English disease!" he said with a huge grin. It's so nice when our English hooligans can put on a spe-cial show for visitors from abroad...

So at last this season I was determined to lay this one to rest. In previous seasons I've always wanted to attend this fixture, but have never been able to due to whatever reasons (I attempted to entice numerous girlfriends with the "a nice day out at the seaside" line, but it never worked). This time, though, noth-ing was going to get in my way. An added incentive was the marvellous price of a fiver (if bought in advance, which I did) due to an outburst of generosity from Pompey's board (they felt sorry for us sitting in an uncovered area - they must have known that it wasn't going to make pretty viewing). On top of this, a ticket stub from this game would give us priority (with a season ticket) for the Southampton 3rd Round Cup match. I was there, dude...

For me this was quite a short hitch, the only doubt being where to hitch from and whether to choose the M3 or the A3. The A3 was more direct, but the M3 was familiar to me. In the end I went for the direct-but-uncharted option. But where to go from? I studied the map and decided there was no sufficiently close tube or railway station within the M25, and as I always desire to put that mon-strosity behind me, I cheated slightly by getting a train from Waterloo to Guildford. The thing is, the train I was on was going all the way to Portsmouth, and temptation was almost too much. I still got some funny looks from the train-operator employees as I asked if this was the "Portsmouth-via-Guildford train" (they obviously had a knowledge of the fixture list and had noticed my

Blades woolly hat). They checked my ticket very carefully and were all hanging out of the doors watching, making sure I got off at Guildford.

I don't like towns like Guildford. Featureless, full of Tories, no football team - just very, very dull. I offered myself the opportunity of a look round too, as coming out of the station I failed to understand the map and went right when I should have gone left (for someone who relies on his wits so much, I have a very poor sense of direction). After walking a mile or two, I took the sensible option of asking directions, and so headed back a mile or three in the opposite direction. Eventually the A3 was located, so out came the yellow shirt. Surely I'll be recognised now, I thought (wrongly) and was stuck there for an hour, and yes it was very cold. I wandered up and down the slip road in an attempt to find the best place to be seen and for cars to pull in, and eventually settled on somewhere up near the top, just in case any passing Blades were whizzing down the A3. By now it was midday, and an SOS text was sent to Maidenhead as a precaution. As usual this proved a winner, because as he was texting his reply saying he'd look out for me, I got my lift.

The chap that picked me up was a twenty-something Southampton fan who was living in Guildford but hated it and was thinking of moving to London. He was travelling down to Wickham for a meeting, so he wouldn't be able to take me into Portsmouth, but I would be early enough to walk into town, and even find everyone else in the pub. As he dropped me off on the A3(M)/A27 he asked me to "stuff the Mushers for us" and I said I'd see him at the Cup match in a couple of weeks.

So, here I was on the outskirts of Portsmouth, and no idea how far I would have to walk, or indeed where Fratton was. It couldn't be far, or so I thought...

After I'd taken off my yellow shirt to ward off any potential batterings, I headed towards the town centre, phoning Musical as I went to establish where he and the London Blades contingent were. They'd just arrived in Portsmouth themselves, and were just getting off the train. "I've no idea how close I am, but I can't be far off, so I'll see you in the pub soon!" I announced, full of confidence.

I walked, and walked, and walked. Let me tell you, Pompey's town centre is very long. At what later appeared to be about the halfway point, I called Musical again to establish what road the pub was on, and then carried on walking. I would have asked the locals, but they seemed a scary bunch to me, reminding me of a southern version of the Dingles. I felt confident that signs for Fratton would soon appear, but even when they did, it was still a fair old trek. And then when I'd found the ground, I still had to find the pub, the Old Canal, recommended by Pommpey Blade (we still don't know where you got your extra "m" from, Pommpey!). I asked the girls in the petrol station, and with the help of a streetmap, we located it. And still I walked on and on. After about an hour and twenty minutes I had found my pub, and mighty relieved I was to see my fellow Blades sat in the corner. Amongst their number were Musical, N6, Warminster, Lords (with the lovely Mrs. Lords), Pommpey (with some junior Pommpeys who were struggling at pool against an 8 year-old girl), Exiled Coal Astoner and others (probably, if I actually took notes on the road all the time, or if I wrote things up a bit more pronto, I wouldn't have these problems).

My aching limbs barely had time to recover before we were off back to the ground, and once in we secured a good spot behind the goal. There was a fair crowd there, probably taking advantage of the fiver offer, as well as wanting to get ahead in the race for a Southampton Cup ticket.

Now, it has to be said that once again it wasn't pretty stuff, as 0-0 draws away from home rarely are. At least it wasn't raining, but it was cold, and a little bit misty. Not much happened in the first half, but that Pompey fan with the bell is so annoying, and his mate with the bugle should know by now where it would be best to shove it. In the crowd at half-time could be seen Shiny and Old Father Shiny, and Murdoch's Neighbour caused a stir in the pie queue by pushing in and then blagging the last hot-dog which, by rights I believe should have gone to Lords.

The second half was a bit better. We could just about make out Sandy's last ditch clearances up the other end, but no-one has yet been able to explain Tracey's save. It involved a post, and all the papers described it as a miracle, but I can't be sure (and I still haven't seen it on the tele). Late on, Dev remembered what he is good at, and started causing flutters in the Pompey defence. A couple of late chances went begging (Quinn and Kelly the culprits as I remember), and that was that. Lords had bailed out about ten minutes from the end after a bit of pressure from Mrs. Lords (they couldn't miss that train to Basingstoke), but he didn't miss too much.

Once I'd put the LBs on the train, I set off walking back down Pompey. Of course, it was just as far, but at least I knew what to expect this time. I passed the time by phoning and chatting with Katrina. She was going round the Millennium Dome, witnessing history before it was too late (I'm proud to say that despite having seen the thing just about every day for two-and-a-half years, I never went in it). By 6pm I was back at the A3(M)/ A27, but couldn't decide whether my LONDON sign should be used or not. In the end, I half used it, which was lucky, because the couple that picked me up fifteen minutes later just about caught a glimpse of it and could take me all the way into the centre of the capital. Before this though, I'd seen United's team coach going round the roundabout and coming off at the junction before mine, which to my mind meant they'd gone the wrong way - some people would do anything to avoid giving me a lift.

So, the irony was that the young couple, students not surprisingly (the smell of their "cigarettes" gave that away), lived in Fratton and had just driven from there. Ah well...

They were going into the centre of London as the young lady's dad lived in an apartment in Waterloo (and very posh it looked from the outside too), and I had a feeling he was involved in politics. Whatever, I reckon he was loaded. They were thoroughly decent kids anyway, and we had a nice chat about music when Radiohead came on his sound-system. She also thought it was "really sweet" when I got all excited upon overtaking United's team coach (obviously back on track).

When at Waterloo I called Musical, and we all met up in the Rat and Parrot on Wardour Street (deepest darkest sleazy Soho folks!). It was remarkably quiet, so much so that we were able to loaf on the sofas. I guess everyone had gone home for Christmas. Anyway, I was treated to the London Blades' tales of the train journey home, involving more than a little Stella. They'd got split into two factions at the station, but assumed they were on the same train. N6 walked the entire length of the train trying to locate the others, but gave up and resorted to his mobile in the end (probably to Warminster).

"Which carriage are you in?" asked N6, to which the reply came something along the lines of, "Near the front and we've just stopped at a station."

N6: "Hang on... we're still moving!" No time delay here, apart from that brought on by the effects of alcohol possibly. Eventually they sussed they were on different trains...

We all eventually drifted off home, me via EasyEverything, the Internet café on Tottenham Court Road where I was able to add my views to those springing up on SUISA. So late did I leave it that I missed the last tube, but no way was I going to walk again. No, I had to settle for the Night-Bus-From-Hell that is the N25, but with those blisters growing on my feet, for 45 minutes it seemed like heaven. And what's more, when I got home I was able to put a nice new red dot on my map.

Chapter 23
'T'Were Neet Before Christmas...

Tuesday 26th December 1989: Sheffield United 2-2 Leeds United

As Christmas approaches I always seem to end up having the same conversation with my dad as regards my travel arrangements over the Christmas period. He always wants to know when I'm coming up and how I'm getting there, and since 1989 it has been either train, lift with a girlfriend or hitching well before Christmas Eve or well after Boxing Day... "Good... so we'll have no repeat of that Peterborough fiasco on the A1," says my dad, and then we carry on with our daily business.

Yes, Christmas Eve 1989... A time of innocence, a time when I thought I'd easily get a lift no matter how late I'd left it, because everyone would be full of the Christmas spirit. Oh dear, oh dear, oh dear...

Back then I was manager of a convenience store in Brackley, Northants (at that time it was Circle K), and so I had the largest say in what days off my deputy and myself had. The trouble with retail is it involves a lot of Saturday working, and the bigger problem with convenience retail was it involved Sundays and late nights too (this was unusual in 1989, kids). The decree from head office was that out of the two managers instore, one of us would have Christmas off and the other New Year. Quick perusal of United's fixture list made my decision easier. On Boxing Day we were playing Leeds at the Lane, and on New Year's Day we were away to Oxford. Now, Oxford was only 20 miles from where I lived, but Leeds was way too attractive a fixture to miss. At the time the Blades and Leeds were scrapping it out at the top of the old division 2, so my dad was duly dispatched to get my ticket.

That year, Christmas Eve fell on a Sunday, and as Sunday was our busiest day of the week anyway, this one was extra special. We took over twice our normal Sunday takings, and even when I left the company four years later, there had still been no busier day in the store. By the time I escaped, it was 7pm and getting late, but before hitching I had to say goodbye to Annie, my long-suffering girlfriend. My plan was to hitch back on Boxing Day evening, so we said we'd exchange presents when I got back. At the time I had no watch, so Annie had bought me one for Christmas. Incidentally, there were no cash machines in Brackley back then, so at 8ish, I set off hitching with no way of knowing the time, and with no money...

After about fifteen minutes of waiting on the A43 at the top of the town I got my first lift. The trouble was, he wasn't going to the M1, but to Peterborough instead. You see, this was also in the days before junction 15a on the M1 which links up the A43, the M1 and Rothersthorpe Services. Back then you either had to go via the A43, A5 and the A45 joining the M1 at junction 16, or you had to get out on the bridge where the A43 passed over the motorway and scramble through undergrowth to get to Rothersthorpe so's not risking arrest by walking on the hard-shoulder.

After much debate with the driver, it was decided that I should miss the M1 altogether and let him drop me on the A1 just outside Peterborough. "There'll be loads of traffic going up north from there," he said...

By the time I was unloaded on the A1, I suppose it must have been somewhere between 9 and 10pm, but of course I had no way of telling. I was dropped off at junction 17 where it changes from the A1(M) back to the A1. I was stood by two houses next to a short pull-in which was well lit by streetlights, but there was only about one car every ten minutes speeding by. In the front room of one of the houses I could see an elderly couple watching TV, and very cosy and

Christmassy it all looked too. As time ticked by I began to get very worried, and contemplated knocking on their door and asking to use their phone (not many mobile phones back then either). I contemplated for too long however, and when I saw them switch off the tele and go upstairs I knew it was late.

I decided I had no choice but to phone my dad, unless I fancied spending Christmas Day shivering by the A1. But of course, I had no money, and even if I had, I had no idea where the nearest phone box was.

I stood there for what seemed an age, trying forlornly to hitch a lift with what few vehicles there were. Eventually though I saw potential saviours. Just by the junction I saw a taxi stop and a load of revellers pile out. They came up the road towards me and as they got level I attracted their attention (not that I wasn't standing out already) and I asked them a series of questions.

The first question I asked them was, "Er... can you tell me what the time is please?"

The loudest chap of the group (a Scot, incidentally) replied, "1 o'clock Christmas morning... happy Christmas mate!"

Christmas Day... brilliant! My next question: "Can you tell me where the nearest phone box is? I need to phone my dad in Sheffield to get him to come and pick me up..."

I was then given directions to a phone box over the other side of the road in a village called Alwalton, and was also treated to a history of local rivalry with the village this side of the road, Chesterton.

My final question was, "Has anyone got 10p they can lend me, 'cos I'm skint?" and bless 'em all, they had a whip round, and very soon they were unloading change into my outstretched palm. It included tens, twenties, fifties and even the odd pound coin!

"There you go!" said the Scot, "ring yer dad and wish him a merry Christmas!" and off they staggered into the night.

So I crossed the central reservation and ventured into Alwalton, eventually locating the phone box. Somewhat pensively I dialled home, wondering just how I was going to word this.

The following conversation ensued when my dad answered.

Adrian: "Hi dad, it's me...!"

Dad (in slightly agitated voice): "And where might you be?"

A: "In a place called Alwalton on the A1, er... near Chesterton, near Peterborough..."

D: "Peterborough?!!! And what do you want ME to do about it?"

A: "I wondered if you could, erm, come and, erm, pick me up...?"

D (very angry now): "I'm going to have to aren't I..? What on earth are you doing in Peterborough?"

A: "Well, I couldn't get a lift, and it's not actually in Peterborough, but just outside... Alwalton... Look for the signs for Chesterton..."

Details were then given of my position, and my dad finished off with, "Right, I'm setting off! Don't move!" (as if I would), followed by a short pause, and then the immortal words, "I've got a family of idiots!!!"

As I heard the phone clunk down I realised I'd not wished him a merry Christmas... ah well.

So I now had a two-hour wait in the freezing cold. Figuring that my dad wouldn't be anywhere near for a while, I stayed in the phone box for shelter, and now I had money! Firstly I phoned the Blades Line, and then tried 0898 followed by random numbers to see what I got. After a few tries I successfully got through to Simon Bates' Our Tune line. I could only stomach so much of that day's tearjerker, so I tried again and ended up with a chat line. All she seemed interested in was telling me it wasn't a sex line.

"I don't care... I'm stuck in this phone box miles from home waiting for a lift, and I'm bored, so..."

"It's not a sex line you know..." she repeated, and then told me she was just wearing a pair of trainers.

"So, if you're not a sex line, then why do you feel the need to tell me...?"

Her last words as she cut me off were, "We're NOT a sex line...!" Clunk.

I knew that, so why did...? Ah well. I was soon out of change, so I slumped in the box and tried to sleep, but then decided that as I had no way of telling the time, maybe I should go and wait by the road.

I ended up sitting on my rucksack by the side of the A1 facing the southbound traffic so I'd see my dad as soon as he arrived. However, I observed from what little traffic there was that I couldn't make out the registration plates from the front, only from the rear after they'd gone past. Added to this, I was in the dark, so he may not be able to see me. I just hoped he'd be going slow enough for me to catch up and flag him down.

I looked carefully at every plate as they went past, and eventually there it was. I still remember the number - A81JAY. Panic seized me as I realised he was going fast enough to leave me behind, and he'd obviously not seen me. I leaped out into the road as he carried on down the A1 and waved my arms around hoping he'd look in his mirror. He didn't, so I started to leg it after the car hoping that I could keep the rear lights in view until he stopped. Sprinting down the middle of the A1, I jettisoned my rucksack in the central reservation and carried on, watching agonisingly as the red lights of the car vanished round a corner in the distance.

Now what? Well, he had to come back, surely, as he would realise he was in the right area. So I went and stood where I'd originally hitched and waited.

Sure enough I saw the car coming back very slowly, so I stood out by the road. To my horror though, I watched as he pulled off and headed up the slip road towards Peterborough. Oh no! Off I sprinted again, hoping to catch him before he reached the town centre.

As I ploughed up the slope in darkness I noticed he'd stopped on the bridge, was turning round and heading back. I was in the dark, so he probably wouldn't see me, so I had to sprint back towards the streetlights before he either drove past me or knocked me over (more likely). I just made it and was able to jump into the road and flag him down. As he pulled up and opened the door he said, "Where have YOU been?"

Out of breath I just about gasped, "Chasing you... up and down... the A1!"

"Get in!" he snapped.

Still puffing and panting I managed, "Gotta... get... my... rucksack!"

"Where is it?"

"Central... reservation!"

"Well hurry up then!"

Once back in the car, we drove in silence for about half an hour until he went to get some petrol. When he came back he was smiling and said, "I said to t'bloke in t'garage, 'I bet there's only me and Father Christmas out at this time!' but he said I were t'forty-third customer!"

I breathed a sigh of relief - "Oh yeah... this Scottish bloke wishes you a merry Christmas!" I said.

Not satisfied with a 5am Christmas Day arrival in Sheffield, I decided I needed more festive fun. By the time kick-off on Boxing Day morning arrived I'd caught up with my sleep and watched a pulsating 2-2 draw with Leeds. Mel Sterland put Leeds 1-0 up with a free-kick from somewhere near the halfway-line before Wilf Rostron equalised, then after a fantastic cross and a delicate nod back (Sir Bob was involved somewhere- did he cross it, or did he nod it back?) Tony-Tony Agana scrambled the ball over the line to have us 2-1 in front at half-time. To think, if we'd held onto that lead we would have finished champions, but it was not to be. I believe it was Carl Shutt who netted the equaliser for Leeds, making three out of the four scorers ex-piggies. Funny how we took to Wilfie better than we did to Terry Curran...

That afternoon I met up with a couple of old mates in the Millstone near Hathersage before wangling a lift to Woodall Services in the evening. There was a lot of traffic about, and getting my first lift was easy. The sad thing was he developed engine trouble, so the car limped into Leicester Forest and I left him scratching around under the bonnet whilst waiting for the AA. "If this thing gets sorted and you're still waiting, I'll pick you up again," he said as we shook hands and bade each other farewell. Sadly, it was left to someone else to, er, pick me up...

Within a matter of minutes a BMW pulled up, and my suspicions were immediately aroused. BMW drivers never stop- they always drive past with their finger raised. Anyway, I got in and the bloke asked me where I was going. My reply of Brackley but junction 16 would be fine was met with just a nod of the head.

"So, where are you heading?" I ventured.

"Oh, I just wanted to get out of the house. I've been stuck in at home all Christmas and I just needed to get out, so I'm out for a drive."

I didn't like this... What's more, he was driving very slowly. Surely BMW drivers liked to show off by driving as fast as possible?

Whatever, I started a conversation and hoped my worries were unfounded. I ended up waffling on about work and how stressful managing a Circle K store was.

"What you need in a job like that is a gymnasium next door so you can just pop in and work-out to relieve the tension," he suggested. Not a bad idea actually, but I had a feeling that the picture in his mind's eye was not the same one I had of some fit young girl working out on a nautilus...

"Anyway, it could be worse," he added, "you could be running a video shop."

"Erm... well we do do video hire actually," I replied, trying to take the conversation my way, not his. I then went on to explain how it wasn't worth it because we hardly took any money on it and it took up too much space, and "the customers are always complaining," I finished off.

"What do they complain about, not enough porn?" he asked.

"Erm... well, we do have a selection of adult titles, but they're not very popular..." I said, in a desperate attempt to avoid his issue.

Too late... "It's all I use my video for now, porn," he mused, as if talking to himself. He then started to describe how he'd been watching a video with his "friend", and as he described what had been going on on-screen, I realised there was one thing missing from his blockbuster movie... women!

Junction 16 couldn't come quickly enough, but because he was driving so slowly we'd not even made it to Watford Gap yet. Realising his video exploits weren't getting him anywhere (my response of, "Er... oh!" wasn't too encouraging I felt), he went for the direct approach.

I glanced to my right and noticed he was driving with one hand on the wheel, the other shoved down his tracksuit bottoms.

"Oh no," I thought, "I'm arousing him!"

His next question was somewhat direct.

"How big's your dick?"

"None of your business!" I replied sharply.

Undeterred he carried on: "Get it out!" he demanded.

"Look, I've got a girlfriend! I'm not into that sort of thing at all, so just leave it!"

"Go on!" he persisted.

"NO!!"

I'm not sure how I came across, but I can tell you that inside I was petrified. For the first time in five years of hitching I realised how vulnerable you can be.

Okay, so he was going slowly, but I still thought that if I tried to get out of the car I'd end up splattered on the M1.

Besides, he probably had central locking, so he'd lock me in, drug me and I'd wake up the next day in a ditch with a sore botty (and yes, this WAS all flashing through my mind as he drove on).

I tried to disguise the fact that I was shaking like a leaf, but from then on we drove in silence until we approached junction 16.

"I think this is my turn off!" I announced. No response...

"Yup! This is it - A45, Weedon, junction 16..."

Still no response, but then just as I had visions of him carrying on down the M1 and a fight breaking out, he turned up the slip road and stopped the car at the roundabout. I got out, grabbed my rucksack off the back seat, said, "Er... thanks for the lift!", slammed the door and ran off to the A45.

For any hitchers out there, he was in his 40s, greying, slightly balding; so now he'll be in his 50s, even greyer and hopefully much balder.

I was still nervous as I hitched, and quite soon I had a lift with a young chap from Brackley who recognised me from the shop. As I spoke, I realised my voice was quavering, so I thought it best to explain what had happened.

"Sh*t!" said the chap, "I don't think I could have handled that," and I said... (boom boom).

Seriously though, I said, "Well, before it happened I wouldn't have thought I could handle a situation like that, but going down the M1 in a car with central locking, I just had to..."

He ended up dropping me off right outside Annie's door, and I was surprisingly early (about 9.30ish). She gave me a big hug and said, "Blimey! You're here early! Safe journey?"

"Yeah... no problems. Good game too..."

Chapter 24
A Visit from the Spin Doctor

Tuesday 26th December 2000: Sheffield United 2-0 West Bromwich Albion
Saturday 30th December 2000: Sheffield United 3-2 Preston North End

As with every year, my Christmas Eve disaster of 1989 was in my mind again as this year's festive celebrations loomed. As usual my mum started asking me in August what my plans were, and as usual I started thinking about it around December 23rd. And on December 23rd 2000 I was sitting upstairs in the Rat and Parrot, Wardour Street with the London Blades, post Portsmouth match. It transpired that Warminster and N6 were both journeying up to Sheffield on Christmas Eve, so the possibility of scrounging a lift was mooted.

On the morning of the 24th as I struggled with the photocopier in Mr. Patel's (making copies of my Sheffield Star appearance) a call from N6 established that it would be Warminster picking me up from some tube station on the Northern Line.

As the rain lashed down on a typically miserable Christmas Eve I felt mighty glad I wasn't hitching in this, never mind looking for phone boxes by the side of the A1 near Peterborough. As it was, the hardest thing about the journey was staggering up the hill to my mum and dad's, rucksack on back, rain blowing in face.

Christmas is a time for the family, and it was with great delight that I visited my sister's for Christmas dinner. You see, her hubby is a W*******yite (I can't call him a piggy, because despite his allegiance to our porcine cousins from S6, he is actually a nice chap), and despite my dad saying it wasn't the done thing to "intrude on the grief of others" I couldn't let the opportunity pass of at least wandering around their house wearing the hallowed red and white.

Yes, a time for the family, which is why my parents cleared off to my brother's in Wheldrake near York on Boxing Day. Trouble is, Boxing Day is also a time for football, which is why I cleared off to the Lane to see us take on West Brom instead. Rather glad I did.

The meeting point was the R&R, and I was the first in there just as they opened the doors. I was happily watching Man United v Villa in the prime seat in the place when all the other riff-raff joined me. As it was the holiday period there was an awful lot in there, far too many to mention, but special mention goes to Putney Blade for telling us that his mate had been the star of the BBC's "Lorna Doone" shown over Christmas.

Now, many of us expected to get a tonking off the Baggies, as they were the form team. Even I, the eternal optimist, was thinking we'd do well to get a draw. As it was we turned in possibly our best footballing performance of the season thus far, and ran out comfortable 2-0 winners, with Kelly being the main tormentor, ironic really as he is a Baggies fan. It was he who got brought down for the first-half penalty (calmly tucked away by Fordy), and he who linked up so poetically with Dev, tucking away an absolute diamond of a goal. Yep, Christmas was pretty merry so far. Mind you, Tesco were to put an end to that...

Tesco have a rule banning holidays in December, and as I was already on a yellow card for absenteeism due to my music and football involvement, I felt I couldn't push my luck on this one. I was due to do a shift Wednesday evening (Dec 27th) so I had to hitch back. The only concession I allowed myself was getting my dad to drop me at Woodall Services.

Within minutes I had my first lift, in a Merc driven by a Southampton fan. His job was picking up vehicles and dropping them off wherever. He wasn't quite a trade-plater, but near enough. He described himself as "the luckiest man in England" as he was a divorcee in his 50s who was about to marry a "gorgeous 25 year-old nymphomaniac". He was heading back to Southampton, which meant he would be cutting across from the M1 to the M40. I decided to go with this as it would make a nice change and I had plenty of time.

I was dropped off at Cherwell Valley Services on the M40, and within ten minutes I had a lift with real rarity value. Getting lifts with females is one thing, but attractive ones...well, now you're talking! To make it even more unlikely she was a Leeds fan (although Leeds fans giving me lifts has hardly been unusual this season), and the impression I got was that she was rather well to do. Her name was Tonya, and she was on her way down to Kent to visit relatives. She'd be back in Leeds for New Year, which incidentally is where I would be...

As she dropped me at junction 4 of the M40, I left her the web address so she could read these stories. Good so far, but now my luck ran out...

I was stuck here for over an hour, and the cold started to bite. I decided everyone had already lost the Christmas spirit. I was just glad I'd got my Tesco uniform with me meaning I wouldn't have to go home first. Eventually yet another young attractive female rescued me. She was in a hurry - something to do with some prescribed drugs she needed for her kid that she'd left behind, though I never quite got to the bottom of her tale - but at least she was able to drop me at Perivale tube station on the Central Line, thus meaning a fairly relaxed trip to Liverpool Street. Before she turfed me out, she told me she'd done some work for the Labour Party and she thought she might have remembered working with my brother, a junior Labour spin-doctor. But before we could go into too much detail I was out, and waving her goodbye, just bothered by the fact that I was going to have to lug my rucksack (the big one) into the changing rooms at Tesco.

Hawkwind will always have a place in my personal history as the main reason why I got into hitching in the first place. You see, it was to see them at Stonehenge Free Festival in 1984 that provided my first ever hitch, and even though it took me and my companion, a black guy called Ben who was an experienced hitchhiker, 24 hours to get from Sheffield to the 'Henge, and we had to sleep rough in a lay-by, I was hooked.. But now ironically it seemed Hawkwind were about to deny me a hitch. You see, they were having their Christmas/ New Year-party gig at the Astoria on Friday 29th Dec, the day before our home match with Preston. I really didn't fancy hitching straight after the gig, or getting up early the next morning. Added to this, the plan for New Year was for myself, a beautiful Czech girl called Michaela, my best mate Ian and his girlfriend Veronika (another Czech) to see in the new year in Leeds where yet another Czech chick, Vendula, lived. Ian asked me if I wanted to go up on the coach on the Saturday morning as it was cheap. Without thinking I said yes as

I thought it might solve a few problems.

When I actually studied it, it was going to cause even more. Yes, I'd be able to watch Hawkwind in comfort (no lugging of baggage into the venue for a start), but the coach was on the day we played Preston and it didn't stop in Sheffield. What's more, I had an away match to get to in Birkenhead on New Year's day, so I wouldn't be able to get the return-coach journey either. Ian had already got my coach ticket, so I had a decision to make. In the end, the weather forecast clinched it. It said it was going to snow, and I could just imagine the accusations if I only changed my coach ticket to take me to Sheffield (one-way) and missed hitching in a blizzard. Besides, I fancied an adventure in the snow, so off I went to get a refund on my ticket. I lost out on £5, but so what? Hitching would probably make things more straightforward in the long run.

Hawkwind came up trumps again. It wasn't quite as extravagant as their Brixton shindig (no Lemmy or Nik Turner for a start) but with numerous Hawk related or inspired supports, it ran from 4pm until 10.30. I also got chatting to a Bournemouth fan who'd been to the Lane once or twice, and had very similar musical taste to me - he even liked Gong and The Enid. He'd not heard Cardiacs but he was instructed to do so at the earliest opportunity, and you know what? I actually think he will!

Afterwards I extracted my rucksack (the big one again) from the cloakroom, and headed on the tube to Brent Cross. Around this time, as I walked to Staples Corner in fact, a series of bizarre missed phone-calls between myself and Katrina started (for those wondering, we were sort of back together at this point, but then sort of not...). Messages were left by both of us, and my phone seemed to develop an annoying habit of ringing off after half a tone. Ah well.

Within 5 minutes of my arrival at my old familiar spot I had my first lift, in a Post Office lorry. This doesn't happen too often (once before I think, plus one occasion whilst at Stonehenge when me and four others had a lift in the back of a postie's van along with all the sacks of mail), but he said he quite often picked up hitchers. He was going up to Liverpool, and told me some good tales, my fave being the one about the hitcher who he threw out onto the hard-shoulder for eating his (the driver's) sandwiches without even asking.

He dropped me off at Watford Gap, and here there was a covering of snow. It was now gone midnight and very, very cold. I had to contend with a rival hitchhiker too, a middle-aged bloke who had no baggage and no coat. I couldn't believe how stupid he could be. I had so many layers on (topped off with the super-visible yellow shirt) that my bulk would make me very hard to miss, and yet he was stood out of the way, and what he was wearing was dark. He was going up the M6 to Liverpool and was most cheesed off when I told him the wagon that had just dropped me off was going there.

"I didn't even bother sticking my thumb out for it as Post Office lorries never stop," he whined.

Tsk! I have a rule, and that is you stick your thumb out for everything, even mopeds...

Eventually I got a lift with two lads on their way up to Leeds, and despite the fact that there was a problem with the oil, meaning at one point we were stopping every half hour to fix it, progress was pretty swift. One concerning thing - at about 4am my mobile rang and Katrina's number appeared on the display. I answered it, but a bloke's voice was on the other end and he said, "Katrina's stopping at Julie-Anne's tonight." I was just asking who on earth he was when he hung up (it turned out he was Julie-Anne's brother and he thought I was Katrina's brother or something - all very strange; I blame Christmas).

By the time I was at Sheffield Parkway it was nearing 5am, and lifts seemed unlikely. Still, a black cab appeared and as I stuck my thumb out he stopped.

"How much would it cost to Struan Road?" I asked optimistically as I loaded my rucksack in.

"About fifteen quid," he replied, so I hauled my rucksack back out saying I'd just carry on hitching. He then said he'd take me into Sheffield centre free of charge. Seemed like a fair deal to me - mind you, I did end up walking from Midland Station to my mum and dad's which even without my rucksack would have been some trek. Kept me warm mind you. At the end of it, my reward was about two hours kip in the caravan and that was cold, I can tell you!

Our family being as dispersed as we are, New Year has always been much more convenient for gatherings of the clan, and so it was this year. Present were my detective sergeant in the British Transport Police brother and his mob, and also the junior spin-doctor with his (including my famous niece, CBBC presenter Angellica Bell). My dad had got most of them tickets in the family enclosure, and from my vantage point in the Laver Stand, through half closed eyes brought on by lack of sleep, I could see them all lined up along the front.

2-0 down after 20 minutes, and I wished I'd stayed eyes tightly shut, curled up asleep in that freezing caravan. To make things worse, the Preston fans were chanting, "Are you Wednesday in disguise?" Cruel... Fordy's penalty before half-time gave us hope, but I still thought the highlight was going to be the appearance of Woodward and Currie pitch-side at half-time. I delayed a trip to the gents just to see that.

But what a magnificent rally in the second half. Kelly nodded a simple equaliser after more great work from Dev, and it was all rounded off when Thomas came off the bench and netted the winner to make Soho's prediction come true. And what did we sing at the now-sullen Preston contingent? "Are you Wednesday in disguise?" It has never sounded sweeter...

The Bell (snr) household was a happy place that evening as we all wandered around grinning stupidly, all except spin-doctor brother, who reckoned we were lucky and Preston must be gutted. My response? "Yeah, but so what?" Ah well, it must be a novelty for him to try and make a sow's ear out of a silk purse for a change as opposed to the other way round.

Six points from these two games were more than any of us could have hoped for. Surely this would boost confidence for the trip to Tranmere. But first I had to get there, via Leeds, and New Year...

Chapter 25
21st Century Schizoid Women

Monday 1st January 2001: Tranmere Rovers 1-0 Sheffield United

It had all the necessary ingredients for a disaster. First of all, the line-up for this year's New Year celebrations was the same as the previous year, i.e. Michaela, Veronika, Ian, Vendula and myself. Crucially though, this year there was to be the addition of Vendula's Bosnian boyfriend, and Katrina had made vague noises about travelling up to Leeds too and meeting me up there. The trouble was, she never announced any definite plans...

Now, you see last year Veronika and Michaela had a huge row as we waited on London Bridge to welcome in the year 2000, so Ian, Veronika and Vendula had gone off on their own, leaving myself and Michaela to celebrate on our own (well, along with about 100,000 others crowded onto the bridge).

So, there was always the possibility of trouble again this year as we once more prepared to see in the 21st Century (depending on whether you're a literalist or a makes-more-sensist...), especially as Katrina was intrigued that Michaela and I had a little history (although sadly not enough to write a thesis on).

I ended up getting a coach to Leeds from Sheffield on New Year's Eve, and as I set off I still didn't know if Katrina was staying in London or heading up to Leeds. Whatever, I met up with Ian and Veronika at the station and we headed back to Vendula's flat (in a rather ghastly tower block) where we found Michaela getting merry along with an assortment of other male and female Eastern Europeans. I ended up eating all the Nik Naks and drinking all the coke before we eventually decided to venture out into the rain, heading for the city centre. I was hoping I might just bump into Tonya, the nice Leeds girl who'd given me a lift on the M40 a few days before, but even more so I was rather hoping I'd bump into Katrina. Was she in Leeds, or was she in London? I left a message on her voicemail, but since she'd had her decent mobile nicked in the toilets at Tesco, she'd been left with her rather unpredictable old one with a very short battery life. I wasn't optimistic...

Anyway, at midnight we all cheered, hugged each other and wished each other a happy New Year. Michaela was trying to text her Aussie boyfriend, and

I was trying to text Katrina. There were a lot of people in that city centre, so hardly surprising that I saw no-one I knew. After a while we headed to the Walkabout and whilst in here I got a text from Katrina saying she was in the Fruit Cupboard in Leeds, so where was I? I sent one back saying the Walkabout and she sent one back saying if we didn't meet up that night, we'd meet up the next day. She then tried to phone me, but I didn't hear it in the noise. She'd left me a message, but it was barely understandable as it kept breaking up. I tried phoning back, but by now her mobile was off, presumably battery dead. I sent a text explaining that I couldn't meet her tomorrow as I had a match to get to in Birkenhead, Merseyside.

I asked everyone where the Fruit Cupboard was, but nobody knew. The misery of it... My sort-of girlfriend was in the same city as me at New Year, but I didn't know where.

So, I watched Michaela flirting with every bloke there, and risked getting duffed up myself because every time she finished with one she'd come back to me on the dance floor and dance suggestively in my direction. I was getting some nasty looks, so I was rather relieved when the whole thing was over and we got chucked out. Trouble was, Michaela couldn't find her bag, but was confident that Ian and Veronika would have it.

"I saw Ian and Veronika leaving an hour ago, and they didn't have it," I pointed out, but Michaela insisted on leaving the building empty-handed. Across the road were stood Ian and Veronika, and they had no bag.

"Adrianko," (my Czech pet-name - sweet, eh?), "please come with me to get my bag back."

So, we went back to the door...

Bouncer: "Sorry, you can't come back in, we're closed."

Me: "She's left her bag in there..."

Bouncer: "All right, in you go."

So, we go in and find the bag.

Upon exiting, Michaela realises she has no coat...

"Adrianko..." etc etc

Bouncer: "Sorry mate, you can't come back in, we're closed."

Me: "She's left her coat in there."

Bouncer: "Okay...!"

In we go, find coat, come out, Michaela has no scarf.

"Adrianko..."

Bouncer: "Sorry mate, you can't come back in, we're closed." (I was rather expecting him to recognise us this time.)

Me: "Scarf this time, mate!"

Bouncer: "All right, in you go!"

By the time we came out with everything, Veronika was rather annoyed with her best mate, and with me for helping her out all the time. Indeed, Veronika kept trying to take me to one side to tell me something, but I kept dragging Michaela with me. In the end Veronika said, "Adrianko! Listen to me! Michaela is such a bitch..."

I just shrugged and said, "I know, but what can you do?"

Veronika continued, "No, listen! Tonight she went too far. Tonight she snogged Vendula's boyfriend! She is no longer my best friend. I want nothing to do with her ever again. And you are stupid for putting up with her and helping her all the time. Goodbye!" And off her and Ian went, leaving me with Michaela who was hanging her head (in shame, no doubt).

"Ah well," I comforted, "she probably doesn't mean it."

"She's right though. I am a bitch," mumbled Michaela.

"Yeah, I know, but it takes two... now come on, let's follow them before they disappear, 'cos I can't remember how to get back to Vendula's..."

So, we followed them, but clever me decided they were going the wrong way and we took a short cut. Except it wasn't. All tower blocks look the same you see, and they are most plentiful in Leeds...and... Oh dear.

Lost, hopelessly lost in the centre of Leeds. We couldn't even remember the name of the block. So we wandered round Leeds aimlessly for hours moaning about girlfriends who turn up in Leeds but only tell you when it's too late, and boyfriends who have the audacity to go back to Australia.

Whilst doing this, at about 4am Katrina called me on a land-line.

"Where are you Adrian?" she asked.

"I wish I knew... Lost in Leeds! Where are you?"

"I dunno," she said. "Hang on...." (goes off... comes back), "Wortley, at a house party."

I was still none the wiser, but I just had chance to tell her I was off to Tranmere the next day so I couldn't meet her, before she hung up. Apparently she was supposed to be phoning for a taxi but sneakily called me first, panicking when the house-owner appeared.

As Michaela and I carried on our tour of Leeds by going under a bridge we saw a couple having a furious row on the bridge above us. It resulted in the bloke climbing over the fence and threatening to jump, whilst his girlfriend and her mate started to panic a bit and tried to pull him back.

Whilst I got my mobile ready to dial 999, Michaela just whistled up to him and when he looked down she said, "Come on then, jump!"

"Don't say that Michaela!" I fretted.

Ignoring me, she tried again; "Come on! Do it!"

"I want to, but they won't let me!" he shouted before climbing back over the fence into the arms of his girlfriend. "Told you he wouldn't jump!" smiled Michaela.

Eventually Ian answered his phone and we got the address, enabling us to get a taxi to Vendula's. I was kipping on the floor and managed about 3 hours sleep. Miserable...

On New Year's Day I left a rather uneasy atmosphere in the flat and headed into Leeds. It was nearly midday, so I abandoned hitching and got a coach to Liverpool.

On days like this I despair, because all the money I save by hitching seems to go on just one disastrous day (like the time I had to get a taxi back from a gig in West Bromwich all the way to Brackley just to get back for work - fifty quid that cost me, in 1992!)

On this occasion, by the time the coach got to Liverpool I was cutting it very fine indeed, so I had to get a taxi, and "going through the Birkenhead Tunnel adds a few quid on you know, mate". Not happy, but at least I was there in time for kick-off. I just had to squeeze my giant rucksack through the turnstile.

Now, if you look in the Blades programme, you will see the away attendance that day as being 1001. Well, I can exclusively reveal it was actually exactly 1000, because the poor turnstile operator had to put my rucksack through, then me. I bet the books didn't balance that day.

We've seen some duff refs this season, but I reckon this guy is up there as the worst. His equally incompetent linesmen ably assisted him, and do I need to say more apart from they were booed off at the end by both sets of fans? Mind you, I think we were the slightly more irate as we'd had a Santos last minute goal ruled out for... why? I don't know; probably offside, but Santos started his run from well behind the defender as Browny crossed it. Whatever, I'm sure the linesman was smiling as he held his flag out. So we lost 1-0. Not a good start to the year 2001.

I'd met up with Halfway Blade in the ground, and I completed a day of total none-hitching by begging a lift with him back to Sheffield. I justified this knowing that on Wednesday 2nd January I'd be hitching back to London and Tesco again.

And so it proved, scrounging a lift with my dad once more to Woodall. It was quite an easy journey as it happened. My first lift was with a music loving small-white-van man (I put him on the Cardiacs trail). He dropped me at Trowell where I swapped with the hitcher already waiting there (both were heading to Birmingham you see).

I then got a lift to Rothersthorpe in a chicken lorry (he could carry 12,000 chickens or something - bit worrying that), but when there I noticed a trade-plater. However, in true trade-plater tradition, he'd got a lift in the time it took me to put my rucksack down and fish out my LONDON sign.

I then got a lift with a young couple from Sheffield, Firth Park no less. They were visiting southerly relatives by going round the M25, so I got them to drop me at Enfield, and from there I got the train to Liverpool Street, Tesco and blissful work.

Whilst waiting I phoned Katrina, and she explained that she wanted to surprise me by appearing in Leeds unannounced, but as the celebrations and alcohol took hold it all went horribly wrong. Too right - crazy women, a Blades defeat, THOSE match officials, and now five-and-a-half hours on the checkout. Grim...

Chapter 26
"I Can See the Pub from Here!"

Saturday 6th January 2001: Southampton 1-0 Sheffield United (FA Cup 3rd Round)

Southampton hasn't always been the happiest of hunting grounds for me. For a start, I've never seen the Blades win there, and three previous hitches for other reasons have hardly been happy. Well, hitching to see Cardiacs in 1996 was okay as I did it in about 80 minutes, arriving in the afternoon thus giving me time to do my usual trick of finding the venue, helping the band unload and so secure a place on the guest list. Except this time I had no idea of the venue address, just the name (The Joiner's Arms). I made the big mistake of asking a vagrant for directions (in exchange for 50p I might add) and he sent me in completely the wrong direction. I spent most of the afternoon wandering around the town, and at various points could see the band's van making regular appearances at the end of every road I was walking down. It felt like a bad dream as every time I got to the end of the road, I saw the van disappearing around a corner before appearing going across the end of the next road I was walking down. It appeared they were having the same problem as me...

The next time was when myself and my then-girlfriend (a German girl called Annette) helped my best mate Ian move out of my house in Brackley and into a house in Southampton with his then-girlfriend. After moving them in, it was quite late in the evening and Ian's girlfriend gave us a lift only so far out and left us to hitch the rest of the way back. I'd been up all the previous night working, and was less than pleased when the Old Bill pulled over and questioned us as we hitched. He was a lone copper, but boy was he officious. Once he found out that Annette was German, he wanted to know everything about the two of us, and I protested most strongly.

"You have to admit that a 31 year-old English guy hitching with a 19 year-old German girl is suspicious," he pronounced, and I'm afraid I lost my cool. And the more I lost my cool, the more he wanted to know. Annette kept whispering to me to calm down as I was only making him worse, but it was a matter of principle now, and I was going down fighting.

He didn't believe I was a Tesco night-manager, or that Annette worked and lived at a home for the mentally handicapped. He also thought the moving house story was rather dubious and asked for Ian's new address.

"I can't remember the number, but it's on Mousehole Lane. Look it up if you like, but you won't find him registered there BECAUSE HE'S ONLY MOVED IN TODAY," I replied in best "You're so thick" voice.

By the time he left us he had more info than was healthy to leave in the hands of the Law, and I had steam coming out of my ears. I seem to remember falling asleep on a train from Salisbury and then hitching from Oxford (I think). I ended up getting some poor sod to go out of his way to drop us both home by dolefully crying, "Everything's gone wrong today..." *Sniff*

And the last time I had to hitch to Southampton was to go to my cousin's funeral on the Isle of Wight, and these events are never the happiest. I was due to meet my mum by the ferry at 11.30 in order to secure my lift over, and duly arrived at 11.25. That was all very good, but hitching back was an absolute nightmare. I ended up getting a lift with a Chinese guy, and as we sped up the M3 the car broke down. It was a borrowed-from-a-mate car and he had no cover. What's more, when he tried to phone the mate on MY mobile, we discovered the battery was totally dead. He insisted on trying to jump-start the car, so I found myself pushing the tin-pot little vehicle along the hard shoulder, in the dark, in the rain. In the end he admitted defeat, and decided to ring for help from the emergency phone, except his English was so bad the phone was ultimately handed to me:

"No, it's not my car... No, it's not his car either... No, I'm not really his friend, I'm just some poor hitchhiker who would rather not be involved but..."

When I told him how much it was going to cost to get the thing towed away he shook his head and muggins here ended up doing another stint of hard-shoulder car-pushing (still in the rain).

He gave up again, so I had to ring the emergency people once more, and eventually the local garage came out to tow him away. I jumped in the cab, but the misery of a garage-man refused to go out of his way to drop me at a train station, so I got dropped off in the middle of nowhere (some poxy town in Surrey) and I had to walk miles (in the rain!) to find the station. I ended up having to bunk the last train into London as I was totally out of cash.

Oh yes, I was looking forward to hitching to Southampton again...

I decided to give myself a head-start by stopping at the delightful Clayre's place in Wimbledon the night before, and was highly delighted to find she had a PC. I was able to introduce her to SUISA and see for myself that DC Blade had responded to my vague plea for help regarding a lift back to London. You see, Katrina had said she may well be up for going out that Saturday night if I got back on time, so I was on the scrounge for a lift. As it happened, DC (thus christened because of his initials, not because he lives in Washington - he actually lives in Doncaster) and his daughter were paying visits in London after the match, so if I wanted I was in. I did want, so I left my mobile number and hoped for the best...

That morning I waved bye-bye to Clayre as she ventured off to work and I got on a train to Sunbury, the station being right next to the start of the M3. Now, the slip road may be long and gives plenty of room for drivers to pull in, but I rarely get a quick lift from here. On this occasion I waited about 45 minutes for my first success, the driver being a leather-jacketed chap wearing a Fairport Convention tee-shirt. Not surprisingly he was a musician playing in a folk band called Only Folk or something like that. He was quite into his rock too, so I put the names Cheese Cake Truck and Human Oddities into his head, then impressed him by telling him how many times I'd been to Cropredy and that I had plenty of Incredible String Band and Robin Williamson albums in my collection. I also waffled on about seeing Alain Stivell at Stonehenge Festival in 1984, which had led me to buying such albums as Renaissance of the Celtic Harp... Greenwich a folkie, eh? Only mildly, honest...

He was able to drop me at Fleet Services, but it was still quite early (about 11-ish) and I was hungry so I popped in for some breakfast. I wandered in and was delighted to see the entire Family Glossop Blade in the restaurant. I went over and cadged a lift and they said that the night before my name had been mentioned, and they'd said that if they saw me they'd give me a lift. Spooky, eh?

After we'd breakfasted I squeezed in the car with Glossop, Dad Glossop, Mum Glossop and Brother Glossop and off we all went. Mum Glossop was dropped off somewhere just outside Southampton to visit a relative, and then as we drove into town, Glossop produced his fan's guide book, which had very precise directions to the Dell. Whilst approaching, FBFD and Halfway phoned me for directions, so rather bizarrely I was dictating them over the phone as I heard Glossop dictating them to Dad Glossop who was driving...

We all arrived safe and sound, and headed for the designated pub, the Winston, right by the away end. We were in there at least two and a half hours before kick-off, and most of the London Blades were already in, including new-recruit Paris Blade, whose refusal to change his alias (so far) has impressed many.

The pub seemed more than happy to have us in there, and the Southampton fans left us alone, even when one guy claiming to be Sandford's cousin (a strange cross between a Pompey fan, a Stoke fan and a Blade) started shouting at them that they were "all a bunch of scummers!" Did I mention he was rather tanked up?

Whilst in the Winston I was delighted to receive a call from DC Blade, so he appeared in there and introduced himself. I wonder how many times he was asked, "So, have you flown over for the match, then?"...

With a quick-but-lusty rendition of the Greasy Chip Butty song, we all decamped to the Dell, and what a pokey little hole it is. The last two times I've been we've been stood on the terrace, but now sitting down it was rather cramped, not helped by my baggage. On our row was the handsome combination of myself, Alty, Radio and Musical, the main topic of conversation being what shirts United would wear (gold or white? important stuff!), and was that bunch of 15 year-olds really the Southampton Firm?

Not much to report on the match really, except that United never looked like scoring, but I was rather fancying a draw. But who was that referee? The programme said not, but it certainly looked like our old chum Mr. Elleray, and his decisions soon had us believing that once more he was going to do us.

At some point in the tedium that passed for a match, Radio spotted the pub outside the perimeter walls. "Hey guys, I can see the pub from here!" And so Alty started the chant... Giggles all round, as it seemed highly amusing compared to what was taking place on the park.

In the second half our favourite refereeing schoolmaster gave Southampton a dodgy penalty and subsequently sent Fordy off for his protestations. Poor old Bobby; he'd probably only said what we were all thinking (and some shouting).

At the end I'd shouted myself hoarse at Elleray, which made me feel a little better. To cheer myself up I called Katrina to secure our night out by telling her I was on my way and I may even be there by 8 o'clock. She said she was too knackered and ill to go out, and then over the course of my gentle whinging her battery went dead. I didn't bother phoning back but chose to chat about prog rock with DC, something which I'm sure delighted Miss DC sat in the back.

DC was most impressed by my ability to reel off the line-up of High Tide from memory (Tony Hill, Roger Hadden, Peter Pavli and Simon House by the way), and I was most delighted in his Rick-Wakeman-with-The-Strawbs story. Prog out!

I was dropped off at Clapham Junction and then got the train in to Waterloo where upon arrival I left a rather vicious message on Katrina's phone. And then I left another one. The London Blades meanwhile had had another in the Winston at the end of the game before catching the train home, or more correctly to the Harp near Charing Cross (which is becoming home). Here I was to join them, and as I entered they were just in the right state to start up, "Na na na na, eeza Blade and eeza Blade," but this was soon quelled by a panic stricken barmaid. The look on her face will stay with all of us that saw it...

So, I was glum. A cup exit, and another row with the sort-of missus. Most of the LBs thought I'd been a little harsh with my messages (don't worry, we made up over a Burger King on the Monday) so now I was feeling guilty too. To make myself feel better, Radio, Woodford Green and I went for a curry (best curry house yet, Lee - now what was it called again?). For once it was an easy trip to and from Southampton, but hey, I had to add a personal disaster to the one on the pitch, otherwise it just wouldn't be the same...

Chapter 27
No Sleep 'Til Stratford

Saturday 13th January 2001: Sheffield United 0-1 Watford

Banks and myself have never got on. They don't seem to like my easy come, easy go attitude, especially Yorkshire Bank in Banbury (I'm sure they won't mind the publicity). Indeed it was they who nearly put an end to my house purchase in 1995 by refusing to believe that the estate agents were going to give me all of my deposit back unless I provided signatures, letters etc from just about everyone involved. The estate agents said that I had one day left to sort it with the bank or the whole thing was off, so there was I without a penny to my name, hitching backwards and forwards between Brackley and Banbury, running from Haarts to Tesco to solicitors and finally to the bank, one minute before they closed. The assistant manager (a more pompous twerp you will never meet) had to shout across to the cashier, "Whatever you do, don't close that till!" and thirty minutes later I was sprinting back up the road to the solicitors with a brown envelope stuffed full of cash.

I never forgot how helpful they were on that (and many other) occasions, and so it was with great glee that I was finally, come January 2001, in a position to close my account with them. And in keeping with tradition, I decided it best to hitch there to put the finishing touches to a 10-year relationship. Trouble was, as usual, I had a rather hectic schedule...

It was the Friday before our home match against Watford, and that night Cheese Cake Truck had a gig in High Wycombe. The good thing about that was that I could stay on the M40, the bad thing being the M40 isn't the best motorway to hitch on. Still, I jumped on the tube, made for the Metropolitan Line, and headed for Hillingdon. As I exited the station and wandered to the A40/ M40 slip road I saw a very interesting pack of cards spread out on the pavement. My attempt at "Fifty-two Card Pick-up" just failed (it was broad daylight, and people were watching), but I was guaranteed some interesting games of Snap! should the day get dull.

One thing I did notice as I stood at the top of that incline - it was freezing, mainly due to a breeze whipping right up the road into my face. After 45 minutes I was getting irritable, so I was mighty pleased when a white-van man stopped. He could only take me one junction to Uxbridge, but it was a start.

I jumped out of his van straight into a muddy splodge, and had to apologise to the businessman-type who immediately picked me up as I squelched into his car and got it dirty. He was able to take me to Oxford Services, and things were looking good again, except I got stuck here, only picking up abuse from teenage joyriders...

Eventually I got a lift in an estate car with a chap whose son was in a band. I gave him Cheese Cake Truck's web address in case his son had a thing about Norwegian weird metal ("He likes allsorts...") before being dropped off on the outskirts of Banbury. A long walk ensued, but the resultant closing of my account was very pleasurable...

It was then off to Tesco in Banbury where I was due to meet Fiona, a lovely young lady who I had the pleasure of working with at Tesco in Brackley. (One of our earliest encounters was when we were dragging cages onto the shopfloor, and I was acting rather dangerously. "You'd better not run me over with that!" she warned. So I did. She ended up getting medical treatment for a badly grazed leg, and I had to sign the Store Incident Book... Surprisingly we developed a firm friendship after that.)

After going back to Fiona's and catching up on all the latest gossip, she was good enough to give me a lift to the M40 roundabout, where hitching was recommenced.

By now it was about 6 o'clock, dark and very cold. Luckily I was soon picked up, this time by a small-white-van man (the van was small, not the man you understand). He was an Oxford fan, so he had plenty to complain about. I told him to cheer up, because things would get better as they had just signed an ex-Blade, none other than good old Andy Scott who'd been banging 'em in for Brentford all season. But this I could not understand - a move to Oxford (probably the one team doomed for the drop already in January) is not much of a career move.

"Well, I don't know what's going on," said my driver chum, "but all of a sudden every player wants to leave Brentford so I've been told." Looks like Mr Noades may be causing a bit of a to-do...

He dropped me at Cherwell Valley Services, and here I found a magazine to keep the pack of cards company (and destined to keep Cheese Cake Truck entertained as they waited to go on stage). Now it really was getting cold, and this is an especially bleak spot - the wind whips wickedly down the slip-road. Added to this, everyone was obviously in a hurry to get home, so no-one wanted to stop, except for three separate people who were coming off at the next junction and whizzing down to Southampton on the A34 (one of these was a most beautiful young lady, and believe me when I say it was mightily painful saying No to her...). So, a little tactical hitching was in order. I may have been heading to High Wycombe, but as I had no sign bearing that name, out came the one saying LONDON. Within minutes I had my lift...

"Where in London, mate?" asked the (Australian) driver.

"Erm... High Wycombe!" came my confusing reply. All was explained, and off we went, talking music. He was more of an Allman Brothers type of guy (you know, ageing hippie, shoulder-length hair), and as usual me entering the uncharted waters of Henry Cow and Magma lost him. Resorting to Yes and King Crimson had us back on track, but he was probably glad to turf me out at the top of that rather steep hill at the High Wycombe junction of the M40.

Now, I'd been to the White Horse twice previously with my other bands, Jesus Underground Band and Human Oddities. But could I remember where it was? I wandered down the hill into town, and then headed in the direction I thought it was. I spied two girls coming the opposite way all done-up for a night on the town, and one of them wolf-whistled at me, followed by, "Oooh, a cyclist!"

"No - a hitchhiker!" I corrected, somewhat puzzled.

"Oh well, never mind," she said, and the moment was lost forever.

As I headed on auto-pilot to Burger King I realised - that fluo-yellow Blades away-shirt from last season must have flummoxed them...

I took my seat in Burger King, and as I settled down about to tuck into the obligatory Double Whopper-with-cheese, I thought I'd better text Mr K, the Truck's rather fabulous drummer, to find out where I was supposed to be. I was just about to hit SEND when in he walked, closely followed by singer Jonas, and violin-player Barney. Now this was spooky, as a very similar thing had happened when I got off the bus in Oxford prior to their gig in Oxford (see Hog Tied story). Whatever, it meant I could relax...

They'd parked the van just round the corner, and were somewhat dismayed on their return to find a parking ticket. We returned to the venue (they'd already soundchecked), me having to slum it in the back of the van in the dark, emerging at the venue feeling a little unsteady and ill...

The gig, as ever, was a triumph. The Truck really do kick ass you know, but to do it whilst wearing natty little tutus is just something else!

After the gig, the Most Beautiful Barmaid In High Wycombe (what a cracker she was boys) tempted me with a packet of tomato-and-mayonnaise crisps, and then I received a text from Ian's sister, Alex, telling me her and her chums had just found a wardrobe on the streets of Deptford and were currently trying to get it home to New Cross. Students, eh?

Upon viewing the lack of traffic on the M40 (it was gone 2am), I decided to get the Truck boys to drop me back in London at my old fave, Staples Corner, and it was from here at 3.45am that I finally started hitching to Sheffield. If I thought it had been cold earlier...

Within 10 minutes my gamble had paid off, and I secured a lift with two London Underground techies from Kettering, one of whom rejoiced in the name of Adrian. They commuted into work every night, as it proved cheaper to live in Kettering and do it that way. Plus they were always finished before the traffic got bad.

In no time at all they had dropped me at Rothersthorpe Services on the M1, and here the really bizarre stuff started. Firstly an Italian woman with a car full to bursting with her family stopped, wound down the window and told me that sorry, she didn't have room to give me a lift. In 17 years of hitching, no-one has ever stopped to tell me they can't pick me up. Quite sweet though...

Then, as I held up my SHEFFIELD sign, a German truck stopped. As I jumped in (on the right-hand side - left-hand drive you see), it became obvious that this chap spoke no English. Not a word. Quite remarkable these days, I should think, but even more so when you remember that exactly the same thing happened to me on the way back from Lincoln earlier in the season.

He just pointed at my sign and nodded, then plonked the map on my lap and pointed at Goldthorpe, near Rotherham, followed by a delivery note for some place on a Goldthorpe industrial estate.

Okay, thought I, I'll be getting out at Tinsley Viaduct then, as by the time I got there the Supertram should be running. But then he started to rummage around underneath the delivery note, and unearthed another one, slapping it down on top of the map. He then shrugged his shoulders and gave me a look that could only say, "Help! No idea!"

I looked at the address, and I'm afraid I didn't feel I was going to be much help to him here. You see, there was a company name (some engine-manufacturing place by the looks of it), an industrial estate (totally anonymous sounding) then just the word "Flintshire" followed by what looked like a Chester postcode. No town was mentioned anywhere.

Now when I was at school they taught us all the county names, and I feel that I have a fairly sound geographical knowledge, but I don't mind admitting I had no idea where Flintshire was. Surely if it was a Chester postcode, it would be in Cheshire? But then this doesn't always follow I know, and eventually after scouring the road atlas around that area, there it was, located in the north of Wales. Thing is, it covered a fair old area, and there was no way I could pinpoint the Faceless-Just-Like-All-the-Others Trading Estate. But as this guy was obviously desperate, I took extreme measures. First off I sent a text to Katrin, my German-friend-who-just-happens-to-be-a-girl. However, she didn't respond (it would have been about 6am in Deutschland), so I phoned Scoot and gave them the name of the company plus the bit of the address that I had in the hope that they would furnish me with a phone number so at least the guy could call them when he was a bit nearer (and hope that they spoke German). Scoot couldn't help me. This German trucker was going to have problems...

I shrugged my shoulders, put the delivery note inside the page with Flintshire on it and said a silent prayer for him. I trust he is still driving round Wales now, poor chap.

At least all this passed the time, and once I'd given up on his behalf, Tinsley was looming. It was just gone 7am when I jumped out, so off I went in search of a Supertram. All doors into Meadowhall were locked, so I ended up going to the tram station near the viaduct and waited... and waited. My, was it cold. Once in Sheffield centre I figured that it would be plain sailing to get to my parents'. Wrong. Another protracted wait ensued at the bus-stop, and it was 8.30 before I walked through their door. It took me as long to get across town as it had to get from Rothersthorpe to Tinsley. I should have hitched...

My mum was up and about, and was delighted to see me march in, announce I was going to get thirty minutes sleep and then head off to Northumberland Avenue where I had to meet the Internet Blades for a nice friendly match. How I got up after half-an-hour I will never know, never mind play a game of football (although those that saw me that morning may wish to comment on this). We were playing a strange combination of Crewe, Wolves and some church team or something. They had nice green shirts anyway.

I was in goal for the first half, and was apparently at fault for their goal. I blame the all-weather pitch - a nightmare to dive on. Meanwhile Stafford was in inspired form at right-back, alternating between Kozzie last season and Kozzie this season, every 5 minutes. He also did a passable impression of Chris Short on Tarrico at Ipswich in the Cup in 1998 as he booted one of their players into the 5-a-side nets at the side of the pitch.

In the second-half Mouse took over in goal, Stafford moved up front and I slotted in effortlessly at right-back, likening myself to John Cutbush at his very best.

With a minute to go, it was 2-2, so thanks must got to Colin who was reffing, as he played about 10 minutes of injury time, thus allowing us to score the winner (from the boot of Stafford's - or was it Radford's? - uni chum.). As soon as they kicked-off, Colin blew for time, money changed hands (only joking!) and we forced our aching limbs down to the Pump to celebrate a rare 'Net Blades F.C. win.

I regaled the London Blades with tales of heroism - you know, Simon Tracey in the first-half, Len Badger in the second... Somehow, my chilli-beef Yorkshire-pud with lashings of Henderson's almost made me believe it all...

And so we were off to Bramall Lane, and there we witnessed a dire match. Because it was so cold, and for that reason alone, I stayed awake. We lost 1-0, with Tommy Mooney netting a late winner for Watford. Boo!

After all that, there was no way I was hitching home, especially as Murdoch's Neighbour was driving back to London. Once we located the car and I was sat comfortably in the front seat, I nodded off to sleep listening to grumbling Blades and whinging piggies on Praise or Grumble. I woke up at Watford Gap as Murdoch's Neighbour filled up with petrol and half-asleep I stumbled into the shop to buy a Yorkie and a can of Red Bull. I rubbed my eyes in disbelief, but there could be no doubting it - there in front of me were two chinless wonders covered in mud having just got out of an OverLander. They had t-shirts on telling the world how proud they were to bother (and kill) small furry animals. Our in-house expert Musical later guessed that these buffoons were probably from the type of hunt where they chase hares on foot (the hunters, as well as the hares before you say). Most people stood and laughed - a good reason to ban hunting, and also a good advert for why you shouldn't indulge in sexual pastimes with close relatives...

In the end, M's N was good enough to give me a lift all the way to my front door, and with what energy I had left I walked to the Chinese Take-Away, once again talking to an Irish Celtic fan about Paul Devlin. Once my Duck Fried Rice was taken home and consumed, I fell into a deep sleep that lasted for about sixteen hours. Not even a Motorhead CD in the background could keep me awake. No Sleep 'Til Stratford... like Lemmy, I never seem to think I'm too old to keep putting myself through this...

Chapter 28
Severe Ribbing

Saturday 20th January 2001: West Bromwich Albion 2-1 Sheffield United

It is a sad fact of life that no matter how many times we think that an embarrassing episode will be the last time we humiliate ourselves in public, we are always just around the corner from making a right arse of ourselves one more time. Whether it be tripping over a paving stone or letting the ball slip through our legs Chris Woods style, it will happen again...and soon!

I have many, like the time I was at my Uncle Billy and Auntie Wendy's on Hayling Island, aged 16. Whilst all my relatives sat chatting round a table in the living room that backed onto the garden, I spent the whole evening, full of youthful exuberance, kicking a football around the garden and running across the patio into the house to get drinks of water and so on. The French doors had remained invitingly open all evening, until... As I ran across the patio one last time, I wondered why everyone had stopped talking to look at me in a concerned way. As I approached the doorway I gave my admiring audience a quick smile to re-assure them, before crashing nose first into the now-closed doors. Once the laughter had stopped, and I'd been peeled Tom-and-Jerry-like from the glass, it was commented on how lucky I was that I'd not broken the glass thus severing arteries and such. I laughed about it later...

So, there I was in Tesco working my shift on the checkout one Wednesday night, three days before our away trip to West Brom. I was bored so I stood up to look around the store for any attractive girls. In order to get a better view, I stood on the metal ring near the bottom of the stool on which we are supposed to rest our feet. As I swivelled round I spied the vision of beauty that is Katrina, and as I waved to her I got my boot caught in said metal ring. In my efforts to free myself, I felt myself toppling over. I made such a commotion going down that by the time I hit the checkout rib first, every customer and every member of staff was watching me. How they laughed, Katrina laughing loudest of all. It hurt - both the humiliation and the rib. I'd managed to land right on a nasty sharp metallic corner and I knew straight away that damage had been done.

The following day I suffered some discomfort at work, and maybe I was just grouchy, but I ended my shift with a row with Katrina, leaving the store for a Cheese Cake Truck gig with the assumption that (once again) it was all over between us, for good.

The gig was at the Garage in Islington with the Truck supporting Sack Trick (Penguins On the Moon - marvellous!), and of the London Blades contingent, Musical, Stow and Lords all put their eardrums in danger by showing up. Also there were those two lovely Truck fans I'd met in Norwich - Spiky Em and Kirsty. By the end of the night we'd persuaded them that they wanted to come to a Blades match with us, and I was feeling the effects of gentle moshing with a suspected cracked rib. Musical said he'd never experienced a gig before where his ears had felt so thoroughly assaulted. Cheese Cake Truck strike again!

By Friday the pain was getting worse, but I was still of the opinion that I could run it off. CCT were playing in Watford (at the rugby club no less - they have a regular Friday-metal-night) that evening, and as I sat in the House of Truck waiting for the van to depart, Musical secured me a ticket for the Baggies match thanks to his credit card. Hooray!

It was a cold and frosty evening in Watford, but in that club it was steaming. It was packed to the rafters with those 14-year-old Slipknot and Limp Bizkit fans that seem to be everywhere these days. This time though, I refrained from joining the pit (carting CCT's bass drum through the door had really finished my rib off this time), so I found a little cubby-hole between the stage and the PA stack, and watched teenagers flying over my head as they continually stage-dived off said PA. Apparently the audience were quiet by their usual standards.

As United were playing in the Midlands and I would have nowhere to go if I got there early, I opted to go home with the Truck boys and get up early in the morning. A sensible move, but it was hard getting out of bed.

Once more I found myself perched at the foot of the M1, Staples Corner, the obligatory one-hour-later-than-I-intended (9am). I wasn't waiting long though, my United shirt once more attracting the attention of a fellow footy-fan. As I clambered into this chap's car he said to me, "Are you Adrian?"

"Er... yes. How did you know?" was my nervous response.

"How do you think?" he replied.

After just over a month, here was the first person to recognise me and give me a lift as a result of my Five-Live 606 exercise. Marvellous!

His name was Nick and he was a Forest fan, but really more of a self-confessed ground hopper. He was on his way up to Leeds that day to add Elland Road to his list (I've still not done that one), and he admitted he'd never been to the Lane. "Maybe this season will be the one," he added with our March 10th fixture in mind. Being a bit of a collector myself, I can see why people like to ground-hop, but to me it only means something if I see the Blades there. On the few occasions I've been to a game not involving United I've felt strangely out of place, deriving very little pleasure from it, hence why those grounds don't get represented by a little red dot on my map until I see us struggling for a point (or worse) there...

Anyway, as we assumed we'd both be zooming around the motorway system some more before the end of the season, mobile numbers were exchanged as I got out at Watford Gap should I be stuck for a lift in the future (another chance to cheat - heh heh).

As I took up my position at the exit, I just had time to add to the "Greenwich Blade on tour" graffiti before a huge left-hand drive Italian truck pulled up. Now, the last thing you expect with a foreign truck is a Brummie accent, but that's exactly what I got. "I can take yow as far as Wednesbury," said the rather large driver.

"Where's that?" I asked, forgetting my confusion for a minute.

"Near West Bromwich!" he replied, and so in I scrambled to plonk myself into what should have been the driver's seat. As I settled in, I now realised just how much this rib was hurting. Extreme discomfort. I then asked the question: Italian truck, Brummie accent...? It turned out (rather obviously really) that he was working for an Italian company which seemed fair enough, but when he started telling me about tax and not officially existing in England it all sounded a bit dodgy to me. Still, we exchanged some very entertaining stories about ex-girlfriends, which served to take my mind off the pain of my rib.

Once we got to Wednesbury he dropped his trailer off then headed for home where I was able to experience a tractor-unit trying to negotiate its way up a tiny road on a West Midlands council estate. Scary.

Whilst he sorted his car out, I sat in his living room watching Rosie and Jim videos with his wife and 2-year old kid whilst sipping cherryade. Bizarre. Now I know I shouldn't criticise children's TV programmes, but the acting in Rosie and Jim was diabolical, and what really got me was every single episode started and ended in the same way. Trumpton was much better (even though that always started and ended in the same way too, now I come to think about it).

One thing though - whilst watching the credits roll I was reminded that the music for this (and Teletubbies) was composed by none other than Andrew McCrorie-Shand who used to play keyboards in a seventies prog band called Druid (who sounded more like Yes than Yes). Hitching to a Cardiacs gig once,

I got a lift with a work-colleague of his who was most amused when I told him Mr McCrorie-Shand's dark secret. "He kept that quiet!" he chuckled. "Prog rock? Oh dear." Hey - there's nothing wrong with prog you know! Greenwich - Prog and proud!

Once he had his car sorted, this wonderfully generous chap gave me a lift all the way to the Hawthorns, and once again concern that I may have left it too late was dispelled as it wasn't even 1pm. Why, I'd even arrived before my ticket, so a bit of waiting around was in order. Whilst strolling around I noticed a food-hut called Auntie Leah's Giant Frying Pan so I sent Princess Blade (christened Leah) a text saying this (and only this). She sent me a question mark back. She'd toyed with the idea of hitching with me to this one, so I felt it only right to let her sample some of the atmosphere.

As I hung around the players' entrance I watched an obviously infatuated teenage Baggy read out a toe-curlingly embarrassing poem to the object of her desires (don't know who he was, but Richard Sneekes was close by looking like a member of Focus).

I then got chatting to a Blade from Northants and his delightful teenage daughter. My (small one today) rucksack gave me away as he asked, "Are you the one that hitches everywhere?" I was only too happy to own up as he shook me by the hand.

Thanks once more to the wonderful technology of mobile phones, Woodford Green and Camden were able to locate me; tickets were picked up and into the ground we went. justoutsidestokeblade and Bert (the legendary) spotted us and joined the throng, with most of the entertainment provided by Bert's anxiety at the workmen wasters who were watching the game rather than getting on with making the Hawthorns a four-sided ground again. With only three sides available and no tickets on sale on the day, there was quite a gathering trying to watch the match from the gates opposite (and even two on a nearby warehouse roof). They may have seen Ully get his marching orders after 20 or so minutes - not a popular decision with us or Mr Warnock. Despite this, United showed much improved attitude than of late, and it inspired us to outsing the Baggies even when 1-0 down. Some ridiculous stewarding failed to quieten us down (why is it that they think chucking "anyone in a red and white shirt" out of the ground will make the rest of us behave like good little schoolchildren?) and when Pesky blasted his standard goal against his former club (I know he's got a lot of former clubs now, but it was his Blades debut too) we all went, er, barmy with me jumping on WGB, thus knackering my ribs well and truly.

Then just as it looked like the "plucky 10-man Blades" were going to get a point, that git Hughes notched the winner. Lucky, lucky Baggies. It all served to make West Bromwich seem even worse as we wandered round to WGB's car (I scrounged a lift on medical grounds), and seeing Unitedites arguing with stewards at the gate was a lasting reminder of their wonderful handling of people. It meant we had to take the long route round to the car, and even without an unlucky late defeat, it was quite clear that this was one grim place. Glad I live in London. Bah!!!

On the way home, in between shovelling painkillers, I phoned my mum to wish her a happy birthday, then fell asleep, sedated.

Once back in London WGB dropped me at South Woodford tube, and I dragged my aching body home. I felt hungry though, so a quick visit to the Chinese was in order. As I looked at the menu, the word RIB jumped off the page at me, so BBQ Spare Ribs it was. Corny I know, but sadly nevertheless very true...

That next day I was supposed to be helping Ian and Veronika move to Muswell Hill but was in such agony there was no way! I went to visit them in their new flat that night, by which time my toothache had flared up again too, so they, fed up with my grumpiness in the pub, offered to lend me the dosh to get dental treatment which duly commenced that week. I also headed for casualty at Greenwich District Hospital after uni on the Monday (after phoning in sick at Tesco), and they said it was probably cracked ribs but they wouldn't x-ray it as it "wasn't worth it" (well thanks!) because all treatment was the same whether cracked, bruised, or broken - nothing! Just suffer and take Nurofen. I wanted better than this - I wanted a wheelchair, I wanted to be tended by beautiful young nurses, I wanted morphine! But no - Nurofen.

But what do I know? It actually started to work, and who knows? There may even have been a chance that I'd be fit for the Internet Blades before Dev (out with a similar complaint) returned to the first team.

As I thought about all this walking home that night, I tripped over a paving stone...

Chapter 29
Lady Luck and Cheese Cake Truck

Sunday 4th February 2001: Fulham 1-1 Sheffield United

There are friends and there are special friends. Clayre will always fit into the latter category. We first met when she was just sweet 16, still at school and starting a part-time job with the newly-opened Tesco in Brackley. I was her section manager, myself just embarking on a career with the UK's number one food retailer, and we spent many a happy evening travelling on coaches to such exotic places as Bicester and Buckingham to undertake our training. After four months in the job, the General Manager was tiring of my antics running the checkouts and decided to boot me onto nights, something I'll always be grateful to him for as I festered there for three-and-a-half years, learning in the process the art of anger-management, restraint and self-control, working thirteen hours a night whilst getting paid for eight... As a souvenir, my final written warning still adorns my bedroom wall.

Working nights didn't stop my friendship with Clayre however, and as the months became years we got closer and closer, developing an unhealthy mutual interest in Teletubbies (she once posted me a cutting from the Mirror instructing me how to make my own Po or LaLa) and discovering a love of football within both of us. Okay, she was a Coventry fan but an indication of how much respect I had for her came when we dumped them out of the Cup in 1998 and I didn't rub it in too much (and I still only mention it every 3 months now). Her revenge has been to send me a birthday card (February 13th) disguised as a Valentine's card on at least 3 occasions. I fall for it every time...

Over the 6 years that we have been mates, the poor girl admitted that she had developed a "soft spot" for the Blades, and kept promising to come with me to see them. Why she felt the need to get involved in this was hard to understand as she had seen first-hand how the passion could affect me. For example, when United were playing Ipswich in the second leg of the play-off semi in 1997 I was stuck at Tesco. I turned up for work that evening rigged up to my Walkman tuned in to Five-Live. My first duty was to drag cages onto the shopfloor, and I always needed the wasters off the checkouts to give me a hand, especially when I was spending more time nipping outside for a quick listen where the reception was better. Things were getting tense at Portman Road as it seemed amidst the crackles and buzzes that Ipswich had just equalised Katchouro's shock opener, and Alan Kelly sounded like he was playing with one leg missing. I re-entered the store to find all my checkout-helpers (including Clayre) skiving by the CDs, so I blew my top, Clayre getting the worst of it. I felt a little guilty the next day and as the Blades had edged through on away goals in the end, I felt good enough to write her a card of apology.

Just short of one year later I found myself in Crewe having just hitched up there for United's vital end-of-season match. It was a Thursday-night kick-off, and I was there with hours to spare so I found a phone box and called friends and family to pass the time. One such call was made to Clayre as gossip had to be caught up on (I was off work with stress and tension and had a recent break-up of a relationship to report). Clayre said she felt absolutely awful, like a really bad 'flu and couldn't see how she was going to get through teaching her impending clarinet lesson (she was now based in Kingston, Surrey at Uni.). I still made her listen to my rants and raves before leaving her to her sickness.

Upon entering Tesco the following week to negotiate my return to work, Darren from the produce department accosted me. "Heard about Clayre?" he asked.

No I hadn't. "She got meningitis." You know those moments where your stomach disappears and you go numb? This was such. I just about heard Darren faintly saying, "I think she's okay now though."

A subsequent call to her family confirmed this, and a week or so later when she came to visit me at home I don't think I've ever been happier to see someone alive and well. It had been a pretty close call by all accounts, but she made a full recovery. Apparently the last thing she remembered was talking to me on the phone. She decided not to do the clarinet lesson, instead choosing to slip into a state of delirium. She tells me I should feel proud of the fact that it was my whinging and moaning that almost sent her over the edge. Whatever, all of sudden United messing things up, ex-girlfriends and stupid jobs didn't seem important. Life did.

With both of us now resident in London, Blades attendance was always looking more likely for the Lady Godiva of Tingewick and Wales, and as she was now proclaiming that after Coventry her two favourite teams were United and Fulham, a wet Sunday lunchtime at Craven Cottage it looked like being. Not only that, but as Katrina and I seemed to have hit one of those little impasses we seem so keen on, I went for broke and invited Spiky Em and Kirsty as well. They had seemed up for it at the Cheese Cake Truck gig, and Spiky even welcomed me texting her the words to the Greasy Chip Butty song.

With no hitch involved it was a pleasure to just sit on the District Line and let the train take the strain. As I buried my nose in the Sunday 'paper I heard a voice from opposite say, "'Ere geezer. Is that a Sunderland shirt?" It was two Tottenham-supporting street urchins. I put them right, told them where I was off to, they wished me luck, and all was well. "I fink you'll do all right there today," one of them said. He was more confident than I was...

An early arrival meant I had time to go on a fruitless search for a cashpoint in an attempt to get a ticket, abandoned in favour of meeting Clayre on Putney Bridge (a strangely protracted affair thanks to confusing directions), followed by a rendezvous with the London Blades in the Duke's Head. Meanwhile Spiky and Kirsty were struggling through London, quite an achievement considering their wild night out the night before.

As the rain continued to come down, we left it as long as possible before venturing out to the ground, although not all were brave enough. Those that stayed in the pub to watch the Sky coverage will remain nameless, but it has to be said that one or two members of the North London massive were able to describe Jaffa's goal in minute detail. Shame they couldn't get Shiny's Fanzone commentary on there too, then they would have been able to tell us how the yellow-shirted one managed to get, "Wednesday are having a pig of a season!" into his broadcast.

More shame was heaped upon the LBs as the majority of them paid extra to sit in the shelter of the stand. Me? Too much of an open-terrace man to betray my roots, so Clayre and I braved the elements (okay, I know the Lane had very little in the way of open terracing, but it may have had something to do with me arranging to meet my two Metal Maidens there).

After a few frantic mobile calls, Spiky and Kirsty made it through the turnstile just in time to see us go 1-0 down. I was slightly concerned when Spiky said, "So explain to us what is going on."

"Where do I start?" I asked.

"How about who's kicking into what goal, who's wearing what shirts..." suggested Clayre helpfully.

"Yep - that basic please!" said Spiky.

In the end it was a lot easier than I thought, and as Jaffa nodded that equaliser on the stroke of half-time, they actually admitted they felt quite emotional as it went in. I was totally overwhelmed myself - there are some games where you just don't expect anything, and this was one. The second half was a bit nail-biting, and we were hanging on at times, but Monty put Lee Clarke in his pocket and Browny looked a class above the rest - the only time he looked worried was when Santos floored him. After about four Blades calmed Big Georges down, Warnock performed the quickest subbing in the history of the game, and as the ref. trotted over to see what all the fuss was about Santos was already down the tunnel and gone. Clayre had meanwhile spent the afternoon re-acquainting herself with her old Coventry chum Peter Ndlovu, making his debut for the Blades. A million plus Nuddy for Curtis? Surely Warnock's best deal yet...

Santos and Brown's spat was the main talking point from Clayre's Fulham-fan friends in the pub afterwards. They seemed to think we were a physical team that had stopped them playing football, and the pitch wasn't suited to them blah blah moan moan. They will make a very good London version of Manchester United...

Spiky and Kirsty had already departed to catch up on some sleep before that evening's Cheese Cake Truck gig, but as they left they said they'd thoroughly enjoyed it. "We want to come again!" said Spiky. That warm glow you get when you introduce someone to the Blades shone through the drizzle, but at the same time I felt a little guilty because being a Blade, you do suffer sometimes...

After three or four pubs around the Putney area, I had to bail out, thus missing the curry. You see, a tube strike had started and I had to scramble across town to the Monarch, Chalk Farm for CCT's last gig with violinist Barney. The poor lad was finding being in Miranda Sex Garden and Naked Goat as well a bit too much when combined with his teacher training. Farewell Barney - never again will we stumble over your slumbering body in the dressing room. Sorely missed... In the event not even a reduced tube service could slow me down, as most people seemed to have stayed at home because of the strike. Never has the Northern Line run so efficiently.

A day of surprises then. After a run of bad results, this one had me really believing promotion was back on again. Deluded, me? Never!

Chapter 30
Safety Net

When I was about 5 or 6 years old, my mum started working at Frederick Pell's, a fish wholesaler on Edmund Road, frighteningly close to Bramall Lane. For whatever reasons, if I was at home when all my brothers and sisters were at school then I would every now and again have to sit with my mum at work. As you can imagine I wasn't too keen, as spending time watching her do the accounts was not my idea of fun. Thank goodness she only used to work in the mornings. Anyway, I was going to take some cajoling on this one, but the way they eventually persuaded me that I wanted to go and sit there all morning was when my parents pointed out to me that from the window you could see part of one of the floodlight pylons at the Lane. This was good enough for me, so large chunks of the morning were spent with me looking longingly out of the window at that one (now sadly scythed down) floodlight.

In amongst all this excitement, rough-looking delivery men who had a whiff of fish about them were heard talking about "t'delivery from Grimsby." So much stigma seemed to be attached to this that in my mind Grimsby became some mythical place of great importance - the Centre of All Things Fish.

Over the next thirty years I never went there, and only ever met one person who claimed to be from there (when United beat Grimsby 4-2 in '96/'97 on the tele - I was watching it in the Green Man in Soho, and the bloke next to me turned out to be a Mariner), so I hadn't had many opportunities to dispel any myths. Until now...

I set off for this one on the Friday night because the Internet Blades had a match the next day against Birmingham's internet team, and even though I may not have been fit enough to play (that rib was still bugging me) I felt I should watch. And I'd said if they were desperate I'd see how I felt.

Within 10 minutes of my arrival at Staples Corner my yellow shirt got me spotted and I was clambering into the back of a van with the word GRIMSBY on the side. I ended up perched on a pile of nets and the van reeked of diesel, making me feel quite ill. The cab was separate from the back, so when the two guys in the front tried to converse with me through the glass it was rather difficult. However, after much shouting I worked out that they were going to stop at Toddington, sort out the front and fit me in with them, which was fine as that diesel was getting to me.

Once I was in the front, they saw my shirt and one of them went, "Ah! He's a Blade!" and then proceeded to rip the p*ss out of me!

Once I managed to get a word in edgeways I asked them who they supported. "We're Mariners," came their unsurprising reply, and they then went on about how lucky we'd been to beat them 3-2 earlier in the season. They also told me they were looking forward to the game with us at Blundell Park in April. "You lot always bring a crowd, and there's always a good atmosphere, but always trouble."

I told them I was looking forward to a weekend in Cleethorpes for that one. "Turn up on Thursday," they advised. "You're guaranteed to pull then - students' night in Cleh-thop-eees!"

"Is that how the locals pronounce it?" I asked innocently.

"Nah - that's just us taking the p*ss out of people from... Cleh-thop-eees!" said the driver, and then they both collapsed in helpless laughter. Mythical, legendary Grimsby (and Cleethorpes) was a fast fading memory, but who cares? These guys were far too entertaining.

I asked about the net in the back. "Our company provide safety nets for building sites."

"Saved many lives?" I asked.

"Oh aye. We've both fallen into 'em quite a bit," said the driver. "Me brother always falls into it."

"Aye, but then he always turns up for work p*ssed," said the other. More laughter all round.

I suppose it makes sense. There must be a lot of nets in Grimsby, and a nice sideline would be to use them for rescuing wobbly builders when all the fishing boats have put out to sea and you have a net left over.

After a very amusing lift, these guys set me down at Woodall services, and a slight cheat took place. It was very cold and quite late, so I'd called my dad on the way, and he motored out there to pick me up. Whilst we drove through Sheffield, Katrina sent me a text telling me she missed me. Was it all back on again? Well, we'd kissed and made up earlier in the week over a drink in the Rat and Parrot, Wardour Street, so let's just say we were good mates again.

On the Saturday morning my mum expressed concern when she saw me leaving the house with full kit. "You're not playing with that rib are you?" she asked.

"Only if they're really desperate," I replied.

As soon as I got to Graves Park Colin said, "How bad's your rib Greenwich?"

"I can go in goal if you want," came my reply. I can take a lot of persuading sometimes...

The match took place on what was possibly the muddiest pitch Graves Park had to offer. In front of me was a very splodgy area, behind me a vast open space with no net for safety. I should have nicked one out of their van last night...

After 1 minute we were a goal up. After their first attack it was 1-1. By half-time we were 4-1 down, with most people blaming the mud and a lack of defence for the goals. It has to be said there were some unseemly scrambles in that goal-area, and my yellow Bob Booker shirt was very brown after 10 minutes, and my defence seemed to consist only of Webbo slogging his guts out at left-back.

In the second-half the defence sorted itself out and we kept a clean sheet, although someone suggested I must have shouted "Boo!" at their attackers a few times because on more than one occasion it seemed easier for them to score, but they screwed it wide.

Most of the entertainment was provided by the ball disappearing regularly down the steep slope into the woods, with both teams losing players for long periods as attempts were made to retrieve it.

Whilst we waited and waited for one Birmingham player to return, one of their attackers asked me if the yeti might have got him.

"Nah - the yeti's over there," I replied as Radford ambled into the area.

The game ended 4-1 to Birmingham, and over drinks and Yorkshire pud in the Pump we told the Birmingham lads that the match that really mattered would see the Blades put the record straight. And did they ever...

As we left the Pump for the Lane I heard Stafford and Radford discussing tactics.

Stafford: "Can we define our policy now?"

Radford: "What's that?"

Stafford: "Curtis. Do we boo him or clap him?"

Radford: "Clap him I think."

And so it turned out. Curtis was given a very warm reception by the Blades, as was Carl Tiler, making his debut for the Blues.

But it was our ex-Blues that did the damage. Dev, back from injury, terrorised them throughout, netting our second from the spot; Nuddy was like a man possessed ("That lad ran his blood to water," commented my dad, although he struggled to pronounce his name correctly - still does in fact); Pesky got the third in the second-half and provided us with a rather revealing celebration. I suppose that one was for the missus then Paul. Murph had got our first after Jaffa hit the bar, and celebrated in the back of the net as if to emphasise that we hadn't had any in the morning. To cap it all, the pigs shipped 4 at Wimbledon and each goal was greeted with huge cheers as the scoreboard announced them. Such a shame we let Birmingham get a late consolation, but really it was United's best performance so far in my eyes. We could have had many more than the 3 we got. Splendid stuff!

That night I attended my sister Deborah's house warming party. Her hubby is a follower of our porcine cousins from across the city, and he and his chums were most despondent. "We're going down!" David kept moaning, and my dad kept coming out with his old line of it being wrong to "intrude on the grief of others."

To try and make himself feel better, David produced an old newspaper cutting of Blades fans looking rather glum the day we got relegated in the last minute at Chelsea in '94. I just kept producing my copy of the current Green 'Un...

I had full backing from Richard Caborn MP, an old family friend (he worked for my dad, my sister worked for him). He agreed with me that it was the best performance of the season so far. I then foisted a copy of one of my hitching tales upon him. "I'll tell you what Adrian - if you get it published, I'll launch it for you in the House of Commons, and that's a promise..." He then gave me his card (and of course, he is now a much more high-profile Minister for Sport: up-to-date Political Editor).

I then got chatting to a girl that had acted as translator for a famous Italian footballer who played for the piggies a few years back (and it wasn't Di Canio). Now I wouldn't want to mention anything libellous here, but there may just have been a suggestion that when the pigs bought him, both he and his former club knew of a bad injury (allegedly). And surely he wasn't just interested in the money, and played for the pigs with passion and commitment throughout? He was also a right arrogant sod. Allegedly.

Sunday evening another big cheat took place. My other sister, Fiona, had been up for the party, and as she lived in Chelmsford a lift back seemed like a good idea at the time. Mind you, after wrong turnings, delayed trains, engineering works etc I was almost beginning to wish I'd hitched. Put it this way, it would have been quicker, but quality time with the family is of course of paramount importance.

As a footnote to all this, a few days later Paul Jewell was sacked as the pigs' manager, which I viewed as a great shame because to me he was doing a grand job. I believe he was quoted in the press as saying he didn't see it coming. Never cross the road with this man. Never mind Paul, I'm sure you had the safety net of a hefty pay-off, and it will be on your CV forever: "Left the pigs up to their necks in it."

Chapter 31
Heat in the Jungle

Tuesday 20th February 2001: Sheffield United 1-0 Wolverhampton Wanderers

I have worshipped at the Court of the Crimson King since buying King Crimson's Starless and Bible Black album at the end of 1981. That album provided me with a soundtrack to my revision for the trial 'o' level exams (most people called them 'mocks', but High Storrs School presumably thought this would make us take them less seriously, so trials it was - I never took exams seriously enough anyway, sadly), and over the next few years my Crimson collection started to fill out somewhat. On their Discipline album there is one song called Thela Hun Ginjeet, an anagram of Heat In The Jungle. On this, amidst the shards of metal flying around the studio, singer Adrian Belew can be heard relating a tale of how he'd gone out into the streets of London and been set upon by some guys round the corner from the studio. Unbeknown to him he was being recorded, and what we hear is a very frightened young American repeating the phrase, "This is a dangerous place!"

Whenever I find myself in a dangerous situation those words come into my head: Stonehenge 1988 - the batons fly, the mounted police charge, I hide - "This is a dangerous place!" Looking out of my window in Canning Town one Sunday afternoon having heard much shouting, I see a bloke go up to a guy who's just got out of a car and he produces a huge kitchen knife, bloke gets back in car, car drives off very quickly - "This is a dangerous place!" Sitting in the pub telling Katrina why I hate Spurs, relating how in 1978 we pulled back two late goals against them to draw 2-2, afterwards as me and my dad walk back to the car a gang of Spurs fans come round the corner and start scrapping with the Blades around us, one Spur turns to us and goes, "You Sheffield sh*t!", my dad just grabs my hand and says, "Was he addressing us?", and if King Crimson had recorded it at that time I'm sure I would have thought, "This is a dangerous place!" (I was indeed a precocious 12 year-old prog rock fan - no wonder the kids at school hated me). As the boots and studs went flying at the Lane this night in February 2001, and Jaffa waged war on Pollet and Muscat, one couldn't help thinking once again, "This is a dangerous place!" But I'm ahead of myself...

Danger was the last thing on my mind as I skived off from Uni. early to cross London once more. And there seemed little danger of missing the kick-off as I soon had a lift, this time with two Fulham fans on their way up to Burnley. My red and white shirt did the trick this time, although they had slowed down to make sure it wasn't a Brentford shirt first. With the words Sheffield United mentioned for the first time, the passenger said, "Hey - are you that bloke that was on Talksport?"

"Five-Live, 606," I corrected, and he turned round and shook my hand.

"That was so brilliant!" he said. Pride...

Considering they were sitting pretty at the top of the table, these guys were still worried. "I feel it could still go horribly wrong for us yet," said the driver, and his mate agreed.

"I think you'll be all right," I comforted, but they said they wouldn't relax until it was mathematically certain. (They lost that night to Burnley, so that would have made them worse, I guess.)

They admitted that we'd given them a fright at Craven Cottage, and then told me that Saha had also had a fright that match. At a corner he'd said something none too complimentary to "your big French bloke" in French, not realising he spoke the same lingo. For the rest of the match, Saha was running scared as either Santos or Jaffa were after him. At the time I assumed it was Santos (he did seem rather angry, as Browny can testify), but after witnessing Jaffa's heroics later that night, I would describe both players as big, angry and French...

As they were going to Burnley I expected to be turfed out at Watford Gap, but they told me that they'd be able to drop me at Leicester Forest because they had their own preferred route. Fine by me...

Time was still on my side as I waited at Leicester Forest, and once again my shirt sorted me out.

"I couldn't leave you there when I saw your shirt," said the bloke wearing a suit, speaking with a broad Sheffield accent.

"Are you a Blade then?" I asked.

"No, my allegiance is at the other side of the city," he replied.

I almost asked him to stop the car, but I thought, no - see it through.

As it turned out, he was a most decent chap (as the majority of people that give you lifts are). He admitted that he wasn't a very big Wednesday fan, so I almost felt I could forgive him. He'd just changed his career, moving into IT, and he was on his way back from a training meeting at Heathrow. Most importantly though, he was able to give me a lift right up to St Mary's Gate.

Just as I was getting out my dad phoned me to find where I was.

"At the Lane!" I replied before going off for a kebab. I still had 2 hours to spare before kick-off, and Musical was coming down from a very conveniently-arranged meeting in Leeds, so the R&R it was prior to the match. Attila, Rob, Stafford, Radford all joined us and after the slaughter of the Brummies, we felt good about doing the same to Wolves.

The Star had quoted Warnock as saying that we wouldn't be out for revenge on Muscat after the encounter at Molineux that saw him accused of elbowing Jon Newby (which resulted in Warnock getting his marching orders). Someone should have told both sets of players this. Bad tempered is one way to describe the entertainment...

Just as my dad, Windy and myself were debating whether we'd actually had a shot on goal in the first 20 minutes, Jaffa lifted the ball over the advancing 'keeper and we were a goal to the good. That's how it stayed, but there was still plenty of action. How Muscat didn't get his marching orders is beyond me, but as someone pointed out, if he'd not been on the pitch, he wouldn't have been able to gloriously send that second-half penalty wide. Poetic justice I say...

Jaffa was also lucky to stay on the pitch, and Warnock subbed him for his own safety in the end. However, at the final whistle he was seen fully-changed into his suit squaring up to Pollet as he tried to leave the pitch. He then dashed off to France to witness his wife giving birth. "This is a dangerous place!"

A lift home with Musical was in the offing, but only if I did my usual trick of standing in front of his BMW with my LONDON card. As we motored home tuned in to Five-Live, we heard how Tranmere had come back from 3-0 down to win 4-3 against Southampton in the Cup, then we listened live as Wycombe disposed of Wimbledon on penalties something like about 11-10, and we agreed that football was indeed a very splendid game.

As we approached central London, traffic got bad and that last Jubilee Line train seemed in danger, but Musical's BMW suddenly became magic, seemingly able to reverse up slip roads and go through red lights at will. He never said anything in the following weeks about a fine, so I trust it was also invisible to the cameras.

The last train was made with minutes to spare so I was able to read my programme happily all the way home, and walk through the streets of Stratford, East London at the only time they are quiet - after 1am. I even saw a fox sprinting across the road from the churchyard into Stratford Park. A dangerous place? Not at this time - even the hunted were safe. Mind you, I wouldn't want to be Muscat or Pollet the next time they play the Blades, especially if Jaffa spears our attack.

Chapter 32
Sentimental Mercenary

Saturday 24th February 2001: Sheffield United 1-0 Crystal Palace

Back in 1983 I headed to Glastonbury for the first time - in fact it was my first experience of festivals in any form. The object of my desire was Marillion, a band who were like a breath of fresh air to a 17 year-old "fresh-faced young hippie" (I think I've done that one before) of a prog rock fan. It was also the first time I'd witnessed Marillion live (having been on a week-long school geography field trip in Scarborough when they played at Sheffield City Hall earlier in the year) so excitement was at fever pitch.

On that warm summer Friday evening I lapped up every word of frontman Fish, but did start to wonder what on earth he was going on about when he starting spouting about "sentimental mercenaries." I should have understood - after all, I was a self-styled 6th-form poet myself. Hmmm...

After this weekend nearly eighteen years later I maybe started to understand...

I've never been much of one for Tesco parties. Over the years I managed to avoid all but one of their Christmas 'dos', the excuse of working nights coming in handy most years. And now I'd managed to use "Blades commitments" to avoid this season's party at Tesco Bishopsgate. However, Tesco had other ideas, and because our store came top in some customer service competition the company rewarded us with another party. It was to be held on February 24th, and a quick glance at the fixture list suggested I'd get out of attending once more, but then Katrina stepped in by asking me if I was going, saying she was but didn't want to be on her own. I said I'd see what I could do, but there was no way I was going to miss United's home game with Palace.

I got to work on it and via emails, texts and phone calls a semi-cheat with Maidenhead was set up. It would mean I'd get a lift as far as Toddington, but then I'd have to hitch to London from there. There was a slight element of risk involved, but I was confident I could do it, so I told Katrina I'd probably be there about 9-ish...

Before that there was the small matter of getting up to Sheffield that Saturday morning, not easy after a night at the Camden Electric Ballroom with Spiky Em and Kirsty. As usual I didn't have long to wait for my first lift, and always welcome on a Saturday morning it took me a fairly hefty chunk of the way, to Watford Gap no less. This chap was a typical Manchester United fan - you know, London accent, didn't get to many matches, and in fact went to more Arsenal matches because he got corporate freebies. He actually apologised to me for being a Man Utd fan. I forgave him purely because he was giving me a lift...

At Watford Gap I once more just had time to add to my Greenwich Blade on tour graffiti before getting a lift. Again it was in a foreign truck (Dutch this time) driven by an English bloke (this one was a Scouser). Quite an interesting chap he was too. He'd been in the army in the late-sixties/ early seventies, but when he got out he was tapped up by the Cambodian government to be a mercenary fighting in the war against the Khmer Rouge. The money was good, so off he went.

As you can imagine he had some quite interesting tales to tell, and some most horrific ones too which not even I can bring myself to repeat here. Probably the least disturbing was the way they got information out of prisoners.

They'd take them up in a helicopter, fly them over the jungle, threaten to throw them out, then carry it out. "Normally by the time we'd chucked two of 'em out, the third was ready to talk."

He also described "the yanks" as being "useless when it came to jungle warfare". Apparently they were "loud, never covered their tracks and left the smell of brilliantine wherever they went..."

He was driving to Chesterfield, but was stopping off at a truck-stop for a few hours at junction 29. Time was on my side, so I decided to get out at the truck-stop and take things from there. A quick survey of the scene told me I'd have been better off getting out at Tibshelf services and hitching from there, but too late now so I wandered around the nearby village trying to work out which way the busses were going. A quick word with a local sorted me, and pretty soon I was on the slow-bus to Chesterfield. Interesting aside - the micro-scooter has made it as far as North Derbyshire. What was once a London thing...

Once in Chesterfield I got on the even-slower-bus to Sheffield. It seemed to go round every street and house in both Chesterfield and Sheffield, and very dull it was too. I kept myself amused by sending texts to Spiky, Katrina and Michaela, receiving a call from Michaela which put a smile on my face (meeting arranged in Camden, Sunday lunchtime).

By the time I got to the Lane things were very tight time-wise as I had to buy my ticket for Crewe away, then meet the London Blades in the Pump and order my chilli-beef Yorkshire pud before they stopped taking orders at 2 o'clock. Once again mobile phone technology triumphed - one quick call to Musical ensured my order was placed at the bar, and by the time I got there it was waiting for me (although I believe the Musical one had a little more difficulty securing vegetarian gravy granules - "Vegetarian gravy granules? Gi' o'er!" said the nice lady). The London Blades contingent were all keen to hear my mercenary tales, but I waited until I'd finished eating.

The match was nothing to write home about. Earlier in the week Palace's chairman had offered their travelling fans their money back after a spineless performance at Barnsley, but apparently he was quite happy with this one despite losing 1-0. It has to be said that they were a tad unfortunate not to come away with something, a last minute bar-rattler causing us some missed heartbeats. In the event, the outstanding moment was Suffo's brilliant debut Blades goal. Didn't stop Warnock from taking him off later though...

So now the dash back to London. Maidenhead was located near Edmund Road and a speedy exit we made. As we raced past Watford Gap at around 7 o'clock Katrina called me to see how much progress I had made. At that stage my ETA of 9pm was looking good. But then it all went wrong at Toddington.

For a start it was very cold, and secondly I had to wait about 45 minutes for my lift. Even then he was only going round the M25 in a Hounslow direction. I was desperate though, so Hounslow it was, then a breathless tube dash across town, arriving at the White Hart, Bishopsgate nearer 10 than 9. The party was already in full swing.

Well, the events of that night probably belong to another story, but basically I ended up going home after forty-five minutes, and Katrina and I had an interesting phone conversation at 1am.

Amends were made as I sat in the World's End in Camden with Michaela the following afternoon when Katrina and I had a more civilised chat on the mobiles, and all was sorted Monday evening when she came in to visit me on the checkout. She bought me a present to cheer me up, and on the receipt she wrote, "Sorry Ad. Katrina. Have a muffin." I still have it (the receipt, not the muffin).

So you see, there may not be too much that is sentimental about a mercenary that chucks people out of helicopters, but after mine and Katrina's mercenary behaviour of the weekend (look, I'm not going to tell you) we both showed our sentimental side. Fish knew what he was going on about after all, honestly!

And as if to prove it, Katrina and I decided to officially get back together on that Monday.

This one could run and run...

PS This chapter was originally much longer, but Katrina and I decided that it wasn't worth going over again what wasn't one of our better nights, so I edited it all out. So don't ask me again, all right?!!!

Chapter 33
Freak Scoreline

Saturday 3rd March 2001: Queens Park Rangers 1-3 Sheffield United

The thing I love about England is its marvellously freaky weather. Now, I won't fall into the trap of going on about it, as that would be stereotypically English, would it not (old bean)? But I have fielded at school during cricket practice with the snow coming down, and I may have mentioned before that I once hitched to United v Arsenal on Easter Monday in a blizzard. So, by its very unpredictability it becomes predictable. Or something. I know the Spring Equinox was still a few weeks off yet, but most of us expect that by March any chance of a decent snowfall will have long since gone, especially in smelly, smoggy London.

So imagine our surprise as myself, Musical, Halfway and Lords sat in a Weatherspoons pub in Islington on Friday 2nd March prior to going to see Beth Orton at the Union Chapel, when it started snowing. By the time we came out (my mind purified by St Beth) it was getting heavy, and once I was in the Portway Chinese Take-Away down the road from my house, the game the following day was looking in danger. I told the beautiful girl serving me about my worries, so she gave me a fortune cookie to cheer me up. It said, "If you have much, give of your wealth; if you have little, give of your heart." This gave me food for thought in more ways than one, because though the weather may be unpredictable, Katrina and I, as expected, had terminated our relationship the day before after only three-and-a-bit days back together. Ah well...

By the next morning all was well in one respect however, as the snow had gone. So as planned I tubed it over to the Bushranger pub to meet the London Blades, and as it turned out just about the entire SUISA message board. On the way I got chatting to two QPR fans. They asked me how I thought we'd get on, and I pointed out we were on a run of 3 straight wins so I was quietly confident. They said they were confident too:

"We've just got Ian Holloway, so I reckon New Manager Syndrome will kick in. I think we'll win today, and it will kick-start our recovery."

They seemed so sure of it I started to believe them too. I entered the Bushranger a little unsure.

I think in years to come this day will still be talked about as the best London Blades day out, with the possible exception of last season's Fulham Monty boat-trip (although on that occasion United ruined it all by turning in one of their most inept performances in my near-30 years of watching them by losing 4-0). Like I said, the turnout was incredible, too many to mention here, but special mention must go to Asa who'd come over from Spain (although she is Swedish), and Copenhagen and Denmark Blade who also clocked up the air miles. Maybe everyone turned up to get on film, as I'd put the word out that I'd be there with a Uni. video camera as I wanted to film the London Blades as part of one of my Uni. projects. As a result I got footage of just about everyone sober pre-match, and not so sober post-match. I even got to test the colour balance with Shiny's yellow shirt. Best of all was Asa's t-shirt ("Don't stare! Buy me a pint!") and capturing the Blades in full voice, belting out the Greasy Chip Butty song and Swinging a Pig.

And the match? Awesome. Near on 2000 Blades made the trip (the ticket stubs from that day were to be used to secure tickets for the pig match at Swillsborough), and what an atmosphere we created. Okay, we were 1-0 down at half-time, but kicking our way in the second-half, the Blades were unstoppable. Dev ran riot having a hand in all 3 goals - his corner was netted by Murph after a bit of a scramble, his chipped cross after a short corner was nodded in by Santos, and the ball he played through for Santos' second and our third was soooo perfect. Santos' finish was quality, and his celebrations in front of us guaranteed hero-status for Big Georges. The chant of "Santos!" was at its loudest that afternoon. We could have scored more, but 3-1 away was good enough.

As the second-half continued I started to feel a little guilty about the stick (oh no, unintentional pun!) being dished out to Peter Crouch. "Freeeeeaaaakkk!" rang out every time he touched the ball. I remarked to Hammersmith (ex-Wolves Blade) beside me that I couldn't see him coming to the Lane if ever we put in an offer for him.

Despite "Santos!" and "Freak!", chant of the day had to go to the one composed by our very own Woodford Green. Right in the middle of the foot and mouth crisis, WGB had the presence of mind to start up, "Peter Shreeve's got foot and mouth disease, foot and mouth disease, foot and mouth disease!" to the tune of Yellow Submarine. Like all Blades that day, truly inspired, and WGB's proudest moment!

After the match I retrieved my camera from the boot of Pommpey's car, and festivities re-commenced in the Bushranger, and very entertaining viewing the video footage makes. We have the NLB doing a trick with a lit cigarette (and Tracey - the lovely Stroud Green Blade - can be heard in the background saying, "Adam! Stop it!"); we have him and Lords kissing; many, many Blades giving the "3-1" fingers to the camera; and many confident predictions that we were going up. We were now in 6th, and for us it was all one way traffic. If only the season could end right there and then...

Outside the pub on the way to the Indian the filming carried on. We had Exiled Coal Astoner (ECA) doing the Santos! chant (with the newly added Santos! dance) and getting a vagrant to join in, followed by some merry-as-newts LBs. Then there is captured for all time Musical chatting up a very attractive blonde girl outside a shop whilst the LBs shout "Freeeaaakkk!!" in his direction from behind me, Cecil B. de Greenwich. As Musical leaves the scene of the crime, he can be heard telling us he hates us all, "every single one of you!"

There is probably far too much footage in the Indian, but at least it meant my defeat at the hands of another killer phal was there for all to see, as well as Alty's now legendary bail-out ("He's getting out of paying!" whispered the cameraman) and Musical's touching message to our absent friend, the stuck-in-Thailand Soho. There was also much chanting of "Santos!" and toasting of Big Georges and "the play-offs" and even to "promotion!"

Sadly the battery ran out, so I didn't get anything of our subsequent visit to O'Neill's where after the Irish jig stopped we were all still in the middle of the floor jumping up and down chanting "Santos! Santos!" much to the amusement of the other customers. It also meant I didn't get the comments of the Bristol Rovers fan we met on the platform who was in town so had gone to the match:

"Your right winger - is it Devlin? - he impressed me."

"Don't forget Big Georges!" We needed no excuse to start the chant again.

Once on the train we somehow managed to get another vagrant to join us in the Santos! chant, even more remarkable when you consider that this one was a total and utter fruitcake (in ECA's words).

Eventually we all went our separate ways, Musical passing into a deep sleep that meant he slept right through the IRA bomb going off just down the road from him at the BBC. Meanwhile long into the night I was still getting text messages of "Santos!" on my mobile.

The perfect day; 3-1 away from home, a curry, all on film (mostly), and as far as we were concerned, the Blades were going up. Very freakish...

Chapter 34
Video Evidence

Tuesday 6th March 2001: Crewe 1-0 Sheffield United

There were many outstanding things about my first ever Blades match. It was October 1971 and we drew 1-1 with Liverpool. I don't actually remember that much about it in all honesty (I was only 5 after all) but I do remember Currie's goal, one that is still considered by many Unitedites to be the best they have ever seen scored for the Blades. I also remember my mum and my sisters telling me that they could hear the roar from the Lane as they watched some University Rag Week boatrace down by the River Don, which was mighty impressive to me. But one of the most memorable things for me was seeing myself on Yorkshire Television's Football Special the next day as they showed highlights. My two older brothers and myself were squashed in at the front up against the white railings on the John Street Terrace; it was only the odd fleeting glimpse, but I knew it was me and that was good enough.

Since then, television appearances have been few, with some less thrilling than others. I was actually rather pleased when at Stonehenge in 1986 a local TV camera crew thrust a microphone at me as I sat in the middle of the road waiting for a police roadblock to move to let us carry on our journey to the Stones.

"What do you think your chances of reaching the Stones are now?" the reporter asked me.

"We've come this far, so we won't give up now. We'll make it!" I confidently predicted.

One minute later the police waded in and arrested 286 out of 400 of us... I escaped, but never made it to the Stones, spending a night in Hampshire, minus my rucksack and tent, instead. Not sure if my interview made it to the news, but I can always dream.

Two years later in 1988 I returned home from Stonehenge to find that someone had kindly videoed the news with TV footage of me sitting outside

Salisbury Magistrate's Court, and, er, that's probably it. Other than that I've appeared frequently on police video, whether it be at Stonehenge or at United matches. Hitching got me on a few times too, like when I was on a routine hitch from London to Brackley, and found myself at some horrible junction near Watford. Round the corner came the plod who told me to move further up towards the roundabout (where I'd be causing more danger I might add, but wouldn't be illegally situated the wrong side of the M1 sign).

"We spotted you on the CCTV!" said the driver gleefully.

"Big Brother is watching you!" added his mate. Funny...

So, it was time to turn the tables, time for me to shoot some footage myself, make my own film, and maybe even get the Old Bill on video. Besides, I needed to do more filming for my project at Uni., so here goes.

I collected the camera from the University of Greenwich (supplied by the gorgeous Jess, everyone's fave lab tech), gave instructions to Ross (an Arsenal fan, so he sort of understands) to pick up handouts from that afternoon's Politics, Ideology and the Media lecture (and to let me have his notes), then skived off for the afternoon. Firstly I went home and filmed myself packing (I broke the zip on my small rucksack, having to fix it with gaffa - riveting stuff, eh?), then concealed the camera in my Cardiacs shoulder bag to lessen the chances of mugging as I walked the streets of East London.

After the disaster of the zip-breakage, I felt my luck was turning when I put my money in the Cadbury's chocolate machine at Bank station and out came two bars. This was both a good omen for my hitch and for United that evening. After four wins on the bounce, and with us currently residing in 6th place, I'd been telling everyone that if we could win at Crewe we'd "be in dreamland!". (Dreamland, a win at Crewe eh? As ECA pointed out, says it all for being a Blade really...)

And so it proved with the hitch at least - two lifts and I was at junction 16 of the M6. The first lift was with a white-van-man who was actually a fellow Blade now resident in London. He didn't go to many matches, but I gave him the SUISA website address as well as my email just in case he wishes to hit the London Blades trail - he hasn't done yet, but who can resist for too long? Anyway, he'd picked me up on the strength of my United shirt and not because I was wielding a nice expensive camera, mainly because the camera was kept in the bag, making only brief appearances to film, as I had a feeling I may attract a lift rather quickly from some dodgy geezer if they saw it.

My fellow Blade was able to drop me at Watford Gap. Here I filmed the ritual of adding to the "Greenwich Blade on Tour" graffiti, sadly a waste of the battery as upon viewing later, I discovered that using the marker pen at the same time as the camera had proved too difficult for me, so we got shots of the sky, the ground, the rest of the graffiti, but not mine...

No sooner had I finished this, the chap sat in his wagon sipping a cup of tea honked his hooter and beckoned me over. He'd spotted my CREWE sign and was heading up towards Blackburn, so I was in.

For the third time in a very short period it was a foreign truck (French was today's nationality) driven by an English bloke. This one was from south London, a Charlton fan no less. He only got to the Valley two or three times a season now, but was a regular attendee in the glory years of the 1950s, reminiscing about how the trams "could shift a crowd" (my dad could have talked to him for hours about this).

The plan (arranged as all good cheats are via email and the Internet) was for me to meet justoutsidestokeblade just outside Crewe, at the White Lion in Barthomley just off the M6. I was told to be there before 7 to secure my lift to the ground, so I was highly delighted by my 6pm arrival in said pub. Oxspring (formerly Kettering) Blade and Bob Hatton's Balding Bonce were already in there (always glad to meet new Blades), with josb and josb jnr the younger not too far behind, so as the rains started I had my lift to the ground secured.

Unlike QPR, this time I decided to risk taking the camera into the ground, getting past the stewards by keeping the shoulder bag (full of camera) well out of sight by my side, carrying my rucksack out front for all to see.

"Can I look in your bag?" asked the steward.

"You can try," I replied, "but it's all stuck up with gaffa," showing him the evidence. "I've only got a sleeping bag in there," I continued, so he waved me through...

As I entered the stand a chap I didn't know said, "Where's the camera then?" so I sneakily gave him a peek in the bag (I later learned that this was We Are Mark Beard).

I watched the match stood at the back next to Halfway and his lad Aaron. As the match started Halfway received a text saying that Carl Asaba hadn't turned up for Gillingham that day, which suggested he may be on his way to us apparently. We were supposed to be sat down, but no-one else was, and the steward stood next to me didn't seem to mind. He also didn't seem too bothered that every time United got near goal I whipped the camera out and filmed away.

United seemed quite positive too with Crewe hardly getting a sniff of goal. The rain really was coming down now, and it was swirling in the wind. Apparently those at the front got a thorough soaking, my soaking coming instead when I queued all through half-time for a hotdog.

In the second-half I ended up with lots of footage of corners being scrambled away, shots flying wide and plenty of "ooohs" and "ahhhs" from the Blades. Crewe's only efforts on goal were the one they scored from, and a couple of wind-assisted goal-kicks that bounced dangerously over Tracey's bar.

Special mention must go to Nuddy's free-kick on the edge of the area which disappeared off-camera (via the top) very soon after leaving his boot, and is probably still stuck on the roof of a railway shed as we speak...

An undeserved defeat and the weather made us all feel somewhat gloomy, but one thing brightened me up visibly, and that was josb's announcement that he'd been sat next to Maidenhead and he'd mentioned he'd be getting petrol at Keele Services, as would josb. Imagine my delight upon entering Keele when we spied Maidenhead already at the pumps, especially as the rain was still lashing down. It's not cheating, it's initiative by the way.

Maidenhead was going home via the M40 - not as busy as the M1, but still leading directly into London. By the time Maidenhead and Maidenhead jnr had dropped me at Cherwell Valley Services the rain had eased off (just the odd bit of drizzle now), but the wind was still giving it some - cold and miserable. Midnight came and went, and there wasn't much traffic about. Then at 1am, here came my chance to get the police on video as they came round the corner. I quickly thought the better of it, realising that I may look a little suspicious hitching with a camcorder, so as they pulled up I left it down by my side, still running.

They gave me the usual, telling me I shouldn't be standing there and I should go round the corner to the lay-by. As usual I pointed out I stood less chance of getting a lift here as that ruled out all the A43 traffic coming onto the M40...

"That's as maybe, but if you stay here you'll be breaking the law."

"Yes officer..."

After they took down my particulars I trooped dejectedly round the corner to witness the virtually-nil amount of vehicles coming out of the services. At least it was a bit more sheltered here so I wasn't so cold. I sat on a rock and fired an angry text off to Katrina saying how I'd been here nearly 2 hours, it was wet and cold and the police had just moved me.

To my surprise I got a call back from her immediately. She told me she was missing me, and that I should take care. Basically it was one of those wonderful conversations that made me feel all warm and glowy inside (and we continued it the next day at Tesco, getting back together once again). Peace of mind returned, and as I ended the chat I saw a car coming towards me. I just had time to switch the camera on, declare undying love for Katrina into it, then stick my LONDON sign out.

On the side of the van were the words BIRMINGHAM MAIL (or was it the Post?), and I expressed my doubts into the camera about the chances of getting a lift with this one. But as I opened the door, a broad Brummie accent said, "If it's London yow want, get in!"

He said he was going to Canary Wharf via Oxford and various wholesale news places in London. I told him I didn't care what route we went because Canary Wharf was on my manor! I sent another text to Katrina telling her of my good fortune, and she sent me one back telling me to thank the driver and to take care getting home from Canary Wharf. Sooooo sweet....

The guy was a Villa fan, and when I told him I'd been to Crewe for the Crewe Sheffield United match (he obviously hadn't read my shirt) he said, "What's a Crewe fan doing living in London...? Unless you're a Sheffield United fan... hang on! Are you that one that was on 606?"

And for all you non-believers, this whole exchange was captured on film. Fantastic.

It was a long but lively journey into London, the high spots being when he showed me an x-ray that his wife (a nurse) had given him of a bloke who had an aerosol can jammed in his rectum, and also a trip up the Canary Wharf Tower (they were now part of the Mirror Group) from where I acquired a free copy of the Mirror, and experienced the wobble (I'm sure it creaked as well).

Actually even better was the bit where he said he would be going from Canary Wharf to Dalston, and I pointed out that this would take him through Stratford. So there I was being dropped off at Stratford Bus Station, walking the mile or so home. It doesn't get much better than this...

I was home for 5am, and up for 8 for another root-canal dental appointment - (misery), then off to Uni. to return the camcorder. Here I sat down and viewed what I'd filmed, and I'm pleased to say that there was about as much useable footage as I'd previously had myself in the spotlight of TV. That'll be about five minutes then...

Chapter 35
Scabs!

Saturday 10th March 2001: Sheffield United 1-3 Nottingham Forest

The year of 1984 was not a good one if you were in Sheffield. Myself, I'd just left school with two 'A' levels, not quite good enough to go to Uni., but the job situation was grim in the city too, so I spent a year on the dole before GT News eventually gave in and took me on in September 1985. Meanwhile the miners' strike had a grip on the area, and I was surprised to discover that the fallout from this was still remembered today. Back then, my only real contact with the strike was when the cricket team I played for, Sheffield Bankers Juniors, were invited to play Renishaw Miners who found playing cricket a good way of passing the time whilst they weren't working.

I went in as opening bat, made a brisk 11 (by my sedate standards anyway - I tried to model myself on Sir Geoffrey Boycott) before holing out to mid-off. No sooner was I back in the pavilion than someone chucked a white coat at me.

"Ever umpired before?" I was asked.

"Nope!" came my reply, which I fully expected to get me off.

"Never mind - you know the rules though don't you? Off you go then."

So there I was out in the middle trying to remember to move the pebbles from one pocket to the other and wishing it would all be over very soon.

Renishaw had a big rough looking fast bowler called Perce, and he was bowling with some aggression. One of his deliveries hit one of our batsmen on the pad and Perce let out a blood curdling appeal.

I'll be honest - I hadn't a clue whether it was out or not; I just remembered my dad's advice which had been to never give lbw at this level of cricket (although he once gave me out when umpiring, only to admit he was wrong afterwards, even drawing me a diagram to show how a left-arm bowler round the wicket couldn't have trapped me).

"Not out!" I said firmly.

"Tha wot?!!" shouted Perce.

I may have seemed calm outwardly, but inside I now had grave doubts.

"Not out," I repeated, realising I couldn't back down now.

"No way!" screamed Perce.

Then his captain stepped in. "Perce..."

"What?"

"It were miles off!"

"Were it? All right. Sorry umpire...." And so the game restarted...

As I headed up the M1 on the night of Friday 9th March Perce and his mates were a long way from my thoughts. Instead in my head was the fact that due to various strange circumstances I'd not been to any United against Forest matches since March 1977. On that occasion we won 2-0 with Edwards netting both our goals. At the end of that season Forest went up, going on to be League Champions, then Champions of Europe. We finished 11th, and four years later were relegated to the Fourth Division...

My first lift soon had Renishaw miners back in my mind. The driver was a Forest fan, so I asked him if he was going to the match the following day.

"I don't go to Forest/ Sheffield United matches anymore," he replied. "Too much trouble."

I admitted I'd not been to one since 1977, so I was puzzled.

"Tomorrow you won't hear any chants to do with the football," he explained. "Instead it will just be Scabs! Scabs! Scabs! from the Blades to the Forest fans." He then reminded me of some long-forgotten (in my mind anyway) history. It was all to do with the miners' strike you see. Whilst South Yorkshire's finest stayed out, Nottinghamshire's worked on, and this still rankled with those from Sheffield, Barnsley, Doncaster etc.

He then went on to tell me that the last time he'd been at the Lane he'd found himself caught up in fighting on John Street quite against his will. He'd been called a dirty scab, and had thought that it wasn't worth it any more. Strangely enough, he wouldn't have minded so much if he had been insulted for being a Forest fan, but this was something that had had nothing to do with him, even 17 years ago.

By strange coincidence, it had everything to do with my next lift. I'd been dropped at Trowell Services, and after 25 minutes I had a lift in a breakdown wagon. He was able to drop me at Woodall, and as it was getting close to the midnight cut-off point, I called my dad and got him to meet me there.

On the way I got chatting to the driver about my conversation on the previous lift, and he told me that he'd been working in one of the Notts pits at the time. He'd been born in Doncaster, so his loyalties were being stretched here. He'd stayed on strike for a long time, but eventually had decided it just wasn't worth it as the vast majority of Notts miners were working, so he went back.

"Looking back now, Scargill should have put it to the vote, then there would have been no questioning..." he reflected. But that was then, I guess...

On another very cold night, a lift into Sheffield with my dad was most welcome. Texts from Katrina put a smile on my face as well...

Saturday afternoon as I walked to the Pump to meet the LBs and feast on chilli-beef Yorkshire pud, I left her a voicemail message explaining that I was bricking this one, as in my mind this was the "most vital match of the season thus far."

And in front of a sell-out crowd, it all went horribly wrong. By the time my dad had negotiated the traffic and found us, United were already 1-0 down. Shortly afterwards Santos went off with an horrendous head injury resulting from a stray Forest elbow, and overall the vibe was bad. As someone said the next day, we huffed and puffed, but it wasn't enough. In the second-half after some dreadful defending we were two down, then Fordy's penalty clipped the bar and flew into the kop. Murph got a goal back, then had one cleared off the line, but late on more shocking defending saw Forest snatch a third. The brightest point was Asaba's debut - he looked a handful and with a bit more match fitness... And true to the driver's prediction the previous night, the Blades chanted, "Scabs! Scabs!" throughout (Musical and Attila - on odd breaks from being Cuddles Blade - being very vociferous).

Afterwards everyone's opinion was that we had been out-fought throughout, Santos going off so early certainly not helping. The feeling also was that promotion was now definitely off...

I had plenty of time to reflect on it, as I opted to stay in Sheffield for the weekend, eventually getting my dad to return me to Woodall late Sunday afternoon.

It was a very easy trip back too, as I did it in one go. The young chap that picked me up had been in Leeds for the weekend clubbing, and was now heading back to his home in Eltham, South London. He'd not slept all weekend, so he was rather tired and uncommunicative at first, but we kept stopping at services where he'd down Red Bull and the odd coffee, and by the time we left

Toddington he was wide awake.

As he was going to head through the Blackwall Tunnel to get home, he was driving very close to Stratford, so he agreed to drop me at Bromley-by-Bow tube station. The trouble was, we couldn't find it, and we spent rather longer than anticipated driving round the backstreets of East London looking for it. When we had found it, I had one more shock as I went to the barrier and realised I'd not got my travelcard. I raced out of the station and flagged him down as he was pulling off, a quick search down the side of the passenger seat revealing my card hidden away...

The next day as I sat in the staff restaurant at Tesco looking at the horrific photos in the 'paper of Santos' injury, I found myself slipping into hard-done-by South Yorkshire mode. "Forest scabs!" I muttered under my breath. Yep, what United could have done with on Saturday was the aggression of Perce and his Renishaw miner mates, then we'd have shown 'em.

Chapter 36
Devlin's Shorts

Saturday 17th March 2001: Huddersfield Town 2-1 Sheffield United

Back in 1995 I had a most beautiful girlfriend who went by the name of Sarah. We met at a Cardiacs gig in Milton Keynes, a gig for which Ian and I had backstage passes, and to my eternal shame I used the line of, "If you stick with me, you can meet the band!" Well, so what? It worked, because I hitched back to Brackley that night clutching Sarah's phone number, and for the next eight months we were an item. We used to hitch together every so often, including the one and only time I dragged her along to watch United. It was the first match of the 1995/1996 season, away to Watford. We lost 2-1 and dire is one word I'd use to describe it. Not surprisingly she never came with me again, but I still live in hope that she may come along one day soon. You see, even after we broke up we stayed chums, and indeed there was a time in 1998 (in fact for most of that year) where we were best mates, proving to be almost inseparable, going to gigs together and driving through London to my then-house in Canning Town from Pinner Green Tesco frequently. She even drove me up to Sheffield for the United v Huddersfield match in December 1998 (Twiss' only memorable moment in a United shirt - that last-minute winner), choosing to go shopping round Sheffield whilst my dad and I went to the Lane.

And once again Huddersfield were the connection here. For the previous two years we'd not been quite so close (my Czech girlfriend and her English boyfriend saw to that), but we still kept in touch, and recently she'd split with her boyfriend, so our harmlessly-flirty text messages started up again.

As I rushed up the M1 on the Friday night before the Huddersfield match, the chap driving the Range Rover that had picked me up from Staples Corner was taking an unhealthy interest in what Sarah's texts had to say, especially when I made the mistake of saying she was "young and blonde." It just so happened that he lived in Milton Keynes you see, and I think he was beginning to wish he wasn't middle-aged and married. He dropped me off at Newport Pagnell, and I suspect he spent the rest of the night cruising round the centre of Milton Keynes looking for a beautiful blonde with 15 ear-piercings, 2 nose-piercings, a tongue-piercing and 2 tattoos (and if I've missed anything out Sarah, I'm sorry).

I had the Uni. camcorder with me again, and I put it to good use to chat up the girls in the service station shop. Then it was out into the rain again and with Sarah's last text warming the cockles of my heart, I stood there getting drenched.

For a change it was the rain that saved me. The chap that stopped admitted that if the weather had been fine he would have driven straight by as he was very tired. His knackered state meant that conversation wasn't too lively, but I did establish that he lived in Baslow and he would be going some strange route round Derby to get there, meaning I was best getting out at Leicester Forest. However, at Watford Gap he stopped and had a strong coffee.

When we got back in his car he announced that he was feeling a lot better now which good for me because he was now prepared to go the slightly longer route home and drop me off in Chesterfield. A quick call to my dad ensured that I would be picked up from here, me selling it to him by pointing out that it was infinitely preferable to Woodall Services.

My lift was more chatty now, and we reminisced about Derbyshire. You see, my dad was born in Hathersage, so I happily related tales of visits to relatives there as well as in Bradwell and Great Hucklow, not forgetting those wonderful Saturdays in the summer when we kids would run riot on the Surprise.

I had to wait longer than anticipated for my dad, but at least it enabled me to get some video footage of Chesterfield bus station...

Webbo had kindly set up a match against Sheffield United's staff for the Internet Blades football team. We were assured that this meant booking office and backroom staff only, with no current or ex-pros turning out. However, that bloke who stuck the ball past me about four times in the first-half did look a little like Keith Edwards (I know it wasn't him, but he did unnerve me). At least I hadn't had far to travel this time as the game was played just over the back from my parents' on United's Abbeydale training pitch. And not only were we playing on a brilliant surface, but the club had kindly loaned us some kit. An unseemly struggle took place in the dressing room as we fought over the shirt numbers. Being in goal meant that I had to settle for Tracey's shirt, but somehow I ended up with Dev's shorts, a fact that made Windy green with envy (she may have only been more envious if I'd had Browny's on). Sadly, I performed more like Dev between the sticks than Trace, which was rather bad as I had given the camcorder to Gleadless Valley Blade with the instruction to capture some footage of me making a save or two. Not one save did I make in that half, so if I could bring myself to watch it, one presumes I would see that Edwards-alike sticking the ball past me rather a lot. In the second half I trundled around outfield and Mouse took over the gloves. I think the final score was 7-4 to United's staff, with this game seeing the start of yet another of my nicknames; Lobbed-Greenwich...

In return for turning out for the 'Net Blades I got a lift to the McAlpine with Gleadless Valley and Mouse, picking up Colin (Gannon's Right Foot) on the way, as well as a rather huge portion of fish, chips and curry sauce. Listening to the radio we learned that England had sensationally won the test series in Sri Lanka, which was rather nice...

Upon arrival at the ground we met up with Dublin Blade who had made a rare trip to these shores, surely much more impressive than a poxy hitch from London...

Once again United blew it. Huddersfield, a side struggling near the bottom, were there for the taking, but we looked tired. The fact that Martin Smith scored against us made it worse, and only Asaba's debut Blades goal gave us anything to cheer about, bang on the stroke of half-time. If we thought the play-offs were a lost cause after Forest, then they were dead and buried after this one, surely. Katrina did her best to cheer me up on the phone afterwards, but it didn't really help.

So, with foot and mouth pyres burning on the hills, we headed back to South Yorkshire. I decided to go straight back to London, so GVB dropped me at Woodall. After 1 hour I began to regret this decision, especially as it started to snow. I knew that Richard Littlejohn was away from 606, with Adrian Chiles on instead, so I thought I may try to ring them up.

It worked, I slipped through and they put me on. I confessed on air that I would even accept a lift with a Wednesday fan the way I was feeling, not that it worked, as not long after a car went past and someone shouted out of the window, "Piggy b*****d!"

Half an hour later I was sorted however, when a Leicester fan and his young lad stopped. They'd heard me on the radio and asked if I'd been on "a few months ago." I owned up...

They'd just come back from Old Trafford where they'd seen Leicester lose to two late goals. They had been in the corporate boxes, and had hated the whole experience. They were none too impressed with the ManUre fans in there. "The whole prawn sandwich thing is so accurate," said the dad. "They hardly seemed bothered when they scored near the end. We'd have been going mad if it was us..."

Leicester Forest Services meant one thing - Burger King. Running very behind schedule now, I was even considering a rough-sleeping session, but much to my delight the first vehicle that came my way stopped. He was driving a tanker full of whey, which meant that due to the foot and mouth crisis he was having to disinfect his truck at every port of call, and boy could you smell it! He was delivering somewhere south of the Blackwall tunnel, so for the third lift home running, I was going to get dropped off in East London.

He was a part-time Forest fan, and as we journeyed south he got chatting to his Notts County-supporting mate on the mobile...

"I've picked up a hitchhiker - a Sheffield United fan. He's not very happy 'cos they've just lost at Huddersfield." Short pause, then, "Is he who? Hang on, I'll just ask." Then to me, "My mate wants to know if you're the one that was on 606..."

In the end the phone was passed to me and we had a good old chat. It turned out that he hadn't heard me an hour or so previously, but remembered me from Barnsley last December...

In the event I was at Bow Road DLR station much earlier than I anticipated, even getting back in time to visit the Chinese (and yes I know it's excessive on top of a Burger King, but there you go).

The house was silent when I entered, but just as I was settling down to sleep, my housemates plus many others arrived and a party broke out. After two hours of trying to get them to shut up I gave up and joined in, choosing to film Pavla, the Czech girl from upstairs, with the camcorder. I also captured a very beautiful girl (another Czech) called Jitka running shyly from the bathroom to the living room. When I returned to my room, Katrina had left me a voicemail message in response to my earlier irate call complaining at the party going on around me.

I don't know, text flirting, video camera flirting, voicemail flirting... could it be that Sarah had been right when she described me as one of the world's biggest flirts? Not at all; I'm just very, very friendly...

Chapter 37
Roast Pork for Sunday Lunch

Sunday 1st April 2001: Sheffield Wednesday 1-2 Sheffield United

Settle down folks, this will be a long one. This was one very full weekend, and ultimately rather a satisfying one, so no time for introductory bygone hitching tales tenuously linked to the current one - let's get straight in there!

It all started late on the Friday afternoon when I called Katrina. Now, over the course of the two weeks since United's last match we'd had a typically up and down time. We were no longer "officially" together, but had spent a most pleasant time shopping on Oxford Street whilst United weren't playing, going for a curry afterwards, then heading pub-wards. So now we were in "sort-of" limbo again, but on the phone she was telling me that she was going up to Leicester for the weekend, and that if we'd thought about it earlier, she could have hitched so far with me. This was the second time this season that our lack of forward planning had foiled us - believe me when I tell you that there is nothing I would have liked more than to hitch with Tottenham's most beautiful part-time fan. As it was, she was just about to set off, and I was going to a gig that night.

I squeezed my huge rucksack into the small café underneath Helter Skelter Books on Denmark Street, central London, and everything felt very 1960s. The gig was by William D. Drake (Bill to his mates), former keyboard player with Cardiacs, so it was heavily populated with Cardiacs' wider family, including a Palace fan I met at a previous gig, and Ian, thankful that he could go home on the tube after this one, unlike me, a late-night hitch in the offing.

Once Bill had finished tickling the ivories (summer is indeed a-coming in), clutching tightly my brand new Organ fanzine so kindly donated by Marina, I headed tube-wards with Ian. For old times' sake we got out at Camden and went to the Hot Rock Café, and the good news is that their garlic sauce is back, better than ever! Once back on the tube we went our separate ways, Ian to East Finchley and me to Brent Cross.

Whilst sitting there minding my own business a very aggressive young man entered our carriage and started demanding money off people. Most just ignored him, but when he scowled at me, "You got 10p?" I shook my head.

"Oh come on!" he snarled. "You MUST have at least 10p."

"Look, if you carry on like that you're not going to get anything off anybody," I advised, all of a sudden feeling about 65-years old.

This made him worse: "I'm not threatening you - I'm not gonna slice your ******* head off with a broken bottle, I just want some dosh!" he shouted.

I felt he WAS capable of slicing my head off, so I produced my SHEFFIELD sign from the rucksack. "Look, I've got to hitch to Sheffield tonight 'cos I haven't got any dosh," I explained.

"Oh - why didn't you say? If I'd known you were on yer arse like me, I wouldn't have asked you," and off he went to bother the rest of the carriage. I was still shaking a bit as I left the station...

By the time I set off hitching it was fast-approaching midnight, but I was soon clambering into a truck (right-hand drive for a change) and motoring up towards Watford Gap. One interesting "fact" I learned from this trucker - he insisted that Stobart's were owned by the Mormon church.

"That's interesting, seeing as I am one and I didn't know anything about it," I said. I made a mental note to ask my dad, but as the midnight cut-off had passed, it most probably wouldn't be tonight (still haven't asked him yet).

From Watford Gap I got a lift with a small-white-van man called OB who was heading up to Bradford. He was of Irish origin, and told me that he worked in London every week, travelling north most Friday nights, so he gave me his number should I get stuck in the future. He also told me about the threats and violence he'd dished out at Leeds matches when anyone had verbally abused his kids. I had the feeling that OB was the kind of guy you didn't mess with.

By the time he dropped me at the M1 end of the Sheffield Parkway, 2am was becoming a distant memory, but a lift was soon forthcoming, and what a lift it was. Young, female, blonde, attractive... This vision of beauty was heading to Niche's night-club in Sheffield, a club that raves on all night apparently. She asked me what I was doing, so I told her about writing this book about hitching to United matches; "You see, you'll be in it now." Good line Greenwich...

"Well, my name's Debbie," she said.

"I'm Adrian," I politely replied.

"There - we are strangers no more," she said, and my heart missed a beat or two...

She went on to tell me she was from Huddersfield, but my reference to our defeat there two weeks previous meant nothing to her.

There was no doubt that if I hadn't been lugging that rucksack around, and that if I wasn't so knackered, and that if I hadn't had an important Internet Blades match against the piggy equivalent from across the city the next morning, I'd have been hopping through the door of Niche's with this delightful young girl. But imagine the headlines if the Cat had been caught in a night-club before such a vital game - "INTERNET 'KEEPER FINALLY HAS EXCUSE FOR HORROR SHOW" maybe?

Full of regrets, I bade her farewell (not even getting a number or email address, so Debbie, if you're reading this...) and was immediately accosted by two Wednesday fans who saw my yellow shirt.

"Whose is the signature on your shirt?" they asked.

"Bob Booker," I replied.

"He's a bit of a hero isn't he, really," they commented (and not sarcastically I might add) then broke into the "Ooh-ah, Bob Bookah!" song. Strange - I mean, I don't know any songs about Wednesday players...

Anyway, we all agreed that it would probably end 1-1 like it nearly always did, and off I went on my early-morning stroll up Ecclesall Road, eventually flagging down a taxi. The taxi driver told me I should have gone to Niche's. "If you go in there on your own with a girl, you've as good as pulled," he explained. Ah well...

My mum had finally trusted me with a key, so even though I didn't get much sleep, what I did manage was warm and comfortable - no more caravan for me! Still far too early for my liking, Webbo was picking me up and we were off over to a mud-bath in Ecclesfield to play the Internet Owls. Considering it was against the enemy, the turnout was most dismal. We were actually short of two players, and the piggies seemed to have hundreds snuffling for truffles out there. To even it up, we borrowed a long-haired Bournemouth fan that they had (and a very decent central defender he turned out to be), as well as one of their own who we took great pleasure in making pull on the sacred red and white!

I gave Gleadless Valley the camera again, and thankfully this time she actually got some footage of me making a save or two, normally wallowing in the mud.

As Mouse and I exchanged shirts at half-time, we were only 1-0 down, and as I trundled around at right-back in the second-half (it was hard work squelching through that mud) we still clung on to our one goal deficit until fifteen minutes from the end. But remember, we'd had the same eleven men on throughout, and with the piggies subbing someone every five minutes in the second-half, it was hardly any surprise that we ran out of energy, and they netted 3 late goals to run out 4-0 victors. They must have been very proud. We told 'em tomorrow's game was what mattered most, and left 'em to their celebrations...

Never satisfied with a quiet life, that night I'd arranged a Human Oddities gig at the Boardwalk on Snig Hill, and mighty fine it was too. The guys played with more power and passion than they had for a long time, and won a few new fans that night. The only distressing thing was the presence of people dressed as Vikings in the audience. To compensate, two of my best mates from my High Storrs schooldays, Sewer and Nige, were there.

Before any match I get a buzz of anticipation, but I think it goes without saying that before a derby match, especially one where both teams are from the same city, then the buzz is that little bit more, combined with excitement, nervousness, anxiety... This was no different, the 2pm Sunday kick-off time only adding to the feeling.

A Sunday lunchtime rendezvous with the just-off-the-train LBs in the Bankers Draft had been arranged, and as I sauntered towards the pub, two piggies came past the other way. One shook his head and said, "Pity United..." They will never learn. You save all that for afterwards. Pride before a fall and all that...

The tram journey from the pub to Swillsborough was as lively as the one for the Worthington Cup match last October. I phoned Katrina and let her listen to our lusty renditions of the Greasy Chip Butty song and Swinging a Pig. I'm sure she was impressed... One Blade caused much laughter as he was stood next to a young Wednesday fan for whom there was no escape (the tram was 99% United); "For you, pig, the war is over," he said, and there was much hilarity.

There was much tension as we entered the ground, although Lords made us all feel better by telling us that he felt certain we were going to win.

Inside the ground our row consisted of myself, Musical, Alty and Radio all sat together, with the Bert family (Bert, Mrs. Bert, Bert jnr - a legend in the making - and H the Enforcer) all sat behind us.

There was nothing in the first-half to worry us unduly, with neither side creating many chances, but I did feel we had the better of it marginally. We were perhaps a little naughty to chant, "He's got foot and mouth, he's got foot and mouth!" as Quinn got carried off for the pigs, but then football fans can be most cruel sometimes.

The second-half though - sweeter than sweet. A long clearance from Trace bounced dangerously in the area, Asaba shrugged off the challenge (with ease) of "You'll never beat" Des Walker, he laid the ball off for Jaffa, and he picked his spot and slammed it past Pressman. Berserk! And that was just Jaffa - boy was he pumped up for this one. Injuries were sustained on chairs as we celebrated, but I don't think anyone was too worried.

Then with around 20 minutes left, heaven. Asaba just got enough on his header from a chipped Dev cross, and it seemed to take forever as Pressman scrambled after it across the line. It sneaked in the corner and once again mayhem ensued on the away end. I think I hugged Alty - in fact I think I hugged anyone that came within a foot of me. I phoned Katrina and left her a voicemail message of the Blades celebrating - again, I'm sure she was touched.

Sibon pulling one back (and we have to admit, it was a cracker) led to a rather anxious last fifteen, so much so that Musical had to spend that time under the stand nervously puffing on a ciggy like an expectant father. Apparently there were about 20 others down there doing the same!

The final whistle brought much relief and glorious celebrations. Chanting, "We beat the scum 2-1," at the Wednesday fans as they all filed out was just beautiful.

It doesn't get much better than beating the pigs on their own muck-heap. Fantastic...

The tram journey back was joyful, although there were as many piggies on it as Blades now, and it was going very slowly. As we went by some little piglets at the bus-stop, they ran up to the window and started cheering and waving their scarves at us in triumph. This was beyond me - when we lose to them, it's sackcloth and ashes for a week. "Ah well, no sense no feeling," I mused out loud.

Then there were the two delightful oinkers who spat on our window once they'd got off (we'd had a rather lively discussion with them on the tram) - they shifted rather quickly when they thought Musical was coming after them... Apparently the LBs just made it back for their train. Meanwhile, I had to go home to pick up my gear. Upon arrival I discovered that my mum had left me a dinner to warm up in the microwave, and do you know what it was? Roast pork! Roast pork for Sunday lunch has never tasted sweeter... I'm sure my mum didn't realise the significance, but texts were duly sent off to the LBs and they all agreed that at that moment, Greenwich's mum was quite possibly the best in the world.

As I left the house with my heavy load ready for the long journey back to London, Alan, a season ticket holder from across the road who hadn't been able to attend, saw me and we had a quick chat. He said he'd seen me as I'd walked up to the door and apparently I danced down the garden path. Not only that, I was grinning fixedly, as if I'd attempted to swallow a pencil sideways

Despite a slow hitch home (which meant I missed the LBs celebrations in the Harp that night), that grin never left my face - for about a week.

Anyway, once I'd bussed it into Sheffield, I cheated a little and got a taxi out to the M1. I didn't care what people said or thought, quite frankly!

My first lift, taking me to Tibshelf Services, was with a thirty-something who was on the managerial ladder with Burger King. He said he was about ready to move on, perhaps working for one of the bigger retail organisations "like Tesco or Sainsbury." I told him how much I'd "enjoyed" my stint as a night manager, and he just sighed.

"There was I thinking I had it all sussed out, and now you've really put doubts in my mind," he moaned. Ah well, no Burger King vouchers for me then...

By the time I got a lift from Tibshelf, darkness had descended. I was wedged into the back of a car with a toddler in a child-seat and tons of luggage. In the front was an Irish couple, the girl looking strikingly similar to my ex, Andrea from the Czech Republic. I kept expecting her to speak in an Eastern European accent, and was still feeling surprise at her Irish accent when we were approaching Rothersthorpe. One thing that wasn't surprising was the driver's name - Paddy

I waited over an hour at Rothersthorpe, thus ending any faint hopes I had of joining the LBs. At least I had time to write "Sheff Wed 1-2 Sheff Utd (D'Jaffo, Asaba)" on the back of a sign.

Just as I was beginning to think a night in the bivvy bag was in the offing, a wonderful Somalian chap called Nasser stopped and took me all the way into

London, and yes, you guessed it, for the fourth time running it was a lift all the way into East London. He whetted my appetite for my forthcoming trip to Cleethorpes for the Grimsby match by telling me he'd just come back from there, and it was so easy to pull, with the beach close by for those little romantic interludes.

Once we'd visited his fave place to grab a chicken burger, he dropped me at Mile End tube station, and home was but one stop away...

The next day I bought every single newspaper, and glowed with pride looking at the photos of Asaba's goal. In Tesco's staff restaurant all 'papers were suitably annotated by myself - you know the sort of thing, on Pressman's shirt I wrote, "FAT GRUNTER," and, "When the ball hits the goal, it's not Shearer or Cole, It's Asaba, it's Asaba!" scribbled all over the place. Childish, I know, but like I said, it doesn't get much better than this. The season could end right now. With promotion hopes all but gone, we had done whatever else we came to do...

Chapter 38
Unfinished Business

Wednesday 4th April 2001: Blackburn Rovers 1-1 Sheffield United

Like most people (I assume) I suffer from recurring dreams. There are the standard sliding-down-a-steep-slope dreams, and the desperately-trying-to-run-fast-but-coming-up-against-a-strong-force ones. But then there are four United matches I always dream about too, all of them night games, and all away from home; Port Vale 1988 (3-3), Watford 1990 (FA Cup - won 2-1), Bury 1998 (FA Cup - won 2-1) and Crewe 1998 (lost 2-1). Then there is my recurring nightmare - Blackburn away 1990. You see, I never quite got there, and it has been bugging me ever since. It was our second-to-last game of the season, and a win would have secured promotion. I had a ticket for both this game and the Leicester one the following Saturday, because no matter what, I wanted to be there when we finally went up. It proved to be a nightmare hitch up, with me getting stuck at Knutsford Services, and then at the St Helens turn-off of the M6. I was still there at half-time, so I turned round and came home. Getting back to Brackley wasn't easy either, and the most annoying thing was that none of the three vehicles I got lifts in had radios that were capable of tuning into the football results. I got to Brackley market place at 3am, and as I ran to the phone-box I remembered that I'd promised Annie I'd call her as soon as I arrived home so she knew I was safe. I rang the Bladesline first... It was a strange feeling I had when I heard we could only manage a 0-0 draw. I was disappointed, but at least I knew if we went up at Leicester, I had a good chance of witnessing it.

So, all this season I'd been determined that I was finally going to lay my Blackburn ghost to rest. When the fixture was re-arranged to a Wednesday night, I eradicated the Tesco threat by booking the night off. Nothing was going to stop me.

I bored my first lift to tears with my tale of Blackburn woe, and I'm sure he was glad to turf me out at Watford Gap. From here a pretty rapid lift was secured in a truck. He could only take me as far as Hilton Park Services (just north of Birmingham) but still had time to tell me about how he'd left his missus. She'd said to him, "You won't go - you still love me! You haven't got the guts to do it!"

"The next day she came home from work, and I'd gone..." he said.

Once at the services, my BLACKBURN sign came out and I soon had a lift with a trade-plater who was delivering a car to Colne, which meant he would be driving straight through Blackburn. Mind you, if you look on the map, it is a fair old distance from Birmingham to Blackburn, but I'd given myself plenty of time for once. Why, we even had time to stop off at a transport café with the driver's fellow trade-plater chum. I ordered a chip butty (not greasy) and soup of the day, expecting a bap filled with a few chips and a mug of soup. Much to my surprise almost as soon as I ordered my food it was being served up next to me. The chip butty was two huge doorsteps stuffed with chips, and the soup was in a dish as big as a bin-lid. I struggled to finish, and Burger King was definitely off the menu when I arrived in Blackburn.

The trade-plater had no interest in football: "I used to drive the coaches, and I saw so many idiots in my time driving to football matches that it put me right off. We used to get free tickets sometimes, but I hardly ever went and if I did, I didn't pay much attention." Weird, some people...

I was prepared to overlook his dislike of football though, as he drove me within spitting distance of the ground. As I walked towards Ewood Park at about 7, a voice shouted "Greenwich!" and I turned round to see Rob stood at the door of the pub, so in I went, and very busy it was too, full of Blades and Rovers.

I couldn't consider my business with Ewood finished until I was in the ground, so I took it easy before going in, and made sure I looked both ways when crossing the road.

Now, tonight's performance was one to make all Blades proud. It would be safe to say that we weren't expecting too much from this one, especially as Blackburn were in good form as they battled for an automatic promotion spot, and when we conceded an early goal, we feared the worst. But we didn't let it get us down, and midway through the first half we were in the ascendancy. Kozzie's rasping shot form the edge of the area was the nearest we got, as whoever it was that was in goal instead of Kelly tipped it over. I really want Kozzie to score for the Blades...

In the second-half we were hanging on a bit at times, but then with around fifteen minutes to go Nuddy chested the ball down and leathered it in from the edge of the area to score his first United goal. Great stuff...

Neither josb or Maidenhead were there (at least, I couldn't see them in the crowd, or maybe they felt I'd cheated enough recently and so were deliberately ignoring their mobiles), so it looked like a "proper" hitch all the way back to London.

As I walked through Blackburn trying to find the M65, I heard one Rover saying to his mate, "They were about the best side we've seen here all season..." Proud to be a Blade.

Eventually on the roundabout on the M65 leading out of Blackburn, my Bob Booker yellow shirt soon got me a lift with a Preston based Blade driving his work's van. He'd been working in Blackburn, so was extra pleased at being able to take in the match. He also asked me if I was the chap who'd been on Five-Live.

He was able to drop me at the junction of the M65 and the M6, and I have to admit, here I started to feel a little worried. For one, it was very quiet, and two, I was technically breaking the law as I was hitching on the motorway, this also meaning the traffic was travelling at quite a speed.

Thankfully, the old shirt got me spotted once again, and the car that had been zooming past suddenly screeched to a halt, so I picked up my bags and ran like the wind. Not surprisingly it was another Blade, this time based in Knutsford, Cheshire. His Internet alias was Rob Kozluk's Lost Locks (so that's where they went), so much 'Net Blades talk was bandied about. Best of all, he was able to drop me at Knutsford Services, and I felt I now really was on my way.

Not so fast, Greenwich! Recent trips back may have been quite straight forward, but this usually means a slip-up is just around the corner. And so it proved this night.

I was stuck the best part of an hour at Knutsford, and there was very little traffic about, so I resorted to re-enacting Nuddy's goal with a Lucozade bottle (until it lodged in a tree). Then the old bill questioned me, taking down the usual details. The cold was just starting to seep through my defences when I got my lift. The guy was a huge Villa fan, and when I say huge, I mean MASSIVE. Not particularly fat, but just a very big bloke! (Actually, now I come to think about it, he was rather fat really.) He dropped me at Stafford Services, which may have been nice and new, but again they weren't very busy. Thirty of forty minutes here, and I had a lift in a Bird's Eye truck. He was stopping off somewhere in the Midlands, and I suggested Hilton Park Services as being the best spot for him to drop me off, but he insisted that the Coleshill junction of the M6 would be better as it was "very busy".

He was wrong. I think I was here for around 2 hours, although my memory may have been dulled by the cold. The thing was, I was due at Tesco at midday, but whatever I did, it wasn't looking good. It was now 3am, so I could either carry on hitching, possibly not getting a lift until 4 or 5am, and not getting any sleep, or I could grab some very uncomfortable and broken sleep down at the bottom of the embankment in my bivvy bag and sleeping bag. Whilst chewing this over, I phoned Katrina who kept remarkably calm considering I woke her at 3 (she likes her sleep does our Katrina). I whinged and moaned about the hitch, but raved about the battling Blades. Poor lass... I told her my choices, and she told me to do whatever I thought best (in between yawns), so I said I could see three vehicles coming over the hill, so I'd try to hitch with those, and then kip down for the night, and with that we signed off (she later told me that all she could think was, "The idiot - he's got to be at Tesco for twelve..."). And what do you know? The last of those three vehicles stopped for me. I know you probably all think I make this up, but any hitcher will tell you, it is amazing how many times things like this happen. And you know the other thing? Yawn yawn - he was driving his truck to East London - Barking this time.

It was so warm in that cab, and I was very, very weary, but this bloke wanted to chat. In the end I had to explain to him that if I nodded off he wasn't to take it personally. All told, as we journeyed south I dropped off three times, each time announcing, "Right, I'm just gonna get my head down for a bit now!" Every time I woke up, off he'd go asking me questions again. Top bloke though.

By 5.30 we were in Barking where he dropped off his wagon and picked up his car, which was all frosted up and fffffreezing. As we drove to Barking tube station I shivered in that bleary-eyed early-morning sort of way...

By the time I stepped off the tube at Plaistow and wandered home it was 6.30am, and the funny thing was, I beat Radford (who had gone home via the most mind-boggling of train combinations) by a good thirty minutes or so, and he was only travelling to Notts. I'd told him at Ewood that he should hitch with me - these kids will never learn!

That afternoon as I sat in the Tesco staff restaurant again, reading the 'paper through half-closed eyes, I circled the score and put a heart next to "Sheffield United", writing underneath the team's line-up, "I love them all!" Yep, a week in which it was great to be a Blade. And what's more, I now have another game to add to my list of recurring dreams, Nuddy's goal featuring prominently, except now he keeps volleying a Lucozade bottle into the back of the Blackburn net.

Whatever, at last my business with Blackburn and Ewood Park was well and truly finished.

Chapter 39
Belch, Barnsley and Bert's Benz

Saturday 7th April 2001: Sheffield United 1-2 Barnsley

Considering the amount of hitches I've carried out over the years, I haven't had too many lifts in what could be considered quality cars. There have been a few bizarre lifts, like once having to go part way round with one bloke on his milk deliveries between Towcester and Brackley, then there was a cement mixer when I was hitching back from Towcester Magistrates Court (I'd just been there about my licence application when I managed my convenience store). The road-sweeping lorry fulfilled a childhood ambition, and possibly the most dangerous was when my friend Richard and I got a lift back from a Poisoned Electrick Head gig in Milton Keynes in the PA Hire company's lorry. The only place they had room for us was in the luggage compartment above the cab...

But posh cars? Well, there was a Jag coming back from a Cardiacs gig at 6.30am once, and then there was a Merc when I was hitching back to Sheffield from the Milton Keynes Bowl in 1986. I'd been down there for Marillion's "Welcome to the Garden Party" and had met up with an old school chum, Jonathon Salmon, or Salm to his mates. Salm had come down on the coach, and his return journey didn't leave until some time Sunday morning. On my recommendation the silly boy decided to hitch back with me through the night, arriving about five hours after his coach would have swept majestically into Pond Street bus station. I'm sure Salm has never forgotten that night, crawling through bushes and undergrowth, standing around for hours on end at numerous points along the M1, waiting for buses in Swallownest, then when we decide to walk to the next bus-stop, one flies past and we miss it... Well, at least he got a lift in a decent car on his first (and presumably only) hitch. You see, that same night Wham! had played their farewell gig at Wembley, and this guy in his Mercedes had attended with his daughter.

"You've got to admit, those Wham! boys put on a good show," said the bloke.

"I wouldn't know, and I don't..." I started, before Salm butted in with some tactful rubbish. He later admitted he was worried that I'd insult Wham!, which would upset the guy, and we'd be out of the car. He also later admitted to one of our mutual friends that he would never "act on one of Belch's suggestions again!" Well, I know I apologised to him almost daily for about a year after that, but here it is in print now - Sorry Salm!

So, where was I? Oh yes, hardly ever getting a lift in a decent car... Well, imagine my delight when one day I sat at my PC at Uni., checked SUISA (as I always do first) and saw a posting from Bert's Official Spokesman offering me the chance to have a lift back from the Barnsley match in the Bert Benz. A chance to cheat in style, duly grabbed with both hands.

But just who is Bert? Bert only ever posts on Blades United (on the official site), refusing to rub shoulders with the "wasters" on SUISA! However, he was kind enough to partly sponsor the SUISA site by donating a banner that exhorted us all to "Get some work done you wasters!" As far as we knew, Bert ran Bert plc, but some people doubted the existence of the Bert Benz (quartz, not lilac don't forget). Well, we got to meet Bert as his season ticket meant he was located in the South Stand just to the right and down a bit from the LBs' favoured position, and we discovered that he was indeed a top bloke with a nifty line in wind-ups aimed at students and Blades from London (or indeed those on SUISA). It might also need mentioning that Bert's Official Spokesman, who appears on SUISA (and on BU when Bert once got banned) bore an uncanny resemblance to josb...

Anyway, it turned out that Bert was heading down to London to catch a 'plane as he was flying out to the Middle East or somewhere.

So all I had to do for this one was hitch up on the Saturday morning, and you know what? It was dead easy! My first lift took me from Brent Cross to Trowell Services, my benefactor being a Scottish chap. He was a Stirling Albion fan who followed Liverpool more now he was living in England. His liking for them came about as the result of a friendly they played against Stirling Albion when he was a kid.

As we chatted about hitching and Sheffield United, he said, "There was this bloke on..."

Before he could finish his sentence, I said, "It was me!"

He said he'd suspected I'd been the bloke off 606, so he'd driven really slowly past me on the slip road to check the badge on my shirt carefully.

As I stood at Trowell the rain started, but luckily I got a lift in no time, once again with a white-van man. Fate had not dealt this chap a kind hand - not only did he have a strong Welsh accent, but he had a speech impediment too. The rain hitting the empty drum-like van only made things worse, and our conversation was punctuated by me going, "Eh?" and "You what?" a lot. He dropped me at Meadowhall, and I had time to get the Supertram in, go to the Lane to get my Gillingham tickets (including one each for Spiky and Kirsty), buy a postcard for Katrina and meet the LBs in the Pump.

After the euphoria of the pig match, and the exertions at Blackburn I guess United's players were pretty wiped out. But enough of that! I expect them to slog it out every match with no excuses, especially when it's against the Dingles. They always seem to beat us, and trust me when I tell you it is always very hard to take. But our lot looked dead on their feet. Barnsley's winner was a cracker, but that was no comfort. Indeed the only real comfort was Asaba scoring for us again. I think I'm going to get to like this boy...

Bert had been spotted in the crowd during the match, and locating the Benz in the car-park afterwards was no problem - not many lilac (sorry, quartz) Mercs in there you know.

As we swept regally out of the car-park we just happened to spot Bert's Official Spokesman sporting a neat Blades umbrella. "You found the waster then!" he commented as Bert wound his window down.

It was a pleasure to travel in such a sporty-but-swish motor. London was soon upon us; indeed at one point as the M1 was petering out we were racing neck and neck with the very train that the LBs were on.

I joined the LBs in the Harp, Charing Cross (did I ever mention that this is now known as London Blades Central HQ?) and eventually it was left to just myself and Radio to uphold the tradition of a curry. I wanted to try and blow away the sore throat I felt coming on, but in the end still had to buy some Strepsils on the way to Charing Cross station.

So, a pretty stress-free day really, apart from United's efforts in the afternoon. And what of Bert himself? Well, sometimes figures of myth and legend deserve to maintain that very mythical-and-legendary status, and so it shall be here. But one thing is for sure - the Bert Benz is very real.

Chapter 40
A Box of Kleenex

Tuesday 10th April 2001: Sheffield United 1-1 Norwich City

There are some things that I wouldn't wish on anybody, not even a Wednesday fan. One such thing is glandular fever. I went down with this monster of an illness in the summer of 1989, just as the football season was about to start. I got it as a result of working silly hours as manager of a Circle K convenience store in Brackley, and wound up having six weeks off work (which, I later found out, wasn't actually that long for such an ailment). In the early days of the illness, the pain was almost unbearable. Those that have had glandular fever will know what I mean; those that haven't, all I can say by way of description is that it was the only time in my life when I've thought that given the option of dying, I'd take it.

And so it was that I was confined to bed when United kicked off the season against West Brom at the Hawthorns, and I was pleasantly surprised to hear the score-flashes on Radio 2: 1-0 to the Blades, 2-0, then 3-0, Deane and Agana doing the business. All of a sudden my pre-season prediction of promotion didn't look so silly.

Ten days later I was up in Sheffield. My mum had suggested that I go up there to aid my recuperation, and who was I to argue? Somehow though, I convinced myself and her that it was a good idea to nip over to Rotherham on the bus to watch United in the League Cup. Now, the doctor had told me to take it easy and avoid stress (he stopped short of telling me to avoid excitement and crowds, but it wasn't far off) so watching the Blades lose at Rotherham, thus making our traditional early exit from that competition, probably wasn't the best thing for me. I went home in a foul mood, thinking that I'd probably added another week to my time off work.

I didn't learn though. Less than two weeks later, I was dragging then-girl-friend Annie up to Sheffield on the train for the Brighton game. I predicted a comfortable win for the Blades, arguing that it would make me feel better, and it would be stress free. As we cruised to a 3-0 lead in the first-half, I felt fully justified; not even a goal just before half-time from Brighton could make me feel different. However, in the second-half, as Brighton pulled level then went 4-3 ahead, my stress level went up a few notches. As Jocky Bryson knocked in a late penalty equaliser, the tension was almost unbearable, and when John Francis headed United's winner deep into injury time (5-4 no less) I knew that that meant I was going to have another two weeks off work...

But time heals, and it is whatever illness you may be suffering from at the time that is the worst ever. I know all women think men are big babies when ill, whinging and moaning whilst moping around in bed. Well, I'm not quite like that - I try to keep going, and have to be almost dead before confining myself to bed (like the glandular fever, or the Burnley away match earlier in the season). But I do insist on making sure that everyone knows just how ill I am, so that everyone is aware how much trouble I've gone to...

It was most definitely the case on my way up to this midweek Norwich match, as everyone that gave me a lift was subject to my complaints, also accompanied by me constantly blowing my nose which was getting redder and redder.

The sore throat I'd felt coming on after Barnsley had raged throughout Sunday, then developed into a nasty cough on Monday. I knew what was coming next, and was not surprised to wake up sneezing on Tuesday, so I popped out to Mr Patel's and bought a packet of Handy Andy's. By the time I left the house to go to the match they'd all gone, so I went back into Mr Patel's and bought a big box of Kleenex which I steadily worked my way through.

Through watery eyes, I almost managed a chuckle at someone else's misfortune when I saw a car and a bus stuck in the middle of the road just outside Brent Cross tube station. The bus had taken a big chunk out of the front of the car, and the driver (a distressed looking young woman) and the bus driver were in earnest conversation whilst the passengers looked thoroughly fed up.

I sniffed and snivelled my way through my first lift, once again a white-van-man, this one a Leicester fan who could remember when the Blades took over Filbert Street for our promotion party in 1990. Meanwhile the traffic was bad around the M25, and with one eye on the clock I fired off a text to Maidenhead. We agreed to update each other of progress, and see where we ended up.

I ended up being dropped at Watford Gap, and pretty soon I had a lift in a stud welding truck. The three lads in there were Forest fans, and they'd just had a day welding studs at West Ham's under-redevelopment Boleyn Ground. They also said they'd been at the Lane earlier in the season working on United's new Family Corner. They also took the p*ss mercilessly out of me for my sneezing and nose blowing. Good lads though...

They dropped me at Donington Services, and here contact with Maidenhead was made. He was about 10 minutes away from me when I got a lift, so the Big Cheat (part 93) was delayed a little longer. My latest lift was with a Bradford supporting taxi driver who'd just come from the airport. He seemed resigned to Bradford already being relegated, and was trying his hardest to look forward to watching Bradford play us again next season...

As we sped up the M1, Maidenhead and Maidenhead jnr whizzed past, both giving me a quick wave. One phone call later and we arranged to meet over a Burger King at Woodall Services.

This good fortune made all the difference. No way would I have made it for kick-off without Maidenhead's direct lift, never mind in time to meet my dad at 7.15.

Once my dad had been met up with (still wearing his bow-tie from work I believe) I made him go on a circuit of the Lane in search of anyone selling The Red and White Wizaaard as there was an interview with me in it. We found no fanzines, but josb was encountered, as was Silent Blade who reported on SUISA the following day that "Greenwich was looking tired and ill. Maybe it's time for him to retire the thumb?"

Well, maybe not long term, but there was no way I was hitching back that night, so good job Musical and his magic BMW had appeared from another one of those miracle-meetings in Leeds (always when United are at home midweek eh, Mr Musical?).

And what a thoroughly depressing match it was. It was one of those draws that feels like a defeat, especially as Norwich equalised so late in the game. United looked lacklustre throughout; not even our goal could cheer us up much as it was an own-goal. The only bright spot all night was the presence of Windy, guaranteed to put a smile on the face of any male London Blade...

Musical had a quiet journey home, as all I was capable of doing was sneezing and a-snuffling all the way back to London, something I carried on for the tube journey home.

As always with me, the next day saw the final piece in the illness jigsaw - the raging headache. At least the cold had pretty much gone, which was a good job as I'd got through the whole box of Kleenex. All I had to face now was another trip to the dentist (nine in three months, resulting in four crowns, three root-canal jobs and countless fillings) and then a night of misery at Tesco. Too daft to call in sick you see - well, at least it was something else to moan about.

Chapter 41
Pound Shops and Slot Machines

Saturday 14th April 2001: Gillingham 4-1 Sheffield United
Tuesday 17th April 2001: Sheffield United 0-1 Wimbledon

I an and Veronika decided sometime last year to get married, and the date was set for June 2nd 2001. After many years of hitching around together (mostly either for Stonehenge or Cardiacs gigs), and having lived in four different shared houses, it was nice that Ian asked me to be his best man. As well as the "announced" wedding pressie, I decided to get them a surprise one. You see, they'd officially got together on August 21st 1999 at a Jesus Underground Band gig at the Boardwalk in Sheffield (Ian was bass player and I was manager), and ever since that day, Veronika had been on to me to find one of the flyers from the gig. Well, getting on for 2 years later, I'd finally found it, so decided to frame it and make that the surprise.

Whilst deliberating where to get a frame from, Katrina suggested that I should look in a pound shop for one ("I know it sounds a bit stingy," she said, "but it makes economical good sense!"). Well, if it's pound shops you want, then Gillingham is the place. If only I'd had time to pop in and browse...

As it was, I was progressing up Gillingham's high street in search of a) a cash machine and b) the LBs who somehow I'd managed to lose as they charged off in search of a pub. Two people I made sure I didn't lose were Spiky and Kirsty who decided, having enjoyed the Fulham experience so much, that they wanted more. Their presence, plus the fact that Gillingham is close enough to London to be considered an LBs day-out, determined that I got the train with not a hitch in sight.

As days out go, this one was lousy, mainly thanks to United's ineptitude. The most exciting thing had been seeing the Orient Express as we left Victoria Station, as well as Spiky's story about a friend and a cigarette that had Stow chuckling for the rest of the season.

Thanks to Musical finally answering his mobile, the LBs were located in the pub right opposite the station, meaning I'd been all the way up town and back for no reason. And Gillingham had a funny smell.

Anyway, we had a good sing-song in the pub - a lusty competition with the friendly Gills in there, one of whom kept coming up to me, shaking me by the hand and telling me that it was "great to see some real away fans for a change". In the build-up to the game, most of the interest had centred on whether Asaba would play or not. Apparently when signing him, there was a gentlemen's agreement between United and Gillingham that he wouldn't play, but Warnock seemed about to dump this and play him. As we sat in the pub, the news filtered through that Asaba wouldn't be playing. Thing is, when we saw United lining up, it appeared that no-one else had come along instead of him. Could it be we were playing with the first ever 5-5-0 line-up? Revolutionary. Kozzie appeared to be in midfield, and United seemed to be elsewhere. 1-0 down at half-time was actually very flattering, not that we saw that much, because 1) the view was crap and 2) myself and Musical spent most of the half waving at the police camera that was constantly trained on us. We couldn't resist a few rounds of, "We'll see you all on May Day..." The rest of the Blades preferred to sing, "You're just a town full of Pound Shops, town full of Pound Shops..." with the odd, "Town full of Pikies..." thrown in for good measure.

The half-time entertainment was provided by the Medway Spiders (I believe that's what they were called, though we re-christened them the Pikelettes) who carried more weight than a troupe of John Hartsons, and the second-half entertainment was provided by Gillingham. Somehow we got back into it though, when Dev chipped a cross and Nuddy headed in, but then it went rapidly downhill.

When the fourth went in Kirsty was heard to say, "This really does suck!" (welcome to the world of the Blades, Kirst) and Spiky was most dismayed that hoards of Blades left before the final whistle (including a few nameless LBs - suffice to say, Murdoch's Neighbour and myself were there to the bitter end, but not many others...).

Whilst waiting on the station platform at the end, a Blade came up to me and said, "That's cheating that is!" The price of fame!

Once back in London, Spiky and Kirsty went off to get ready for a night of clubbing and M's N shelled out for a taxi to the Harp. Before long we were drowning our sorrows in curry, me going for broke with a phal that Crouch End described as a "nutter's curry" (at least I finished this one off, but I did suffer the next day).

As I waited for the tube going home, I saw an Exeter fan (resplendent in red and white stripes) marching purposefully down the platform, whereupon reaching the end he started banging out a military tattoo on an electronics box whilst staring straight ahead. I think he was on something...

For some reason, United's Easter programme stretched to Tuesday evening, but as I was totally bored at home, I decided to hitch to Sheffield via Brackley on the Easter Monday. Sometimes it's nice being able to just do something on impulse...

I was delighted to see on coming out of Brent Cross tube that the Abandoned Car Count had returned. It was only one car, but the cool thing was, it was the very car that I'd seen the previous week that had been in collision with a bus. In true Brent Cross fashion, it was now on bricks and all the wheels were missing.

Bank Holiday traffic is notoriously bad for hitching, and here I had one of my longest waits of the season, approx. 45 mins. Whilst waiting, I saw my first rival hitchhiker at Staples Corner of the season; amazing when you consider how popular it used to be. The thing was, this guy was on crutches, and as I had come to feel that the slip road was my very own, I was well up the way, so he was perched a long way in front of me. I felt that he would get the sympathy vote - I mean, how can I compete with crutches? But then, who on earth would be daft enough to hitch on crutches? I don't know, you get some right weirdoes out there.

If he was pulling a fast one, then justice was done when a car finally stopped next to me, and the chap on crutches hobbled up only to decide that as he was going up the M6, and my benefactor was going straight up the M1, then he'd wait for the next one.

This guy lived in Castleton, Derbyshire, and ran an amusement arcade in Cleethorpes (that place again - it all helped build anticipation in advance of my looming visit there). He told me about "professional" slotters, bent programmers and how you have to eradicate this problem by paying those that know how to fiddle these machines so they will tell you the secret. He also said that there were an awful lot of women in Cleethorpes who were "slot addicts".

He himself had just been to visit his brother in London who apparently used to play for the pigs. When I asked who he was, he said I wouldn't have heard of him as he only played a few games, then got injured and his career ended. He mentioned his name, and he was right, I hadn't heard of him, and I forgot it immediately, not bothering to even make a note of it. Sorry!

They'd been thinking of going to watch the pigs that afternoon as they were away at Fulham, but had wisely decided against it. Instead we tuned in to Five-Live and I was highly delighted to hear that Fulham got a last-minute equaliser.

He dropped me at Rothersthorpe Services, and from here I very swiftly got a lift with a young chap that looked like Nick Drake, for those that know who he was (have a look in HMV).

So, I had a very pleasurable stop-over in Brackley, heading to the Plough with Princess (Leah) and Alex, Ian's sister. I ended up kipping on Alex's parents' sofa, then going in the next day to say a quick hello to all my old mates at Tesco before resuming my journey north.

I made it from Brackley to Sheffield in one lift, a real rarity when I was doing this trip regularly. He was a trucker taking a load of steel to Bradford, and other than that it was pretty unremarkable, except he didn't know what all those lilac pipes are that are emerging worm-like at the side of the motorway (I don't know either - does anyone?).

In fact, that sums up everything about our Easter period - unremarkable (bordering on the downright bad). United's performance that night was one of the most woeful of the season, with just Windy keeping my spirits up (we met in the Banker's Draft beforehand).

The most noteworthy thing to happen at or in the stadium was when the stewards searched my rucksack on the way in (a minute before kick-off I might add, and about the only time they had bothered to search it all season). I was not happy as they felt for lumps and insisted on taking my can of Lynx off me. When they felt the bump that was my packet of Homewheat they got even more excited.

"What's this?" one asked.

Removing them I said, "Biscuits. There - have them too. In fact, help yourself, they're very nice," thus handing them to a steward. As I stormed indignantly through the turnstile I was tapped on the shoulder, and the stewards were handing me back both my Lynx and my biscuits, saying, "It's all right pal, you can tek 'em in."

I shoved them in the side pocket on my rucksack, only for the Lynx to fall out and start rolling towards Bramall Lane, so there was a rather unsightly moment as I chased it down the slope, baggage and all...

As the rain teemed down, I was rather glad of the chance of a lift home with Bill, a life-long Blade who has sat in front of us all season without me realising that he lived in London. Good job I left it until so late in the season to make this discovery, as what I really didn't need was another excuse to cheat...

With United's season now well and truly over it was a miserable journey south, so in the morning I felt like a trip to Stratford Shopping Centre (which admittedly doesn't normally cheer one up). I had a look round the Pound Shop, but Ian, you'll be glad to know that I eventually bought your photo frame from WHSmith. I still had my pride you see, even if United's seemed to be on the way out.

Chapter 42
Fish Out of Water

Almost exactly four years ago now (it was the night Chesterfield played Middlesbrough in the FA Cup semi-final replay for those of you that can be bothered to check up on it) I discovered a band that were to change my life considerably. I'd travelled down to London on the train from Banbury to see Poisoned Electrick Head and Sleepy People at the Bull and Gate, Kentish Town. However, upon arriving at the venue, Sean from the Organ, who was putting on the gig, told me that Poisoned Electrick Head had cancelled.

"Ah well," I said, "so what time are Sleepy People on?"

"About 10.30," was Sean's reply.

"Good! I can watch Chesterfield on the tele in the bar then," I announced.

"No... you must see this band!" said Sean, motioning in the direction of the strange looking crew (trumpets and saxophones - diverse!) just having a quick soundcheck.

"What are they called?" I asked.

"Jesus Underground Band," said Sean, and I was suitably intrigued.

So, I watched from the back of the room with one earphone plugged in trying to listen to the football. I eventually gave up...

Never had I seen anything like it. Half the band were covered in what looked like mud and slime, there was a cool sax player wearing shades who every now and again blasted into a trumpet, and then there was the singer. This madman entered the stage, also covered in the slimy stuff, screamed into the mic, dismantled his mic stands, threw them into the audience, picked up a member of the audience, started bashing him against the side of the stage, then picked up a trumpet and let rip on that.

There was no way I was going near the front - this band scared me more than anything I had ever seen, but the music had me transfixed - was it industrial, was it hardcore, was it jazz? Just when I thought I could be surprised no more, the singer and keyboard player had a ritual fight on the stage to the manic pounding of drums which led to the keyboard player being dropped from a great height and landing on his back. He didn't get up for the rest of the gig...

I had to find out more about these guys, so off I went in search of more info from Sean. To cut a long story short, just over a year later I was the band's manager and as a result moved to London.

The adventures we had on the road are probably worth a book in their own right (now there's an idea), but sadly in December 1999 they played their last gig, most of the band disappearing back to their homeland of Slovakia (now do you all realise where the Eastern European connection comes in?). However, Martin - that madman of a singer - was determined to make it with his music, and so got stuck behind a computer and slaved away at it for 18 months, and now in April 2001 he was ready to do his first gig on his own as JUB-Noise, at the Pit in Witney, Oxfordshire.

I felt I should be there, although I realised that hitching up to Cleethorpes either through the night or the next day would be a problem. Added to that, before the gig I had some problems with Katrina to iron out. Now, we'd been officially split for a while now, but had just started to get on better than ever and an understanding was developing. Then it all went belly up one Thursday. We were both at fault, but it was thoroughly unpleasant and I didn't sleep much that night.

The next day we met up in the afternoon and failed miserably, most of the time just sitting in the pub silently. So it seemed that was that, over forever this time...

I journeyed up to Oxford on the Oxford Tube in sullen mood that Friday evening, sent Katrina a text of things I'd meant to say in the afternoon, then whilst waiting at Gloucester Green bus station in Oxford for the Witney bus she called me and we had the chat we should have had all along. We decided to put an end to it, but try and stay friends... quite emotional really (could it be that big tough Greenwich shed a few tears whilst waiting for that bus, or was it just the exhaust fumes?).

Whatever, I got to Witney, had a kebab and went to the gig, and it was rather good actually; industrial, theatrical techno this time. It seemed at the end that I was working for him again. I could live with that.

I decided the best thing to do was get a lift back to London with Martin and his driver Rado (who kept calling me Andy), then I could grab a few hours sleep before heading back north in a Grimsby/ Cleethorpes direction early Saturday morning.

Do I really need to say that I intended to be at Staples Corner for 7.45, but got there at 8.45? And is it necessary to mention that by 8.46 I had my first lift? It was a typical lift really - oldish car, middle-aged bloke... the most outstanding thing to happen on the way to Watford Gap was when I received a phone-call from my landlord. Apparently some rent had gone astray in February, so my first job on getting home was to have a look at a few bank-statements. Oh dear...

As we approached the car-park I felt last night's Witney kebab taking hold, so I dashed straight to the gents on getting out of the car, but on the way into the services I saw a family of Blades coming out. I asked if they were going to Grimsby, and they said yes, but when I enquired as to the possibility of a lift they said they had a carful, so it was not possible. In a way I was quite glad of this as I could now slip into the gents and let nature take its course...

Once at the exit, I added something like the ninth bit of "Greenwich Blade on tour" graffiti before having to wait twenty minutes for my next lift. It was in a nice black Merc with a fairly elderly couple. The chap driving said he had to pick me up because of my Blades shirt. It turned out he was from Worksop and he'd managed Worksop Town at the same time that Neil Warnock had managed Gainsborough Trinity. Small world, eh?

He was able to drop me at junction 31 just before the M18 in the hope that there'd be plenty of Blades going this way. And so it turned out, except that the Blade who almost immediately picked me up wasn't actually going to the match. He was going to Doncaster instead, but he at least had time to tell me that he'd been one of the gorillas at United's promotion party at Darlington in 1982. He'd had his head nicked during the celebrations, but just as he was worrying that he'd not get his deposit back off the fancy dress hire shop, he saw someone wearing it in Sheffield so he claimed it back.

He dropped me at the M18/ M180 junction and here I saw plenty of full cars of Blades who all drove past gawping. Eventually I got a lift with a Grimsby fan who wasn't going to the match, but was going to the bus station to pick up his missus at 1, so he dropped me here and told me to get a bus to Blundell Park.

The young lads in Grimsby shirts getting on a bus were obviously going the same place as me, so I followed them on and went upstairs with them.

"Have you just come from Sheffield then?" asked one of them.

"No, I just hitched up from London," I replied.

His face lit up and he asked, "Hey - are you that one that was on 606?" Guilty...

"That was dead funny - you were wearing a yellow shirt weren't you?" The yellow shirt was dutifully produced from my rucksack.

Upon arrival at Blundell Park I found a cashpoint, bought a postcard for Katrina, bought a huge portion of fish and chips, went for a stroll, saw the sea then a beach strewn with rubbish. Lovely...

As I stood around in the ground talking to Gleadless Valley, Mouse and Oxspring Blade I received a text message from the scarily-similarly-named Katrin from Germany. It said "hi adrian, how are you? i'll come to england. please... could you send me some flyers of some techno - uplifting hardhouse events? please please. 1 ." Not sure what the "1" was for, but I thought it was rather sweet, and with the Katrina situation being what it was, Katrin coming to England was just the tonic I needed, except it turned out I'd have to wait until June. Ah well...

After all the recent shocking performances, and because Grimsby were still in danger of going down, none of us expected much, but we won thanks to yet another Nuddy headed goal, and an even bigger shock was that we actually played very well, with Fordy and young Ben Doane especially looking good. And the Blades at the back of the stand were very noisy.

After the match Glossop Blade made the big mistake of deciding to come with me for a "night on the pull" in Cleethorpes. We went for a stroll along the seafront, then found a quiet pub with a Grimsby Blade in it. We then wandered back to the station with the intention of checking the train times for Glossop before heading for the town, but here it all went horribly wrong. We'd not even got into the station when the police rounded up all stray Blades and told us to wait in the station.

"But I'm not getting the train. I'm hitching back to London!" I objected, but they just laughed and escorted us to the station, saying that it had "all kicked off in town, so it is for your protection, so you should be grateful."

Well, I never wanted to get the train, so I certainly wasn't going to pay. Meanwhile, while we waited one or two Blades tried to escape but the plod soon had 'em cooped up back with the rest of us. All we needed now was Patrick McGoohan and some big white balls...

The unexpected train journey to Sheffield passed through some stupefyingly dull "scenery", so Glossop and I passed the time by chatting to We Are Mark Beard and his Stockport supporting mate. Other entertainment was provided by the young Blade who got chucked off the train with his girlfriend for calling one of the coppers a "sad Dingle b*****d!"

Once back in Sheffield we went to the Globe with WAMB and mate before Glossop had to dash off to get the last train home (I believe he failed to get back to Glossop, but had to settle for Manchester from where his mum picked him up) and I got the bus to pay my parents an unexpected visit...

After a pleasant stay (I even met a nice female Exeter fan at church - now there's something that doesn't happen every day) it was out to Woodall and a hitch back in the evening. Once again I did it in one lift, this time with a Kosovan guy who had been brought up in Germany. He kept telling me that he liked his car, but if it got up to 140mph then he didn't feel in control. Erm...

As if to prove his point he got it as fast as 120mph, but heavy rain and traffic slowed him down. He then watched in amusement as I struggled with my mobile trying to send texts to all and sundry - it kept switching off you see. He produced a box of small screwdrivers and told me to take the phone apart, then tighten all the screws. He watched my pathetic attempts for a while before he took it off me and did it himself. He finished the job eventually after pulling over onto the hard shoulder, which relieved me a little as he had been trying to fix my mobile whilst pushing 100 (by the way, it worked perfectly after this).

Shortly afterwards, after we put the M25 behind us, he got the car to 135mph (I kid you not). He wanted to get it to 140, but we ran out of motorway...

I was quite relieved to get out at West Hampstead tube station in one piece, and I was soon on the underground heading home (via an Internet café).

So, just another uneventful weekend following the Blades. I'd finally got to visit Grimsby (all myths now exploded) and sample the fish (legendary, and rightly so), but as I plodded the wet streets of London I felt something akin to a fish out of water - could my almost-season-long relationship really be over? Could a new one be starting? Could United actually be starting to play well again now it was too late? Could it be that Greenwich, world famous hitchhiker had actually been spotted on a train? Fish out of water indeed - when he cheats, he normally does it in a big posh car.

Chapter 43
In the Box

Saturday 28th April 2001: Sheffield United 2-0 Burnley

Back in the early seventies (I think it was 1973) I attended an open day at Bramall Lane with my two big brothers and their friends. This was before the building of the South Stand, and I remember us all gasping in admiration at the plans for said building. I also remember being very surprised at the amount of trophies on display, considering we hadn't won anything worthwhile since the FA Cup in 1925 (I seem to remember one trophy resembled a totem pole, but then my memory could be playing tricks on me). We had a tour of the dressing rooms (under the John Street terrace back then) and we met Alan Hodgkinson. He spotted my curly hair and passed comment, something along the lines of, "You eat your crusts, don't you?"

One of my brothers said to me, "Adrian, he's talking to you!" but I was all shy and couldn't think of a response. So if you read this, sorry Alan (and now you know why I keep my hair very short these days, folks).

We went into the Director's Box and the press-room, found a phone and called my dad, then we went up on the roof and found Ian Ramsey's hut and a roll of bus tickets which we unravelled everywhere. Then we went in the gymnasium where I watched with amusement as the lads threw a medicine ball at each other. We ended up playing football against some Blades from Handsworth and my brothers ordered me to go in goal (you see, I was once the Kitten). But the highlight of highlights was walking out onto the pitch. I ran up the tunnel onto the hallowed turf, and I felt just like Alan Woodward. I remember looking around at the Bramall Lane stand and the Kop and thinking, "This is IT!"

Since that day, I never got on the pitch again (not for me running on the pitch after a victory, even if it is an FA Cup quarter-final win over Coventry - my dad would disapprove, even though there is no cricket square at the Lane any more), until this memorable weekend.

The last home game is always one for reflection, especially if it is a mean-ingless fixture when we have no promotion or relegation to worry about (though it has to be said, we've had a fair few of those in the last 20 years). And so it was as I set out from Staples Corner for Sheffield for the last time in season 2000/ 2001on the Friday evening.

For once I set off early, a good job as I had a fair old wait before my first lift. Eventually it came in the form of a large West Indian chap called John. He was driving up to Manchester to visit a friend as he was feeling a bit down. You see, he'd just split with his wife, and she had broken into his house with her new bloke and taken a load of stuff. "I've been married to her for eighteen years," he moaned, "and I'm only just beginning to know the bitch."

After taking a swig from his can of Carlsberg he carried on, "What really hurts is, they broke my guitars..." I sympathised with him on this one. Whenever I have had an argument with a girlfriend, I've immediately thought about my records and CDs, and hoped they wouldn't do anything silly to them.

He was one of the nicest blokes you could ever meet, and it was impossible not to feel sorry for him. However, things took a turn for the strange as we approached Northampton. He asked me what time I needed to be in Sheffield and I told him midnight was my cut-off. He then asked if I wouldn't mind if he paid a quick visit to his best mate who lived in Northampton. I felt I couldn't object, but pointed out that I really did need to be in Sheffield at a reasonable hour. He told me not to worry, he wouldn't be long.

I then went quiet, largely because I was sending and receiving texts from Windy, but I think he thought I was concerned (okay, I have to admit that I would rather not have been taking this detour, but I wasn't that concerned), so he reiterated, "There's no need to worry," then adding, "I'm not bent - I like girls. And I'm not a murderer or a rapist!"

I know he meant well, but I really wish he hadn't said this! As it turned out, his mate was out, but instead he decided he wanted to visit his cousin, who was also out. His cousin's wife wasn't though, and I found myself in one of those bizarre situations that I'll keep thinking about for years to come. There I was drinking orange squash in a complete stranger's kitchen, listening to stories that had nothing to do with me. When John went upstairs to the toilet, his cousin's wife made polite conversation: "So are you a friend of John's then?"

"No - I'm just an innocent hitchhiker who's along for the ride," I replied.

"What, so your not even a friend of his?" she gasped, seemingly quite shocked.

When I told John this as we headed back for the M1 he just said, "Oh dear, you shouldn't have said that! Ah well."

When I'd set off from home I'd made contact with WGB who I knew was driving up with Paris Blade. They had been about an hour and a half behind me, but after my enforced trip to Northampton I felt they would be close. I got out of John's car at Watford Gap and rang WGB. They said they'd be stopping for a sandwich at Watford Gap in about 45 minutes, so I said if I was still there they could pick me up.

I tried to get a lift, honest (and yes, the graffiti is there to prove I stood at the exit) but after about 20 minutes I sent WGB a text saying, "Sod it! I'll see you at the petrol station!", so I went in, bought some chocolate and chatted up the girl serving in there (a lively young thing). When those two turned up, we took great delight in showing her the new London Blades flag. She didn't seem that impressed - can't think why...

And so it was a nice easy trip to Sheffield for a change. I was home well before midnight, which was good as I needed a good night's sleep for the morning's Internet Blades match against the Internet Piggies at Abbeydale Sports Centre (famous for me once scoring 55 not out for Sheffield Bankers juniors against Sheffield Collegiate juniors on the old top pitch there; they built houses on it - is nothing sacred?).

We were playing on the all-weather pitch, which was a good job as it turned out. But first we had to find the dressing room (I think it was a cottage round the corner), and then as I took to the pitch I met the very beautiful Norton Blade who said to me, "So, the legendary Greenwich Blade..." This girl will go far.

Which is more than I did. I was in goal for the first-half, and had a 'mare. I only let two in, but then I think I only saved one. To rub salt in my wounds, when reading the report on the piggies' website they said I was "badly positioned", and then said that the second-half replacement 'keeper was "much better than the first one." Thing is, on this showing there wasn't much arguing. The nickname "Lobbed" Greenwich was heard again as the ball sailed over my head for that second goal. Mouse kept a clean sheet in the second-half, which was a good thing as it enabled us to stage a comeback. I was put at right-back again and equipped myself very well, I thought (although one grunter cut me in two like Roy Keane on Alfe Inge Haaland - he apologised afterwards, saying it was my change of pace that had done him - flattery will get you nowhere, mate!).

Meersbrook Blade scored a splendid solo goal to bring it back to 1-2, then we had a goal disallowed when in a goalmouth scramble, Wednesday's Pressman-a-like in goal got kicked in the head. Boy, did he squeal - however, we all felt a bit guilty for trying to claim the goal when by the end of the match his eye had swollen to the size of Pressman's gut...

With the score still at 1-2, I performed an inspired substitution, allowing myself to be replaced by Copenhagen (over for the Internet match, but having to fly off before the real thing - stranger and stranger) just as a violent hailstorm started. I sheltered in the nice little Perspex thing (whilst Radford's mobile drowned) before bringing myself back on as the hail eased off...

Stafford achieved nearly-hero status by equalising near the end, and even though we didn't win, 2-2 after being 2-0 down seemed quite good really. Now, if only we'd had a real goalie in the first half.

Josb had performed for the 'Net Blades (and looked quite useful really, although he hobbled around for the rest of the day) so he gave me a lift to the Lane, even allowing me to leave my giant rucksack in his car. I then went off to get my season ticket for 2001/ 2002 (oh yes, I want MORE!).

This time there was to be no meeting up with the LBs in the Pump as they were all in a corporate box for the day, courtesy of Titanium Blade. The only ones who refused to go in were myself and Crouch End, who was at the game with a lady friend, but we did manage to spot them and give them a wave. A few drunken phone calls came my way - you know the sort of thing - "Greenwich - where are you? Stand up and wave. Ah, there you are! Waaaayyyyyyyy!"

Sadly, they had been asked to remove the LBs flag as it was covering up some ads, but they did manage to wave it in defiance as the teams came out. Meanwhile, Burnley - who still had a sniff of promotion - were creating a top atmosphere thanks to their rather good fans.

But on the pitch it was to be the Blades day, largely thanks to miss of the century from ex-Blade Gareth Taylor. Dev missed a first-half penalty (we all knew he was going to miss it), but Nuddy netted the rebound, so it was 1-0 half-time.

Right at the end of the match, Asaba stuck another away, then on the final whistle the inevitable pitch invasion took place. Meanwhile I left the ground, met josb and picked up my rucksack. As I walked back towards the ground, the rain started to come down. I was supposed to be meeting the LBs in the Sportsman, but as I looked in to the John Street stand, I could see the light in their box was still on. I sheltered under the bridge that takes you into the South Stand and sent a text to WGB telling him so, and to look and wave. Pretty soon, all the LBs were out on the balcony and a chant went up of, "There's only one Greenwich Blade..." It brought a lump to my throat.

They then started urging me to go on the now-empty pitch. I just had to, so I slipped past security and wandered around the Bramall Lane end penalty area. "Look, the Cat's in goal for United!" shouted the North London Blade as I wandered along the goal-line.

As I scrambled over the seats to try and join them in the box, Musical shouted down, "Wait there, we're coming to join you," and they all disappeared.

While I waited I noticed Neil Warnock being interviewed by the tunnel, so I ran round there. When the interview was over, I attracted his attention as he went back to the dressing room.

"Can I shake you by the hand Neil?" I asked, feeling 7-years old again.

"Aye - I thought you were gonna punch me!" he quipped.

"No, not this time," then as we shook hands I told him I was Greenwich Blade, the idiot (or barmpot as my dad would say) who hitched to all the games.

"Ah... you kept me entertained all night when you were on 606!" he beamed.

I swear I floated back across the pitch to join the LBs just emerging from a door somewhere in the John Street stand.

Watching grown men running around a football pitch was rather touching in a way. Musical stood in the centre circle and did his Mary Poppins impression whilst NLB dribbled to the edge of the area and before long had netted a hat-trick, milking the applause from all four stands. Hammersmith and WGB were wide-eyed with wonderment. "This tops it all," Hammersmith was heard to mutter.

The general consensus of opinion was that it was spine-tingling with all the stands empty, so imagine what it must be like to play for the Blades in front of a full-house.

We all ended up in the Sportsman where we purchased copies of the new BBC (Blades Business Crew) book, the LBs unsettling the author who thought they must be CID as they were all wearing suits...

It gave us all something to read on the train back to London... Ahhh... did I mention the train? Hmmm, well I had a problem you see, because that night Martin had a JUB-Noise gig at the Bull and Gate, and now I was his manager again I felt I should be where it all started for me with those Eastern Europeans. And anyway, the season's home games started with a train journey, so it is only right that they should end with one, or something.

Anyway, back to the BBC book. Reading it made me realise that I stood a very good chance of getting my stuff published. If he can, then so can I! Oh yes!

I was trusted with the LBs flag as at that point I was the only one who could confirm that he was going to Bolton for the last game of the season. Once at the Bull and Gate I chucked it in the dressing room for safe keeping, then flung myself at the beautiful Sarah (remember, my pierced and pouting ex from six years ago) who I hadn't seen for about eighteen months. And guess what? She was as gorgeous as ever.

At the end of the gig I retrieved the flag only to find it had collected some of JUB-Noise's fluorescent green paint; you know, the stuff that travels around little Perspex tubes onstage whilst he's performing (what do you mean no - well, you do now, all right?). It didn't come out in the wash either. I knew I'd have some explaining to do, especially to WGB who'd got it done (although everyone put cash to - actually Chris, did I ever give you the dosh - I'm sure I did, but...).

I put my flag concerns to one side for the rest of the weekend as I reflected on a lovely end to the season at home (well, I thought about the football in between spending Sunday with the lovely Jitka from the Czech Republic). The Internet Blades had got a decent result, United had won, I felt I had the respect of my fellow London Blades (as well as United's manager!), but best of all, I'd been on the hallowed turf, and in such a way that wasn't going to earn me a ticking off from my dad.

Chapter 44
Nurses Whispering Verses

Sunday 6th May 2001: Bolton Wanderers 1-1 Sheffield United

I don't know about you, but I think Sunday is a rather lame day to end the football season on. Call me old-fashioned if you like, but to us in England football will always be a 3-o'clock-on-a-Saturday-afternoon thing. Indeed some of United's most historic moments have occurred on the last day of the season on a Saturday. For one, who can forget THAT match against Walsall in 1981? For those that don't remember (or know), we needed a point to avoid relegation to the old Fourth Division whilst Walsall needed a win. We were at home, and I really thought we should be all right. It was 0-0 and quite dull (but tense) when Walsall got a late penalty which they tucked away. We then got a last minute penalty, and I can still remember the feeling of relief (and disbelief) I had when the ref pointed to the spot. John Matthews refused to take it, so up stepped Don Givens - he scuffed his shot and Walsall's 'keeper saved it easily. He raised his fist in triumph before booting the ball upfield, the final whistle soon followed and United were a fourth division side. As the fans swarmed on the pitch and fought with the celebrating Walsall players, my dad booed very loudly, and the whole thing was pretty miserable really. But at least it was a Saturday.

You want more? Stamford Bridge 1994 brought more last-kick-of-the-season fun and frolics. We were drawing 2-2 with a minute to go, and as the other results stood, that was enough for us to stay up. Everton had been 2-0 down against Wimbledon, but we then heard they were 3-2 up, so they were safe. Meanwhile Ipswich were drawing 0-0 with Blackburn, and as that last minute ticked away and we all worked out the permutations from the table in the programme, the bloke behind me said, "Well, let's hope Ipswich don't score against Blackburn."

"Or Chelsea score against us," I added. Then we all watched in silence as Wise crossed, Hoddle flicked on and Stein scored. We were down, and I wished I'd kept my gob shut. How I laughed the following Saturday when Chelsea got stuffed 4-0 by Man Utd in the Cup Final.

Just to cheer us all up a little though, we must remember that fine fine fine Saturday May 5th 1990 when we stuffed Leicester 5-2 at Filbert Street and went up to the old Division 1, whilst the pigs messed it up at Swillsborough and replaced us going down. Has there ever been a better headline than BLADES GLORY - OWLS DOWN...?

So here I was 11 years and 1 day on from that perfect of days hitching to an end of season match that had no importance to us regarding promotion or relegation, and early on a Sunday morning it felt rather strange too.

At Staples Corner I noticed a few Fulham fans going by, but after only a short-ish wait I had my lift. The chap was going all the way to Manchester Airport, so I knew I'd break the back of it with this lift. He was boarding a 'plane back to Germany which had been his home since 1978. After asking me what a Bolton fan was doing living in London, and I'd pointed to my badge and told him I was Sheffield United, he confessed to knowing nothing about football. "Do they still have the FA Cup Final, at Wembley?" he asked. I pointed out that the FA Cup Final still happened, but it wasn't played at Wembley at the moment...

He also admitted that he was very out of touch with all things in England, and it was quite bizarre to listen to his surprise as I told him that Muller yogurts were now huge over here, and that he'd been sent a tape of Red Dwarf by his son which he really liked. "When I'm at the airport I'm going to see if I can pick up any more of those videos," he said. When he expressed a keenness on further alternative comedies, I felt it only right to point him in the direction of the League of Gentlemen.

Before I set off, I sent a text to both Stow and Radio knowing that they were coming up, just in case I got stuck in the early Sunday morning mist. As me and my ex-pat mate trundled up the M6, Radio called me. They were somewhere on the M1 but making rapid progress, so I decided to cut my losses and arranged to meet them at Stafford Services (WGB was also in the car).

After I was dropped at the services, a very embarrassing episode took place. As I wandered round I thought, "Strange - coming back from Blackburn, I thought Stafford looked quite new." You see, this place was all a bit run-down and scabby looking. I put it down to the fact that then I'd been coming south, but now I was on the northbound side. They must have built this side first. It seemed logical, believe it or not.

So, then the phone call. It was Radio; "Where are yer?"

"Petrol station. Where are you?"

"Petrol station. Can't see yer," said Radio.

Ho hum... Eventually we established that somehow me and the driver had both sailed past Stafford and ended up at Keele. I have no idea how I did this, but as I put the phone down I heard Radio saying to the others, "What a...". There's a prize for the best suggestion as to what he said after the phone went dead.

So, I had to wait a bit longer for my lift, just thankful that I'd got out one service station late rather than one early. The most traumatic thing from then on was trying to find a pub near the ground where we could park. We drove round one pub car park, but it looked like we would be disturbing a christening party, and besides, Radio pointed out that one vanful looked like "the Alty family" (it had to be said that most of the occupants bore a scary resemblance to our friend from Sevenoaks).

Anyway, we ended up in the Reebok Stadium car park and headed to a pub in the shopping centre.

Now, ever since I went into the Fulwood Annex to have my wisdom tooth removed under general anaesthetic aged 15 in 1981, I'd had a thing about nurses in uniform (the one that turned up for work in bike leathers did it for me) (and while I feel like reminiscing, two days after coming out, I watched Ian Botham knock the Aussies for 118 at Old Trafford - swatting Lillee for six again and again - with a swollen cheek and in considerable pain as a result of said operation). So, imagine my delight when a girl dressed as a nurse approached me as I leaned on the bar and said, "Which one's Greenwich?"

I owned up (and the others were pointing vigorously anyway!) and she said, "Come with me for a thorough examination!" Who was I to turn down such an offer? Round the other side were two other similarly dressed girls and a grinning Greenhill Optimist (for it was he who was responsible for pointing the four of us out). The nurses turned out to be none other than Boozy Bladette (a Blades United Viewpoints legendess) and mates Scary and Posh Blades (I believe), and a good laugh was had by all. When Boozy explained to Scary that I was the one who hitched everywhere, she got on her knees and genuflected. I could get used to this. Before returning to Radio, Stow and WGB, they administered drugs (Smarties) and gave me a Wallace and Gromit plaster in case of emergencies.

Talking of emergencies, just before Lords joined us (with his shocking new bleached blond hairstyle), Radio went off to the gents. After a long time (longer than necessary anyway) WGB's mobile rang, and before he could even look to see who it was, I said, "Lee's stuck in t'bogs!" And indeed it was Radio, but when WGB tried to answer, he was cut off. Eventually Radio showed rather red-faced. He'd gone into the disabled toilet and had somehow got stuck, and then because he couldn't get through to WGB (bad signal in there you see) he'd had to pull the distress cord, so they sent someone to get him out.

And so into the Reebok. Those four were sat in the posh seats upstairs, but I slummed it in the lower tier with the likes of Radford and Bradway. At least I managed to get the London Blades flag up this time.

As I queued for a pie I heard a monotonous droning noise coming from somewhere up to my right. I looked up and saw a TV screen, and for a minute I thought I was back in 1979 watching Tiswas with Bob Carolgees and Spit the Dog, but no, that drone was from under the moustache of none other than Sam Allardyce being interviewed on Bolton TV or something.

It was hard to get excited about the match as Bolton were already in the play-offs so fielded almost a reserve side, and of course all we had to play for was pride. And this we did rather well. We were far and away the better side, and should have wrapped it up long before the final whistle, Nuddy being the main culprit for missed chances. As it was, all we had to show as we entered injury time was a well-taken goal from Asaba, courtesy of yet another assist from Dev. But then United let in that almost-traditional last kick of the season goal. Good job it didn't matter really, but we were still disappointed.

At the end we watched a Blade run onto the pitch and try to congratulate Warnock. Neil escorted him back past the stewards and tried to persuade them to be lenient and let him back in with us, but as soon as Warnock's back was turned, accompanied by boos, the stewards carted him off. Upon seeing this, Warnock ran over, and to cheers now from the Blades, gave the lad his shirt. Mr. Warnock received a ticking off from a police officer, and we were all left wondering about just how petty it all was.

Afterwards, as we sat glumly in the car-park, WGB spotted Paul Warhurst walking by, so he shouted through the window, "Wednesday reject!" and joy of joys, Mr Warhurst heard, turning round sharply, and he even had a semi-grin on his face (just visible under that crime of a "haircut").

As we drove home, we heard that Palace had dodged the drop along with Pompey, and we were quite happy to hear that Huddersfield had bitten the dust.

So, I ended the season with one last big cheat in Stow's car, but I didn't really care too much. After all, most people have never hitched to one single match in their lives, never mind 30-odd (or whatever it is, probably nearer 40, I'll do a proper count soon) (it was 39, if you count Norwich) in one season, including sleeping rough after Lincoln away, staying up all night coming back from Blackburn, hitching to Norwich with Katrina but arriving five minutes after the final whistle etc etc. Yep, I feel my credentials as a hitchhiker and a Blade remain in tact.

As WGB, Radio and myself (Stow had dropped us all off near his home) all bid farewell at Stratford station, it was time to reflect on what might have been. When we beat QPR at Loftus Road, we were going up - no doubt about it. Then when we capitulated against Forest and then Barnsley we realised we weren't! But then beating the pigs on their own muckheap had made the whole season worthwhile. When you miss promotion by as much as we did, that sort of thing is very important, and don't let any Wednesday fan tell you that it isn't (just like you mustn't believe any Blade that tells you he wasn't bothered about losing to them in the Worthington Cup).

So, there we were, all three of us with new season tickets already secured. And I'll leave the last word to WGB (who really loves the Blades, he does you know!) as we stood around on Stratford Station, the old season barely over, already discussing what the future had in store: "I can't wait for next season!" And so say all of us...

Epilogue
Absolutely Curtains

Friday 27th July 2001: Exeter City 2-1 Sheffield United

I've never been one for pre-season friendlies. The closest I got in the past was playing cricket for Sheffield Bankers on the top pitch at Abbeydale Park whilst a United team (largely juniors and reserves one suspects) slogged it out on the football pitch just down a bit and to the right against Sheffield Club (the oldest football club in the world, you know). Other than that, I once tried to persuade Annie that we should holiday in Skegness, until my evil deputy-manager mentioned to her that I'd heard a rumour that United might be playing a friendly there, so we went to Wales instead, and it rained all week. Ha! Bet Skeggy basked in sunshine that week...

Oh yes, then there was the time that the manager of Brackley Town FC popped into my convenience store for our daily chat about all-things footy. He'd told me previously that he'd gone to school with 'Harry' Bassett, and now he had some splendid news. He was going to make that old school-contact pay-off and get Sheffield United down to the other other St. James' Park (home of Brackley Town) for a pre-season friendly. It never happened, so I never got to share a drink in the Bell with Deano (did I ever mention that in the toilets in the Bell on Brackley High Street, on one of the cisterns is scratched "SUFC" and "BBC"? No? Well, I have now, and it wasn't me that did it either...).

This friendly proved too attractive though. A trip to Devon, a ground I'd never visited (and the way Exeter had performed in recent years, it could be a last chance to do so), and a fabulous London Blades day-out to boot. Except in the end they all wussed out, opting for Brighton the following week instead. I had to give that one a miss as it coincided with Cardiacs at the Whitchurch Progressive Rock Festival in Hampshire. Well, it serves the LBs right that due to their drunken state they managed to lose the London Blades flag on the train home from Brighton. As the only sober one, I could have looked after it (who mentioned green paint?) and we'd still have it now. That's what you get for arranging trips without me, boys...

Well, no matter what, I was going to Exeter, and I was going to hitch! Oh yes...

As I left the house I felt a huge surge of relief. You see, I wasn't going to have to write about this one. I felt liberated, but then as I closed the door I thought, "But what if you have the biggest adventure of your life? You'll have to write something then..."

And within twenty seconds of my journey commencing a dodgy car pulled up next to me and an Irish geezer was leaning out of the window trying to sell me a Camcorder. "It's not stolen, and it works perfectly," he lied. I'd barely had time to reject his kind offer when they were speeding off again. 300 yards down the road I saw the car abandoned, windows still open...

Then there was the Aldershot fan who thought I was hitching to see the Blades reserves take on the Shots ("Do you think I'm mad? No, I'm off to Exeter to see a pointless pre-season friendly"), the lovely girl serving ice-cream at Fleet Services, the police officer who gave me lift all the way into Exeter ("It's been a pleasure to meet a Christian Copper!")...

Just for good measure as I stood on the terrace I got a phone call from Jitka, my new Czech girlfriend, then a text message from Katrina (ah yes, on best-mates terms again), and United were woeful (Asaba's penalty rivalling 'Chico' Hamilton's against Millwall that troubled the pigeons in the Bramall Lane Upper Tier). At least while the fans were having a ruck with the stewards over missing balls, the players were replicating it on the pitch, Santos and Devlin really getting stuck in (er, this was supposed to be a friendly, lads!).

Then there was the lift to a service-station in Shiny's open-topped sporty-job, sleeping atop a grassy-hillock at said services on a warm, starry night, then hitching to Sheffield the next day for my dad's 70th birthday party (caring children that we are, my brothers, sisters and I bought him a Sheffield United season ticket, so I won't be suffering alone).

Here we go again, then...

So far this season we've had United at Grimsby on the day of the World Trade Centre atrocity, a late arrival at Stockport (at least I made it for the last forty minutes...), a chance meeting with Stow at Watford Gap, and the small matter of a hitch to Munich for some game that England won 5-1...

Anyone for a sequel...?

Did I ever mention
I went to Munich?